W9-CFC-043

HEROES

in training

Vicki Redden

HEROES
in training

REVIEW AND HERALD® PUBLISHING ASSOCIATION

Since 1861 | www.reviewandherald.com

The author assumes full responsibility for the accuracy of all facts and quotations
as cited in this book.

Unless otherwise noted, Scripture notations in this book are from the New King James
Version. Copyright © 1979, 1980, 1982 by Thomas Nelson, Inc. Used by permission. All
rights reserved.

Scriptures credited to NCV are quoted from *The Holy Bible, New Century Version,* copyright © 1987, 1988, 1991 by Word Publishing, Dallas, Texas 75039. Used by permission.
Texts credited to NIV are from the *Holy Bible, New International Version.* Copyright ©
1973, 1978, 1984, International Bible Society. Used by permission of Zondervan Bible Publishers.

Edited by RosAnne Tetz
Copyedited by Delma Miller and James Cavil
Art Direction by Patricia Wegh
Cover design by Kelly Butler Coe
Cover illustration by Extraordinair Art, Inc./Gary Fasen
Interior design by Candy Harvey

Typeset: 12/14 Sabon

Printed by Pacific Press® Publishing Association
PRINTED IN U.S.A.

R&H Cataloging Service
Redden, Vicki, 1976-
   Heroes in training.

   1. Children—Religious life.   2. Devotional literature—Juvenile.   3. Devotional
calendars—Seventh-day Adventist.   I. Title.

242.62

ISBN 978-0-8280-1843-2

February 2021

For Ron

God's hero . . .
and mine!

Dear Boys and Girls,

Do you have a hero? I'm not talking about one of the action figures on the floor in your room, or those animated characters with X-ray vision that save the world every day on Cartoon Network. I mean a real live person. Is there someone you look up to and admire? Why? What makes them so special to you?

Heroes come in all shapes and sizes—big, little, short, tall, old, and young. They can be boys, girls, moms, dads, grandpas or grandmas, aunts or uncles, friends, neighbors—even animals can be heroes.

Do you think God has heroes? What do you think it would take to be one of God's heroes?

Did you know that YOU can be God's hero? In this book we'll learn about 12 things that will make you a hero for God. We'll read about all kinds of heroes—from Bible times, all the way up to our times—and each day we'll look at something God wants us to learn from His heroes. By the time we're finished, you'll know just what it takes to be God's hero.

So put on your cape. And get ready to become a hero for God!

Dear caring Adult,

Thank you for reading with your young person and being interested in their spiritual well-being. Kids today are growing up in a world with too much emphasis on the wrong kind of role models. People like you, who care about every aspect of their lives, are the real heroes. This book is written in the hope that it will encourage your children to look around to see the "everyday heroes" in their lives, and to become a hero for God.

It is meant to encourage kids to get into the Bible, to help them see it as an exciting, relevant book, and is by no means meant to replace Bible study. Please study with your child and explore more deeply the biblical stories and principles presented here.

Most important, ask God for direction and guidance as you and your child study together. God will bless the family that is earnestly seeking Him and will, through the Holy Spirit, help us each day to become a hero for Him!

Always Faithful

How long can you go without doing something bad? I don't know about you, but it seems that some days I can't go very long at all before I think, say, or do something I shouldn't. I need God's help to be good.

Did you know that Jesus never sinned? Not even once! Not in His whole, entire life. That's hard for me to believe. I know it's true, because the Bible tells us so.

In everything He did, Jesus was faithful. Whether He was helping Joseph in the carpenter's shop, playing with His friends, or studying the Bible, He did what was right. He didn't lie, cheat, or steal. He believed in God and was faithful in His religion, but His faithfulness didn't stop there. He was faithful in everything He did. Because of Jesus' faithfulness during His life on earth, we know that we can trust Him to do what He says. I need God's help to be good, and to be faithful in the things I say and do. What about you?

Let's say a prayer right now: *"Dear God, thank You for Jesus' faithfulness. Please help me today to be faithful in everything I do. Amen."*

Great is Your faithfulness.
Lamentations 3:23.

FAITH

2
JANUARY

Captain Noah

Noah did everything just as God commanded him.
Genesis 6:22, NIV.

Noah was one of the first human heroes for God. He and his family were the only people in the whole world who obeyed God's command to build an ark and get in it. His neighbors laughed at them for spending so much time building the big boat when they were nowhere near water. Maybe sometimes even Noah began to doubt that what God told him was true. But still he trusted, and kept on building.

After many years it was time, and God told Noah and his family to go into the ark and to take the animals with them. Then an angel shut the door behind them. Can you imagine waiting for that rain to come, sitting there in the ark with the elephants and tigers, chimpanzees and turtles?

Then they heard it—slowly at first: *pit-pat, pit-pat.* Then louder and louder, faster and faster, until the rain was *all* they could hear. It rained for more than a month while Noah and his family and the animals floated in that big boat. I'll bet Noah was glad he'd listened to God!

They were on the big boat for a long, long time before it was dry enough for them to come out. When an angel finally opened that door, the animals were as happy as the people were! I can just see the lambs jumping in the meadow, the horses running in the fields, and maybe a brown, shaggy dog beside Noah, rubbing its back in the brand-new grass.

It can be hard to serve God when we don't understand or when others make fun of us for our beliefs. But we can be brave like Noah and trust in God. He'll be faithful to us, just as He was faithful to Noah and his family.

FAITH

A faithful Friend

Bobby couldn't understand why people were putting his friend in the ground. His doggy brain just didn't understand death, and he howled and howled. All he knew was that he couldn't get to his friend.

Even though there was no marker of any kind on the grave, the little black dog spent every night for the next 14 years sleeping on his master's grave. At first people tried to chase him away, or bring him inside when it was rainy or cold. He always came back, though, and put up such a fuss when he wasn't allowed to be near his master's grave that they would give in and let him back out into the cold, dark night.

During the day Bobby usually stayed near the graveyard too. No matter what the weather, he was never far from the spot where his master lay. Today, standing near the old Greyfriars Churchyard in Edinburgh, Scotland, there is a statue of faithful Bobby, who never forgot his friend.

Jesus is our faithful friend too. No matter how bad things get or how dark and scary things might be, He will always be right there beside us. He will never leave us or forget us. He promised!

I will never leave you nor forsake you.
Hebrews 13:5.

FAITH

Roadside Baptism

I believe that Jesus Christ is the Son of God.
Acts 8:37.

God told Philip to take a walk on a desert road. Philip didn't know why God was sending him, but he followed God's directions. As he walked on that road, he saw a chariot in the distance. Sitting in the chariot and reading the Scriptures was a man from Ethiopia. God told Philip to talk to the man.

When Philip walked up to the chariot, he heard the man reading from the book of Isaiah and asked if he understood what he was reading. The man said, "How can I, unless someone guides me?" (Acts 8:3).

So Philip climbed into the chariot, and they started to talk about the Scriptures. Philip told the man about Jesus—how He came to save whoever believes in Him and will come back one day to take all His friends to heaven.

Soon they came to some water, and the Ethiopian asked to be baptized. Right there by the side of the road they went down into the water, and Philip baptized his new friend.

We may not always know why God asks us to do a certain thing, but He has a plan for each of us. If we ask Him to help us follow His plan, He may even use us to teach someone else about Him.

FAITH

Different Gifts, Same Giver

Growing up, Rochelle always felt different from the other girls. She didn't like to wear dresses or play with dolls. She would much rather play outside or take things apart and see if she could put them together again. The kids at school made fun of her and called her "weird" because she wasn't like everyone else. Because she was shy, she didn't have many friends, either.

After Rochelle grew up, she was still very shy and still felt different from others. She still loved to be outdoors and was really good at mechanical things. She could fix cars and air-conditioners better than almost anyone, and she was great with animals and plants. But she felt as if she didn't have anything to offer God or her church because she didn't like to get up front, sing, cook, or lead out.

One day Rochelle came to realize that God had made her the way she was—that she was special—and that God could use her to do things other people couldn't do. Today she happily serves her church by helping out with maintenance and keeping the grounds pretty—a very important job. She's doing what she can to help God rather than worrying about the things she *can't* do well.

God made you special too. He gave you certain gifts that other people might not have. So you can be a hero for Him in a very special way—a way that no one else on earth can be.

Each one should use whatever gift he has received to serve others, faithfully administering God's grace in its various forms.
1 Peter 4:10, NIV.

FAITH

6

JANUARY

So Abram departed as the Lord had spoken to him.

Genesis 12:4.

A Leap of Faith

Imagine leaving your home—and not leaving just your home but also your toys, friends, pets, and parents.

Now imagine leaving them and not knowing where you were going—or when you would get there.

That's what happened to Abram. (You can read about him in Genesis 12.) God spoke to him and told him to go to a place that God would lead him to. Abram didn't know where he was going, but he trusted that God would lead him and take him to where He wanted him to be.

Abram knew that God would keep His promises. And He did! God made a great nation from Abram's family, and Jesus was a direct descendant of Abram's—like a great-great-great-great-grandson. Abram was a blessing for the whole world, just as God said he would be.

It is easy to get too comfortable with the way things are. If you want to follow God's plan for your life, you might have to be willing to give up some things or make some changes. Trust Him to lead you to bigger and better things, and to show you what is best for your life.

FAITH

Stormy Faith

Rina's heart was sad as she put one tired foot in front of the other. "Lord! Please be with my children!"

She had been away on a trip when a strong storm ripped through her village. As soon as she heard of it, Rina started home. Each time she stopped to ask of her village, the people told her they had heard it was very bad there. Her heart sank, and raindrops mixed with the tears on her face as she wearily trudged toward home, begging God with every step to protect her family.

Finally she came over the last hill and stared wide-eyed at her village. The place where her hut had been was empty! All that was left was a pile of rubble, and she knew her children couldn't have lived.

As she ran through the village, people accused her of causing the trouble. They said she had made the village's gods angry when she began serving the God of heaven. Rina tried to ignore their ugly remarks and began digging through the rubble. Some men came to help her, and Rina was surprised when they uncovered one tiny brown leg. A man pulled out Rina's youngest child. She was fine! Rina's tears of sadness quickly turned to tears of joy as, one by one, all her children were pulled, unhurt, from the ruins of their home.

God heard Rina's prayer, and He will hear the prayers of everyone who believes in Him. Sometimes the answer He gives isn't what we want at the time, but God always knows what is best for us and will honor the faith of those who believe in Him.

Take up the shield of faith, with which you can extinguish all the flaming arrows of the evil one.
Ephesians 6:16, NIV.

FAITH

8
JANUARY

The Fiery Furnace

Our God whom we serve is able to deliver us . . . , and He will deliver us from your hand, O king. But if not, let it be known to you, O king, that we do not serve your gods, nor will we worship the gold image which you have set up.

Daniel 3:17, 18.

The huge golden statue stood surrounded by all the rulers of King Nebuchadnezzar's kingdom. He had given the command that everyone should bow to his statue when the music played, and no one dared to disobey. Or did they?

As the last notes died away, people looked up and noticed that there were three men standing tall. Were they crazy? Didn't they hear King Nebuchadnezzar when he threatened to throw them into a fiery furnace if they didn't bow down?

The king called the men and gave them a second chance. Shadrach, Meshach, and Abednego told him that they could not worship his statue, no matter what. They worshiped the one true God and wouldn't disobey Him by bowing to another. They knew that God could protect them—but even if He didn't, they knew He was still God.

Nebuchadnezzar was angry. He wasn't used to being disobeyed. The furnace was heated seven times hotter than usual, and the three friends were tied up and thrown in. Then the king noticed something strange—the three friends were walking around in the fire, and Someone else was in there with them! He called to them, and when the three men came out, there wasn't a mark on them. They didn't even smell like smoke! Truly their God was powerful.

The three friends didn't know if God would deliver them from the fire or not. All they knew was that they wouldn't worship anyone but Him. Would you be willing to stand up for God the way Shadrach, Meshach, and Abednego did?

FAITH

A Hard Decision

The oldest of eight children, Erin came from a big family. Her parents taught her about God, and they went to church together. They were a happy family.

Then Erin met Brian, and they began studying the Bible together. They had different beliefs, and they wanted to see who was right, according to the Bible. The more they studied, the more Erin felt that Brian's beliefs were true. But she didn't want to make her family angry with her. She prayed and prayed about it.

Erin's family didn't want her to study with Brian. They were afraid that she would turn her back on her family. They had a lot of arguments. Sometimes Erin felt that she should just stop studying with Brian so that her family could be happy again. But she couldn't turn her back on what she felt was right. She didn't know what to do. She loved God and wanted to do the right thing, but she also loved her family very much and didn't want them to be angry with her.

Recently Erin was baptized. Her family is still unhappy with her decision, but they love her and have allowed her to do what she feels is right. Erin loves her family very much, and she finds ways to show them that God has changed her life.

We should always treat everyone with love and respect, no matter what their beliefs. And like Erin, we should always use the Bible as our only guide for what we believe.

You shall love the Lord your God with all your heart, with all your soul, and with all your mind. This is the first and great commandment. And the second is like it: You shall love your neighbor as yourself.
Matthew 22:37-39.

FAITH

10
JANUARY

And Enoch walked with God; and he was not, for God took him.

Genesis 5:24.

The Man Who Didn't Die

The Bible doesn't tell us very much about Enoch. We know that he was the son of Jared and was 65 when his son Methuselah was born. The Bible also says that he had other sons and daughters and "walked with God" for 300 years.

But the last verse that talks about Enoch is the most interesting. It says, "And Enoch walked with God; and he was not, for God took him" (Genesis 5:24). He never died! Somehow—we don't know how or why—God took Enoch directly to heaven.

What about you? If someone were to write about your life today, would they be able to say that you walked with God? Are you following His plan?

Ask Him to help you live your life today as His hero and friend so that one day you can live in heaven with Him. You might even get to say hello to Enoch there!

FAITH

The House That Prayer Built

And whatever things you ask in prayer, believing, you will receive.
Matthew 21:22.

George Müller was worried about the poor people in his town. Most of them didn't have enough to eat or warm clothes or a chance to go to school. George knew that they could live better lives if they had an education, so he began to think about how he could help.

George gathered together as many children as he could and began teaching them to read. Soon there were more than 450, and he treated them all as if they were his own children.

George was most interested in the orphans. They lived as best they could by stealing and begging. He didn't have the money to build an orphanage, so he decided to pray about it. Even though he never asked people for money, he was able to raise enough to start an orphanage. He was so thankful to God!

By the time of his death in 1898, George's orphanages had helped more than 10,000 children. He had been sent more than $5 million for the orphanages. Yet George had never asked for any money to build or run them—except in prayer. When he died, George owned little more than his clothes and some furniture. He had given everything to his children.

God has given us everything too. We are His children. The Bible promises that if we ask God for anything in faith, He will give it to us.

God may ask us to do things that we think are too big or too hard for us, but God is always there to help us. Together we can do it.

FAITH

12
JANUARY

Me and My House

Joshua had been the leader of the Israelites for many years. After Moses died, Joshua led God's people into the Promised Land. Through battles and peace, through famine and plenty, he had led them. Now Joshua was old, and he wanted to speak to the people one last time.

He gathered them together and reminded them of all the times God had protected them and helped them. He made sure they understood that God was always with them. He wanted to believe that they would follow God even after he was gone—but he knew that they were stubborn and weak. This made him sad.

Joshua knew that God loved His people and wanted to be with them, but he knew that God wouldn't force Himself on them either. Joshua knew that the Israelites would be tempted to follow the gods of the neighboring countries rather than worshiping the true God. He knew that that would be a bad decision.

Joshua knew that God always lets us choose whether or not we will serve Him. And Joshua told the people that he and his family had decided to serve the Lord, regardless of the decisions of the people around them. That can be a hard thing to do. Whom will you serve today?

FAITH

A Wretch Like Me

For much of his life John Newton was definitely not a nice person. But God never gave up on him, and John ended up writing one of the most famous hymns ever.

At a young age John went to work on a ship, and he was influenced by the sailors he met. He had a foul mouth. His language was so bad that he sometimes even made the sailors blush! He was a heavy drinker. He was a deserter; he ran away from his responsibilities on the ship. He even piloted a slave ship.

But God never gave up on him. Through all of this, God was working on his heart, waiting for John to accept Him. And eventually he did. John Newton, blasphemer, drunk, deserter, and slaver, became John Newton, minister and hymn writer. He preached to thousands of people and wrote "Amazing Grace," one of the world's favorite hymns. It amazed him that God would love and save even someone with a past like his.

God always, always, always loves us, no matter what we do or say. God wants what is best for us and will forgive us of anything, no matter how bad, if we ask Him to. And He can use our experiences to help others, too, just as John Newton's hymn has blessed untold thousands of people.

If we confess our sins, He is faithful and just to forgive us our sins and to cleanse us from all unrighteousness.

1 John 1:9.

FAITH

14

Eliezer

O Lord God of my master Abraham, please give me success this day, and show kindness to my master Abraham.

Genesis 24:12.

Eliezer was on a mission. Abraham had sent him to find a wife for Isaac, Abraham's son. In Bible times parents often picked out a wife or husband for their child. But Abraham was too old to go, so he sent his trusted servant, Eliezer.

Eliezer went to Nahor and stopped beside a well. He prayed that God would help him choose. He asked God to show him the right woman—she would be the one who offered him and his camels a drink. Camels drink a lot of water, so the woman who did this would be kind and generous.

Soon Rebekah came to the well and offered Eliezer and his camels a drink. Eliezer was thrilled because Rebekah was not only kind but beautiful! He spoke with her and her family and made arrangements for her to come with him and marry Isaac.

Eliezer had learned about faith and God from Abraham; that's why he asked God for guidance in this important decision. What are your family and friends learning about God from you? Be like Abraham and set an example of faith. And be like Eliezer by asking God for guidance in your decisions. He'll help you make wise choices.

FAITH

Twice-bought Freedom

Amanda Smith was a former slave with only three months of formal education, but she loved Jesus and did big things for God.

Amanda's life was a witness to others. She enjoyed passing out papers, talking to people, singing, and speaking to groups. She became well known and spoke all over the world. It was unusual for women to speak in public in those days, and most people had never met a former slave, so her speeches gained a lot of attention. Through it all she remained humble, preaching God's love to anyone who would listen.

One of her favorite sayings was that she had been freed twice: once from slavery and once from sin. We too have been freed twice: by the people in our armed services who protect our freedoms and also by Jesus, who died on the cross to free us from our sins.

Both freedoms are a gift. Let's say thanks today to someone in the armed services and to Jesus for giving us freedom.

Therefore if the Son makes you free, you shall be free indeed.
John 8:36.

FAITH

16
JANUARY

Surely I will be with you.

Judges 6:16.

outnumbered

By the time God had finished sending soldiers home, Gideon's army of 32,000 men was down to 300. It was obvious that if Gideon's army was going to win this battle, God would have to do it.

Even though God had told Gideon he would win, Gideon was still afraid. He looked at his 300 men and thought about what God wanted them to do. He couldn't see how they could win the battle with just torches and trumpets.

But they had more—each man had a torch, a trumpet, and God. There was no way they could have done it on their own, but God followed through on His promise and gave them the victory when they followed His directions. You can read the story in Judges 7:1-21.

Sometimes our problems, like Gideon's, can seem too big for us to handle, but that's because we're trying to solve them on our own. Ask God for the victory, and He will help you win the battle!

FAITH

Big Faith in a Little Girl

The little girl was a long way from home. She worked for Captain Naaman's wife in Syria. Naaman and his family didn't worship her God.

One day Captain Naaman found out that he was sick with leprosy, and the whole family was very worried. Leprosy was a disease that everyone was afraid of because there was no cure. People who had leprosy had to leave their homes and families.

The little girl told Naaman he should see the prophet Elisha, who lived in Israel. Since Elisha served the one true God, the little girl knew he could help.

Captain Naaman was willing to try anything to get rid of the leprosy. So with his soldiers and horses he headed to Israel. Elisha told Naaman to dip himself in the Jordan River seven times and he would be healed. At first Naaman was angry. He thought that was a silly thing to tell him to do. But his soldiers talked him into trying it, and it worked! When he came up out of the water the seventh time, his leprosy was gone.

We don't know very much about the little girl who worked for Naaman's wife. We don't even know her name. However, we do know that God wanted to use her where she was, and she was faithful. Because the little girl spoke to Naaman's wife about her God, Naaman was healed and his family began worshipping the one true God.

Look around you today. Where has God put you? No matter how small you are, God can use you to show His love to others.

Now I know that there is no God in all the earth, except in Israel.
2 Kings 5:15.

FAITH

18

Present your bodies a living sacrifice, holy, acceptable to God, which is your reasonable service.

Romans 12:1.

offerings

Boyman watched as the people around him went forward with their offerings. The large wooden bowls at the front of the church filled with money, rice, oil, and even chickens. Whatever the people of his village had to bring, they placed in the offering plates.

Boyman wondered what he could give. He was a leper living in Africa, and he was very, very poor. He didn't have any of the things that the other people had, and he was ashamed, because he wanted to give something. He thought and thought.

Finally he had an idea. Slowly he made his way down the aisle to where the large wooden bowls were. He found one that was empty and carefully picked it up with his crooked hands. He laid it gently on the floor and placed the only thing in it he could think of to give—himself.

Boyman climbed in and sat down in the bowl while the people watched. He didn't have any of the things that the others were giving, but he gave what really mattered.

God wants us to give ourselves to Him. We don't have to sit in a bowl to do it, but He is happy when we give Him the best gift of all—ourselves.

FAITH

Believing Thomas

Thomas wasn't with the other disciples when they first saw Jesus after the Resurrection. When they told Thomas that Jesus was alive, he had a hard time believing it. He knew that Jesus had died just a few days before. To think that He was alive now was too good to be true. He wanted to see Jesus for himself.

Later Jesus did appear to Thomas. He showed him the nail-prints in His hands and the wound in His side, and He asked him to believe. And Thomas did! Along with the other disciples, Thomas helped to spread the good news about Jesus all around. After seeing the proof for himself, Thomas believed. And he spent his life telling others about Jesus.

It's OK to have doubts and questions about things. Look for the answers yourself; don't just believe what others tell you. Find out why things are done. Ask God to help you find the answers to your questions by reading the Bible and talking to adults that you trust.

Do not be unbelieving, but believing.
John 20:27.

FAITH

20
JANUARY

The effective,
fervent prayer of
a righteous man
avails much.

James 5:16.

The Power of Mom

Every day Emma prayed for her son. She hadn't seen him for 20 years, and she didn't even know if he was dead or alive. That didn't stop her from worrying about him and hoping and praying for his safety.

In her heart she prayed that God would be with her son, wherever he might be. She spent her time sharing her faith with people, and she always prayed that God would work in her son's heart too.

One Christmas Emma told God that the only thing she wanted for Christmas was a postcard from her son telling her that he was well. As December passed, she watched the mailbox, but nothing came.

Finally it was Christmas Eve. It was her last chance to get her Christmas present. Emma's sister went out to get the mail and came in with one small, dirty postcard in her hand. Emma grabbed it and read it quickly. It was from her son! He was well! Not only that, but he had recently accepted Jesus and was coming home. Her prayers had been answered! He had spent time in prison and had been terribly sick, but God had been with him, and now he was coming home.

Even though Emma didn't see the answer to her prayer right away, she kept praying and asking God to send her son back home. God answered her prayer too. God always answers our prayers. Sometimes He says "Yes," sometimes it's "No," and sometimes it's "Not right now." But He will always answer our prayers in the way that is best.

FAITH

Hearing Aid

John Kitto tried hard to keep up with the other workers, but because he was small and sickly, he just wasn't able to. One day as he was carrying some heavy shingles up a ladder, he started to get dizzy. Then everything went black.

When John woke up, he was in a hospital. Several weeks had passed, but all that time John had been unconscious. His first words were to ask for a book; he couldn't understand why no one answered him. He asked again, but still nothing. Then the doctor wrote him a surprising note—he was deaf! When he had fallen off the ladder he had lost his hearing. John was devastated. Now how was he supposed to make a living?

He tried working for a shoemaker, but the man was mean, and he beat John with a whip. John didn't know what to do.

But that isn't the end of the story. John was good at painting, and he loved to read. He became a famous writer and illustrator of Christian books. His picture books have led thousands of people to Jesus.

We are asked to be faithful—not just in religion but in every part of our lives. Even though John wasn't strong enough to do some jobs well, he did his best at what he could do. God blessed John and helped him find a way to be faithful. He'll do the same for us.

I have glorified You on the earth. I have finished the work which You have given me to do.

John 17:4.

FAITH

Ellen White

If they do not speak according to this word, it is because there is no light in them.
Isaiah 8:20.

When Ellen was a little girl, an older girl threw a rock that hit her in the face. It hurt her badly and changed the way she looked. But God used Ellen in a mighty way. She became God's messenger.

Ellen's whole life was dedicated to God and to spreading His Word. God gave her messages for His church, and she delivered those messages—by preaching, by writing letters, and by writing books.

Sometimes people twisted the things Ellen said, or tried to turn her into someone she wasn't, but Ellen's faith helped her to keep doing the job that God had given her. It would have been easy to give up when people said bad things, but she trusted that God had a job for her to do, and she did it the best she could.

Sometimes people claim to have a message from God. The Bible says that we should compare what these messengers say to what the Bible says. If what they say doesn't agree with the Bible, we shouldn't listen to them. Ellen White's messages support the Bible—you can read them and see. We should use the Bible as the highest guide for our lives.

FAITH

Kata Ragoso

He has sent Me to heal the brokenhearted, . . . to set at liberty those who are oppressed.

Luke 4:18.

During World War II the island on which Kata Ragoso lived was occupied by an army. One day an army officer commanded Kata to do something that, as a Christian, he would not do. The officer was angry that someone dared to disobey him, and he ordered Kata flogged. He was ordered to obey the officer two more times, but two more times he refused. He was beaten again and thrown into prison, where he was left to die.

Kata's friends could have fought their way into the jail to rescue him, but they trusted in God to help. They gathered to pray and asked God to protect Kata.

That night, just as the moon peeped over the mountain, a tall man came to the gate of Kata's prison. He turned a key in the padlock and opened the gate. He called, "Ragoso!"

Kata came to the gate, and the man called his friend, Lundi. Then the tall man reached in, took them both by the arm, and led them outside.

The man shut and locked the gate, then led the men down a path to the edge of the beach. He stopped and told them there was a canoe on the beach; they should take it and go home.

Kata and Lundi crept across the beach. There in the water, just as the man said, was a canoe with paddles. They turned to thank him, but he was gone. He was never seen again. God had sent a special messenger to open the prison doors for Kata and Lundi.

God is always bigger than any problem. He can help those who have faith in Him. He'll open the door of our prison of sin and lead us to freedom.

24 JANUARY

Purple Woman

Now a certain woman named Lydia heard us. She was a seller of purple from the city of Thyatira, who worshiped God.

Acts 16:14.

In Bible times purple cloth was rare and very expensive. Only people who were royalty or very rich could afford to wear it. Lydia was a seller of purple cloth, which means she was probably rich, too, because her cloth sold for a lot of money.

When Paul and Luke came to Lydia's town to preach, they went outside the city gates to worship near the river on Sabbath. Lydia was there, and when she heard what they had to say, she wanted to be baptized right away. She believed what they were telling her and wanted to be a follower of Jesus. So, right there in the river, Lydia was baptized. She realized that knowing Jesus was more important than having money.

There are many things that Satan uses to try to keep us away from Jesus. Be like Lydia and remember that Jesus is more important than money or anything else.

FAITH

Storekeeper for Jesus

When Stella was baptized as a teenager, her decision to become a Christian helped to start a church in Stearns, Kentucky. She didn't realize that her decision would affect many people in the future. Because of her baptism and faithful life, many members of her family chose to follow in her footsteps and become Christians too.

Stella ran a small store in her town, and she shared her love for Jesus with almost everyone who came through her doors. Once, while she was working at her store late at night, a car pulled up outside. Stella thought it might be people planning to rob the store, and she began to pray. Within seconds the car left in a hurry, tires squealing. She didn't know exactly why they left, but she always said that she thought an angel had come to guard her store.

Stella's faith affected many lives. The decisions we make in our daily lives may seem small; however, our choices may affect many people both now and in the future for God.

Let your light so shine before men, that they may see your good works and glorify your Father in heaven.
Matthew 5:16.

FAITH

35

26
JANUARY

Secret Agent

For the Lord your God, He is God in heaven above and on earth beneath.

Joshua 2:11.

Rahab's home was in the city wall of Jericho, so she could probably look out her window and see the Israelites camped around her city.

One day two Israelite spies came to her home, and she agreed to help them hide. She told them that the entire city was afraid; they had heard stories about the things God had done for His people. Then she told them that she believed in their God, and she asked them to spare her and her family. They agreed.

When soldiers came looking for the spies, Rahab had hidden them on her roof. After the soldiers left, she let the spies down over the wall by a rope.

When the Israelites came to capture Jericho, they spared Rahab and her family because of her kindness to them and her faith in God. Even though she wasn't an Israelite, God still used her to bless His people. He loved her and honored her faith.

God can use us, too, no matter who we are or what our background is. He loves us all and will honor our faith in Him.

FAITH

Missionary to the Indians

By the time he was 14 David Brainerd was an orphan. He knew God as his Father, though, and he wanted to work for Him.

When he was 24 he went to work with the Native Americans in Massachusetts. There he built a school for the children and preached to the adults. His home was a room made of logs with a dirt floor. His bed was a pile of straw. He ate boiled corn and bread baked in the ashes of his fire. He didn't mind this hard life, though, because he felt that he was doing God's will.

David spent the rest of his life working with different Native American tribes. God had given him so much to be thankful for that he wanted to do everything he could to tell others about God's love.

David knew that following God's will isn't always easy—God doesn't always offer a way full of wealth and comfort. Sometimes He calls us to do what is hard, too. God will help us to have faith and follow Him no matter where He leads. His way is always the best, even when it's not the easiest.

Teach me to do Your will, for You are my God.
Psalm 143:10.

FAITH

28

Nothing to fear

Be of good courage, and He shall strengthen your heart, all you who hope in the Lord.

Psalm 31:24.

Franklin D. Roosevelt was the president of the United States during the Great Depression. Millions of people were without jobs, and many banks were closed. Things were not good, and people were afraid of what the future might be like.

President Roosevelt knew what it was like to go through hard times and be afraid. He had been very sick with polio, and now he had to walk with crutches. He told the American people, "We have nothing to fear but fear itself." He worked very hard to change things, and within several years things started to get better.

When things look bad, it's natural to be afraid. But as Christians we too have nothing to fear. God is on our side! By dying on the cross, Jesus has already done the work needed to change things.

And when He returns, He'll take everyone who loves Him to a much, much better place. Will I see you there?

FAITH

Twice Saved

Ice skittered across the dark deck as the *Titanic* slammed into an iceberg. Everyone thought this ship was unsinkable, but they were about to be proved wrong.

John Harper and his 6-year-old daughter, Nana, were on the *Titanic* that cold night in 1912. John was a committed Christian. When it was clear that the ship would sink, he hurried Nana to a lifeboat. He could have gone with her to safety. Instead, with tears running down his face, he kissed her, told her how much he loved her, and promised that they would see each other again someday. Then he turned and ran back into the crowd to help others to safety.

Soon there was a loud groaning sound as the ship snapped in two. John was one of those still on board who had no choice but to jump into the dark, icy water. John swam from person to person in the freezing waters, leading them to Jesus.

At one point he swam up to a man floating on one of the broken pieces of the ship and asked him if he was saved. The man told him no, and he didn't want to listen to John. John took off his life jacket and said, "Then you need this worse than I do," as he put it around the man's neck.

After talking to others about Jesus, John came back to the man he had given the life jacket to. This time the man listened and gave his heart to Jesus. Because of John's witness, the man's life was saved, not only here on earth but for heaven, too.

If we have given our hearts to Jesus, we can have total faith that we are saved, no matter what happens. We don't have to worry about the future, because we can spend eternity in heaven with Jesus!

Believe on the Lord Jesus Christ, and you will be saved.
Acts 16:31.

FAITH

A Big, Big God

With men this is impossible, but with God all things are possible.
Matthew 19:26.

Imagine that you are taken out of school one day and told you have to go hide because someone wants to hurt you and your family. Now imagine that, even though you're just a kid, you are forced to become a soldier in an army. Then, instead of going back to school when they let you out of the army, imagine you have to drop out because your family doesn't have the money to pay for your tuition. What would you be when you grew up?

If you were Philip Emeagwali, you'd become famous as one of the "fathers of the Internet." All these things happened to Philip, but he eventually went back to school.

It was Philip's dream to make 64,000 computers "talk" to each other to help predict the weather all around the world. People told Philip that it was a crazy idea. Everyone knew it was impossible.

Philip kept quietly working on his dream. One day the government asked him to try to fix a problem for them, and he programmed 65,000 computers in New Mexico while he was in Michigan. Not only that, but together the computers could do 3.1 billion calculations per second, which was a lot faster than anyone had ever thought could happen.

The people who had told Philip he was crazy now thought he was a genius, and they gave him many awards. He is considered one of the fathers of the Internet because he helped computers talk to each other.

Some things may seem impossible to us as humans. Remember that God is much bigger and smarter than all the computers and all the scientists in the whole world combined. No project or problem is too big for Him.

FAITH

Angel Soldiers

On the dark hillside hundreds of Indians were beating drums and yelling. Everyone knew what that meant. Death would come to their village that night. The Indian soldiers were about to attack. The little group of Christians huddled in the church and prayed for protection.

Suddenly everything became quiet. The Indians were gone. The Christians in the mission thanked God for protecting them.

The same thing happened every night for four nights, with more and more Indian soldiers on the hill each night. When the people in the church prayed, the hillside became quiet and the Indians went away.

No one could explain it until several weeks later when some Indians came to the mission and asked where they kept their soldiers. The missionary told them they didn't have any soldiers. The Indians wanted to see for themselves, and they looked in bushes and houses.

When they didn't find any soldiers, they told the missionary that when they had come to attack, they saw soldiers hiding in the bushes. The more Indians they brought, the more soldiers they saw protecting the mission. The fourth night they saw a strange ship in the harbor. It unloaded so many soldiers that the Indians turned and ran away.

God had sent His own army to protect His friends at the mission. You can be sure that all the Christians said another big prayer of thanks to God for His amazing protection.

When we are God's heroes, we don't need to be afraid. He tells us in the Bible that He'll send His angels to watch over us and protect us—just as He protected the people at the mission.

The angel of the Lord encamps all around those who fear Him, and delivers them.
Psalm 34:7.

FAITH

Love Is a Verb

God is love.

1 John 4:16.

Do you know what a verb is? It's a word that tells about an action, such as *run, walk, sit, jump, dance,* or *wiggle.* Did you know that *love* can be a verb? Love isn't just a feeling; it also is the way we act. We can show people that we love them by the things we do.

Jesus loves you. In fact, the Bible says that God is love. The reason He does everything is that He loves you. He created the world and all the good things in it because He loves you. He made flowers, puppies and kittens, lakes, sunshine, families, and Sabbath just for you. Jesus came and died on the cross for you because He loves you. Right now He's in heaven preparing a place for you. One day soon He'll come back and take you to heaven with Him because He loves you.

We can show God and the people around us our love by the way we act. Even obeying can be a way to show love. When our parents ask us to clean our rooms and we obey, we can show our love. When we love one another and follow God's commandments, we show our love.

Another way to show our love for others is by doing nice things for them. Bringing someone food or flowers, being kind, playing fair, sharing—all of these are ways to show people that we love them and that we love God.

Let's pray that God will help us to show love to everyone we meet today and this year.

LOVE

Big Mac Attack

Greater love has no one than this, than to lay down one's life for his friends.
John 15:13.

Mac and his partner, Robert, had worked together for nearly a year when the call came in. They were to go to a tavern where a burglary was in progress; the thieves were still inside. It was pretty routine stuff, and they responded quickly.

When they got to the scene, Robert lifted his bullhorn and told the people inside to come out with their hands up. Then they waited. No one came out, which meant that Robert and Mac had to go in.

Cautiously and carefully they made their way to the door, pushing it open with a creak. Mac crept ahead of Robert. The shadowy room appeared empty. Continuing through the building, they found no one, so they inched their way down the dark stairs. Just as they found a light switch and turned it on, Robert heard a sound to his right. It was the burglar—and he had a knife!

In a split second Mac sprang, taking the full force of the blow for his partner. That gave Robert enough time to disarm the thief, but it was too late. The big dog, Mac, gave his life to save his partner just one week before they were to receive their second citation for outstanding K-9 performance. Instead, along with that award, the Citation for Valor was awarded during a burial service with full honors to pay tribute to the brave dog that saved Officer Robert Parrish.

Jesus paid the ultimate sacrifice for us by dying on the cross. He jumped between us and Satan to take the blow of sin's consequences so that we could escape. He saved our lives, just as Mac saved Robert's. That's how much He loves us!

LOVE

Set Free

For God has not given us a spirit of fear, but of power and of love and of a sound mind.

2 Timothy 1:7.

Mary Magdalene loved Jesus with all of her heart. He had ordered seven demons to quit bothering her, and ever since then she followed Him gladly. She traveled with Jesus and His disciples and helped care for them.

Mary was one of the few people who followed Jesus all the way to the cross while most of His other friends were hiding. And the Bible tells us that she was the first one Jesus talked to when He rose from the dead. How happy she must have been to see Him again!

Many people thought that Mary was a hopeless case because of the demons that were living in her. But when she gave her life to Jesus and began to follow Him, she became a different person.

God loves each boy and girl just as much as He loved Mary Magdalene. Will you show your love for Him by following Him as boldly as Mary did?

LOVE

Brotherly Love

Even though Michael was only 3, he was excited that soon he would be getting a baby sister. Every morning and every night Michael sang to the baby in his mom's tummy. He loved his sister even before she was born.

But when Michael's sister was born, she was very sick. She had to be taken to a special hospital that cares for sick babies. The doctors told Michael's parents that the sick baby girl couldn't have any visitors. Michael was sad and worried. He loved her, even though he hadn't been able to meet her.

One day Michael's mom decided to take him to see his sister anyway. When Michael saw the tiny baby hooked up to wires and beeping machines, he began to sing to her, just as he had before she was born: " 'You are my sunshine, my only sunshine, you make me happy when skies are gray.' "

And guess what happened? The baby's pulse rate became calmer and steadier. Michael's mom told him to keep singing. " 'You'll never know, dear, how much I love you; please don't take my sunshine away.' " As Michael kept singing, his sister's breathing became smoother. As Michael finished his song, the little girl fell asleep.

You might not believe it, but the very next day—yes, the very next day—Michael's little sister was well enough to go home.

Michael loved his baby sister before she was born. God has loved us since before we were born too, and He shows us in big and little ways every day. What can you do today to show your love to the people around you?

My little children, let us not love in word or in tongue, but in deed and in truth.
1 John 3:18.

LOVE

The Choice Is Yours

I have set before you life and death, blessing and cursing; therefore choose life.

Deuteronomy 30:19.

Hundreds of years ago Ulrich Zwingli was the leader of a place called Zurich. In those days many places had kings and other rulers, but the real boss was the head of the church—the pope. The pope told people what to think and how to worship, and he wasn't to be questioned. Often those who didn't obey the pope were killed.

In spite of this, there were some who were brave enough to think for themselves. Zwingli had once been a follower of the pope, but then he started reading the Bible for himself. He realized that the way he had been living wasn't God's way. He wanted to follow God instead of human beings, and he started to preach to others about it.

That didn't make the pope happy. The pope didn't want people to read the Bible for themselves. He wanted people to listen to him instead. But Zwingli and others like him preached the truth of the Bible anyway. Thanks to people such as Zwingli, now anyone can study the Bible and find out what it says.

God won't ever force us to follow Him. It's up to us. God gave you a brain, and He wants you to use it. He created us to think and make choices. It makes Him happy when we make good decisions and sad when we make bad ones, but He'll always let us choose.

LOVE

The Disciple Jesus Loved

John described himself as "the disciple whom Jesus loved" (John 21:20). Jesus loved all of His disciples, but John felt that he and Jesus had a special friendship. John realized that he was sometimes angry and selfish, but he knew that Jesus loved him anyway.

John was with Jesus through most of His ministry. He walked with Jesus through all of the miracles and stories in the Gospels. Wouldn't it have been wonderful to be with Jesus as He healed people, taught the crowds, and walked on water?

And at the darkest, most frightening time, John bravely showed his love for Jesus by staying with Him throughout the Crucifixion.

If we are truly heroes for God, we will show it by our love for God and for those around us. And when we get to heaven, Jesus will tell us that we are the heroes He loves!

Beloved, let us love one another, for love is of God; and everyone who loves is born of God and knows God. He who does not love does not know God, for God is love.

1 John 4:7, 8.

7
FEBRUARY

REACHiNG out

Inasmuch as you did it to one of the least of these My brethren, you did it to Me.
Matthew 25:40.

In the town where I live, there is a company called REACH that helps all kinds of people. If someone needs a visit, a ride to the doctor, or help cleaning their house, the people of REACH find help for them. In the winter, when it is cold, wet, and snowy outside, REACH works with some of the churches in town to run a cold weather shelter for people who don't have a place to live. The homeless people can come to the shelter to get hot food and have a dry, warm place to spend the night. To me, the people of REACH are heroes for God.

When Jesus was here on earth, the people He spent most of His time with weren't rich or popular. Jesus didn't worry about what other people thought of Him. He loved every person the same, and He helped whenever and however He could.

Jesus told His friends that when we do something for other people, it is as if we are doing it for Him. Jesus looks at the way we treat other people, and He hears the words that we say to them—and it is as if we are doing it for Him and saying it to Him. I want to ask God to help me treat people the way I would treat Him, don't you?

LOVE

Tramp for the Lord

Corrie ten Boom was the first female watchmaker in Haarlem, Holland. When Hitler's army attacked Holland in 1940, she and her family turned their home above the watch shop into a hiding place for Jews. They helped many people hide, but after several years she was caught and sent to a concentration camp with her sister.

Even though they were in a terrible place, Corrie secretly led prayer meetings and encouraged her fellow prisoners with her faith and hope. She would tell them, "Never be afraid to trust an unknown future to a known God." She believed that no matter what happened, God was always in control, and He would always be with them.

Eventually Corrie was released from the prison camp. She spent the rest of her life talking about the love and forgiveness of God to anyone who would listen. She even opened a rehabilitation center for the people who had been her captors. She traveled around the world for more than 30 years, telling people her story and how much God loves them. She called herself a "tramp for the Lord" because she wanted to go wherever He wanted her to go.

Sometimes forgiving people who have treated us badly is hard, but God has asked us to forgive one another and show love to everyone we meet.

Love your enemies, do good to those who hate you, bless those who curse you, and pray for those who spitefully use you.
Luke 6:27, 28.

LOVE

The Hero of the Water

Speak each man the truth to his neighbor.
Zechariah 8:16.

James Chalmers and his friends were always getting into fights with boys from other schools, and James was usually the leader of the fighting. One day as they were walking along the riverbank, someone shouted that a boy had fallen into the river. James, although he was only 10 years old, ran to the bridge, where he was able to catch the boy and, with the help of his friends, bring him to shore. The boy he'd saved went to one of the schools that James and his friends often fought with, but they put aside their differences when someone was in need.

Later in life James put aside his own needs when he went as a missionary to the islands of Fiji. The hero who had saved someone from the water sailed across it to share the story of the true Hero and Savior, Jesus.

Although that is one way to share Jesus' love with others, we don't have to sail across the ocean. We can share the story of Hero Jesus with people in our homes, schools, churches, and neighborhoods, too.

LOVE

Haven of Love

*Love does no harm
to a neighbor.*
Romans 13:10.

People were not happy with Yasujiro Aoki. They didn't care that he was working with the lepers. What they didn't like was that he was teaching the lepers about Christianity. Christianity was not welcome in that area of Japan at the time, and Yasujiro suffered for his faith. People did everything they could to make his life difficult. They tried to force him to leave, but he knew that what he was doing was right, and he stayed in spite of it all.

The place Yasujiro set up for the lepers was named Haven of Love. It had a hospital, gardens, clean dormitories, and a chapel. Because of the love shown to them at this hospital, many of the lepers who went there became Christians.

There may be some people in our lives who don't like the fact that we are Christians, but we should always do what we can to make our home a haven of love too.

LOVE

The Gift of Love

For I am persuaded that neither death nor life, nor angels nor principalities nor powers, nor things present nor things to come, nor height nor depth, nor any other created thing, shall be able to separate us from the love of God which is in Christ Jesus our Lord.

Romans 8:38, 39.

Rachel was frustrated. Her husband, Jacob, had had children with one of his other wives, Leah, who was her sister. But Rachel didn't have any children. She thought that Jacob would love her more if she had children. She was too upset to realize that Jacob loved her whether she had children or not. She thought she could earn something that had already been given to her freely.

We sometimes do the same thing with God. We don't understand what the Bible tells us. Maybe we think we're good enough to earn God's love. Or maybe we think we're so sinful that we can never have God's love. Neither is true.

God loves us more than we can imagine. He loves us so much that Jesus came to earth to die for our sins. God's love can't be earned—just accepted. His love is patient and has no beginning or end. Nothing can change God's love for us.

LOVE

Jesus' Friend

I am the resurrection and the life. He who believes in Me, though he may die, he shall live.

John 11:25.

Jesus liked to go to the home of Mary, Martha, and Lazarus. He spent a lot of time with them, and they were very good friends.

One day Mary and Martha sent word to Jesus to come quickly to their house because Lazarus was sick. They knew that Jesus could help him, and they thought He would come quickly because they were friends.

But Jesus didn't come quickly. He waited for two days. And Lazarus died. Mary and Martha were so sad. They didn't understand why Jesus hadn't come to help them. They thought He was their friend.

When Jesus finally did come, Mary and Martha asked Him why He hadn't come sooner. He basically said, "Trust Me." He asked them to take Him to where Lazarus was buried; then He asked that the large stone at the entrance to the tomb be rolled away. In a loud voice Jesus called, "Lazarus, come out!" Everyone was amazed. Was that a noise they heard in the tomb? Could it be? Did they see movement?

Lazarus was alive! He shuffled out of the tomb still wrapped in the graveclothes his sisters had so lovingly dressed him with a few days earlier.

Jesus tells us in the Bible that He is the resurrection and the life. When He comes again, He will raise all of His friends who have died believing in Him. He will give us eternal life. We will be able to be friends with Jesus, just as Lazarus, Mary, and Martha were.

LOVE

A Song for Home

He has put a new song in my mouth—praise to our God; many will see it . . . , and will trust in the Lord.

Psalm 40:3.

The dark night was torn apart by the blasts of the cannon and the fiery red trails of the rockets. Francis Scott Key was trapped behind enemy lines, a prisoner on his own ship. He could only wonder what the morning light would show him of his home.

He'd come with another American, Colonel John Skinner, to a British ship that was docked in the Baltimore harbor. They had come to arrange for the release of an American doctor being held prisoner there. The British had agreed to release the doctor, but none of them could leave until after they had attacked Baltimore. So Francis Scott Key, Colonel Skinner, and the doctor had to wait out the attack behind the British ships. The battle went on for more than a day, and Francis and his friends couldn't sleep that night. They were worried about their city, their loved ones, and their homes. Would they be there in the morning?

That morning Francis wrote his thoughts on paper. Later this poem was put to music and, in 1931, this song became the official national anthem of the United States—"The Star-Spangled Banner." His worries turned into a patriotic song that most Americans know by heart.

Francis Scott Key's song has inspired millions of Americans through the years. As God's hero, what can you do to inspire others with love for their heavenly home?

LOVE

Win or Lose

By this all will know that you are My disciples, if you have love for one another.
John 13:35.

Thick fog covered everything and made driving dangerous. The women from the Indiana University of Pennsylvania rugby team couldn't see very far in front of their cars as they drove toward their game in Shippensburg, Pennsylvania.

Suddenly they saw an accident in front of them. An SUV and a tractor-trailer had crashed and were on fire. Erin Harkins, who was driving the first car, had time only to yell, "Fire!" before slamming on her brakes. The car behind her wasn't able to stop in time, and it hit the back of Erin's car. The people in those two cars were all right, but, because no one could see through the fog, there was a chain reaction, with 21 cars hitting each other.

Erin and her friend Justine Metzger jumped out of their car and ran to safety. They got in a ditch with guardrails so the cars wouldn't hit them. They jumped up and down, yelling at cars to stop before they became a part of the wreck. Then they and other team members spent the next three hours helping people who had been hurt in the accident. Many of them knew first aid, and their training was put to the test that day.

When they finally made it to their game, two hours late, they lost. But by showing kindness to others and helping at the accident, they showed their love for God. And that made them real winners.

You too can be a hero for God by showing your love for Him and others when you help people in need.

LOVE

19
FEBRUARY

Street Doctor

I have come that they may have life, and that they may have it more abundantly.

John 10:10.

If you just looked at him, you might not be able to guess that he's a doctor. Wearing ripped jeans, he searches the streets and alleys for people who need help. Dr. James Withers has been doing this for more than 10 years. In that time he has treated homeless people with broken bones, heart attacks, colds, and many other illnesses. No matter what their problems are, Dr. Withers tries to help.

That's how Operation Safety Net got started. Today doctors, nurses, and other medical helpers work together with people who used to be homeless. In the big cities of the United States and Canada they look for people who need their help. By letting people know they care, these workers have helped people get well and get their lives back on track.

Because Jesus loves us, He has offered to help us get our lives back on track. His help may not always come in the way we might expect, but if we ask Him, He will help us make our lives better.

LOVE

Super Mom

Let each of you look out not only for his own interests, but also for the interests of others.

Philippians 2:4.

What is your mom like? Is she kind? Does she work at home or away from home? Is there something special you and your mom like to do together?

Today's story is about my mom. In my opinion, she is definitely a hero for God. Even though she struggles with health problems every day, she's thoughtful, kind, and generous. No one who has ever been to her house would say they weren't welcome. Someone told me once that my mom was the only person he knew who really meant it when she said, "Stop by any time; you're always welcome."

Growing up, my brother and I knew that our friends were always welcome—it didn't matter when or why. Some friends feel so at home they still walk into her house without knocking and help themselves to whatever is in the refrigerator! And Mom loves it. She says she has been given so much by God that she wants to share what she has with others. I think she's a special hero for God.

Whether you're a kid or a grown-up, it's easy to be selfish with toys, clothes, friends, or anything. But as God's heroes we need to remember to share God's blessings with the people around us.

LOVE

21
FEBRUARY

We All Need Jesus

For there is no other name under heaven given among men by which we must be saved.
Acts 4:12.

Brother Gimeno is a kind, loving, and happy man today, but he wasn't always that way. He used to be the dreaded Commander Bocay—known throughout his country for hunting and killing Christians. He was arrogant and proud, and he thought he didn't need anyone else. He hated Christians so much that he had the number 282 tattooed on his leg for the number of Christians he'd killed.

Finally he was captured, put into prison, and sentenced to death by a firing squad. On the day he was to die, he and two other men were lined up in front of a ditch. Gimeno prayed that, somehow, he would be spared. He had finally realized he couldn't save himself.

Somehow Gimeno was spared at the last minute. The jailers questioned him for hours, then sentenced him to death by the electric chair. Once again he was miraculously spared from death, and he was sent back to prison, where he stayed for 20 years.

While in prison, Gimeno took Bible studies and gave his heart to Jesus. He had learned that he couldn't save himself and that he needed Jesus. The man who used to kill Christians now works to help other prisoners know Jesus. More than 300 people have given their heart to Jesus and been baptized because they studied with Brother Gimeno, and many more are studying for baptism.

No matter how smart we are, no matter how much money we have, we can't save ourselves. Everyone needs Jesus. Will you ask Him into your heart today and let Him give you eternal life?

LOVE

The Love of a Brother

Things looked bad for Chris's sister. She was very, very sick, and the doctor told her family that unless she got a blood transfusion, she would die.

Unfortunately, she had a rare blood type, and no one in the family was a match—except Chris. The gift of his blood could save his sister's life. When the doctor asked him if he would help, with a trembling lip and a tear in his eye Chris said yes.

A nurse led Chris down the hall. She helped him onto a table and got ready to draw some blood. Chris's eyes got big as he saw the needle, and a tear slid down his cheek. He tried to be brave, but he was so afraid. He asked the nurse if it would hurt, but she ignored him. He asked again, a little louder, "Will it hurt?"

The nurse was frustrated, and she snapped at him, "Maybe a little, but it will be over soon." With that, Chris started to sob. The nurse felt bad for yelling at him, and she sat him up to explain exactly what would happen. When she told him that she would just take some of his blood and then he could go back out with his family, Chris looked so relieved.

Poor Chris had thought that he would have to give all of his blood to his sister. He had been asking the nurse if it would hurt to die. Giving her a little of his blood wasn't such a big deal if he could keep some too.

Jesus gave His blood to save us from the disease of sin. Because of His sacrifice on the cross, we can live with Him forever in heaven if we choose to.

You were not redeemed with corruptible things like silver or gold, . . . but with the precious blood of Christ.
1 Peter 1:18, 19.

LOVE

23

FEBRUARY

African Mother

For God so loved the world that He gave His only begotten Son, that whoever believes in Him should not perish but have everlasting life.

John 3:16.

If you had been in Africa about 100 years ago, you might have heard the people talking about someone they called "mother." They wouldn't have meant their real mother; they were talking about a woman who had become like a mother to them.

Malla Moe came to live in the jungles of Africa. Her kindness and love for the people of Africa were known all around. The people knew she loved Jesus, and they knew she loved them, too.

Five women, who knew about Jesus because of Mother Malla, came to her because they needed something to wear. Mother Malla had only enough clothes for four of them. The fifth woman was so disappointed that there was nothing for her to wear that she began to cry. When Mother Malla saw that the woman was crying, she took off one of her own skirts and gave it to her. The women were amazed at the love Mother Malla had for them. She gave them her very own clothes!

When we know and love Jesus, we will show His love to others in everything we say and do. People may be amazed at the love we show, but the love God has shown us is even bigger. He gave us something of His very own that was much more important than clothes. He loves us so much that He sent His only Son to earth to live. Jesus died for our sins so that He can take us to live in heaven with Him. Now, that's amazing love!

LOVE

Everyday Hero

R on is my husband, but he is also my hero. You may think I have to say that since I am married to him, but I'm not the only one who thinks he's special.

Ron works at a hospital and spends his days helping people. Whether it's the sniffles, a broken bone, or a heart attack, he knows how to help. His kindness in treating people helps to make their hospital visits a little easier.

He doesn't just help at work, though. Anywhere he is, if he sees a need he tries to help. When someone needs help moving, when they need an extra deacon at church, or when I can't get a jar of spaghetti sauce open, Ron is there to help.

He is always pleasant and kind—ready to help with a smile on his face. He shows his love for me, others, and Jesus by his kindness. The more time I spend with Ron, the more I wish I were like him.

It's the same way with Jesus. The more time we spend with Him, and the more we get to know Him, the more we'll want to be like Him. Ask Him today to show you ways that you can become more like Him.

Love is . . . kind.
1 Corinthians 13:4.

LOVE

Tuned In

If anyone ministers, let him do it as with the ability which God supplies, that in all things God may be glorified through Jesus Christ.

1 Peter 4:11.

What kind of thing do you like to listen to most on the radio? Talking? Music? Stories? I don't know about you, but I like to listen to all kinds of good things on the radio.

H.M.S. Richards liked to listen to the radio too. However, he was a pastor, and he didn't want to just listen. He wanted to talk on the radio. He knew that lots of people listened to the radio—lots more than came to his church—and he wanted to reach as many people as possible with the good news of Jesus.

He started recording his radio programs in a remodeled chicken coop at the back of his garage. His idea grew and grew into a huge network of programs, broadcasting in many languages around the world.

Pastor Richards was known for helping people to know Jesus better through his sermons on the radio, at camp meetings, and at evangelistic meetings. He was a well-known preacher, but he didn't want fame for himself. He always pointed people to Jesus.

That is what a hero for God does. God gives us our talents, but because we love Him, we should give them back to Him by using them to help others know Him better.

LOVE

A Brand-new House

Frank Lloyd Wright liked to design things—especially houses. His designs weren't like everyone else's, though. His houses were different.

Houses are expensive, so Frank looked for ways to make them more affordable. He also liked to make the houses he designed look nice. He especially liked to make them blend in with their natural surroundings. He wanted to make them look like they belonged wherever they were built.

One of his most famous houses, Fallingwater, is in Pennsylvania. Can you guess from its name what it looks like or what is nearby? He built it over a stream and waterfall. It looks as though the water flows right out of the house!

Frank Lloyd Wright wanted to make housing affordable for everyone, but houses still cost a lot of money. How would you like to live in a house that has been built just for you and is free? Does it sound too good to be true?

God is building special houses just for His heroes in heaven, and these houses won't cost a penny. All you have to do is ask Jesus into your heart, and He'll welcome you into your house when you get to heaven.

In My Father's house are many mansions. . . . I go to prepare a place for you.
John 14:2.

LOVE

No Matter What

But when he was still a great way off, his father saw him and had compassion, and ran and fell on his neck and kissed him.

Luke 15:20.

Jesus told a story about a man with two sons. The younger son got tired of working and hanging around home, so he asked his father for some money. When his father gave it to him, the young son left. He went far away from home and started spending his money on wild parties. While he had money he had lots of friends. After a while, though, the money ran out, and so did the friends. There were no more parties. He didn't even have enough money to pay rent or eat.

He finally found a job feeding pigs. It was a dirty, messy, smelly job, and he had to share the pigs' food. He started to think. Maybe leaving his father's house hadn't been such a good idea. His father's servants were treated well; it would be better to work as a servant in his father's house. He left the pigs and headed for home.

It was a long trip, but eventually he could see home in the distance. He rehearsed the speech he would give his dad. His stomach turned in knots as he got closer.

Then he saw someone coming toward him. He squinted against the sun. Who could it be? As he got closer, the son saw that it was his father. He had been watching and waiting for his son all along. When he saw his son coming, he ran to meet him, threw his arms around him in a big welcome-home hug, and kissed him. He'd missed him so much!

Sometimes, when we are stubborn or lazy, we leave our heavenly Father, too. But He is always watching and waiting, hoping we'll decide to come back. He'll welcome us with open arms!

LOVE

A Lot at Stake

The frightened girl struggled as the strong men tied her hands tightly to the post. As they piled the straw on her hands and a law official struck a match, she cried softly.

Just before the flame touched the straw on her hands, another man stepped between her and the men from the village. She watched with surprise as this man, whom she didn't even know, quickly untied her and put his hands where hers had been. She was even more surprised when this stranger told the village men to burn his hands instead. The official protested; the girl was the one who had stolen, not the stranger. She was the one who deserved the punishment.

They didn't burn his hands—the village men were too amazed. What kind of man would be willing to take punishment he didn't deserve for someone who did deserve it? This simple act gave Aaron Holmes, an African-American missionary to Liberia, the chance to share Jesus with the people of that village.

Jesus took our punishment. He didn't have to. He was sinless and didn't deserve the punishment. We did. But because He loves us, He died on the cross to save us from our sins.

He was wounded for our transgressions, . . . and by His stripes we are healed.

Isaiah 53:5.

LOVE

Everyone Is Equal

Have we not all one Father? Has not one God created us?
Malachi 2:10.

The woman was desperate. Her young daughter was possessed by demons, and the poor mother didn't know how else to help her. She must try to find Jesus. She didn't know if He would help her—after all, she was not a Jew—but she had to try.

When she found Him, she fell at Jesus' feet and begged Him to help. He wanted to help her, but He also wanted His disciples to learn a lesson, so He acted as if He didn't hear her. When she continued to beg, the disciples asked Him to send her away. Finally, Jesus could see that the disciples had seen her faith, and with love on His face He healed her daughter. The woman left, praising God for answering her prayer.

Jesus helped the woman even though she was different than He was. The Jews of His time thought that they were the only ones God loved. Jesus wanted to show the disciples that He loves everyone and that He expects us to do the same.

Heaven isn't only for certain people. It is for all those who accept Jesus as their Savior—no matter what they look like or where they live. God does not want us to treat people differently because they aren't like us. He is God and Creator of all, and He wants everyone to accept His love and promise of eternal life.

Do you treat people who are different as the disciples did? Or do you want to follow Jesus' example? Try to do something today for someone who is different, and show them how much Jesus loves them.

COURTESY AND RESPECT

Fearless Adventurer

*Honor one another
above yourselves.*
Romans 12:10, NIV.

U nexplored." How David hated seeing that word on the maps he studied in school! He couldn't understand how, after all this time, so many places could be unexplored. Africa especially interested him, because only the coast of the continent had been explored. He promised himself that one day he would go to Africa as a doctor to help the people and remove the word "unexplored" from the maps.

That's just what he did. After becoming a doctor, he went to Cape Town in South Africa, on the southern tip of the continent. As he made plans to travel into the unexplored regions, everyone told him he was crazy. No White man had ever done that before and lived. But off he went.

In his medical work with the different tribes of Africa, David made many friends. At each village, the people told him that he couldn't go to the next village, because those people were not peace-loving and kind, as they were. David explained that they felt that way only because they didn't know the people who lived there. And off he went again to make more friends. Many people who had been former enemies were united in their love for David.

Dr. David Livingstone's heart was with the people of Africa, and he spent the rest of his life working for peace and health among the tribes.

Dr. Livingstone gave his love to Africa and its people. He gave his life to God and let God use him in a mighty way. God will use any ordinary person who asks to be a hero for Him in a mighty way. Will you let God work with you to be a hero for Him?

COURTESY AND RESPECT

3

MARCH

Therefore submit to God. Resist the devil and he will flee from you.

James 4:7.

Sceva's Sons

Paul spent a lot of time traveling and preaching the gospel. Over the years he spoke to thousands of people. In addition to preaching, he also healed the sick. In fact, the Bible says that "God worked unusual miracles by the hands of Paul" (Acts 19:11).

One day seven brothers, sons of a Jewish priest named Sceva, came to hear Paul. They noticed that whenever Paul spoke to someone who was sick, he used Jesus' name, and the sick person was healed. They wondered if the words were magic and would work for them, too. They decided to try it out.

In the crowd there was a man who seemed to be possessed by a demon. Sceva's sons walked up to this man, used a phrase similar to what Paul had said, and told the demon to leave.

The brothers were in for a big surprise! The demon did not leave. Instead it talked back to them. It said, "Jesus I know, and Paul I know; but who are you?" Then the man attacked them.

That day those brothers learned an important lesson. We should use the name of God in a reverent, courteous, and respectful way—not as a joke or a curse, but as the precious name of our Savior. The brothers weren't able to heal the man because they misused Jesus' name. God did not reveal His power because they had not asked reverently and prayerfully.

The demon was afraid of Jesus and Paul because it knew their power came from God. But the demon wasn't at all afraid of Sceva's sons, because they weren't connected to God, the power source. I wonder—is the devil afraid of you?

72

COURTESY AND RESPECT

No More Pain

Dr. James Simpson hated having to watch surgeries when he was in medical school. The poor patients were awake throughout the entire surgery. At that time, surgery was used only as a last resort. And many patients chose to risk death rather than have surgery.

Dr. Simpson wanted to find a way to make the patients sleep safely through the surgery so they wouldn't feel pain. He ran many tests and experiments over the years, often putting his own life in danger. Finally he discovered a way for people to sleep through surgery. Many thousands of people have him to thank for saving their lives by making surgery easier.

God's heroes respect other people and care about their needs. They do what they can to ease the suffering of those around them. God is anxious for us to make life better for others here on earth. And when He comes to take us to heaven, He will take away all pain and suffering for good.

Show mercy and compassion everyone to his brother.
Zechariah 7:9.

COURTESY AND RESPECT

Mother of the North

Let nothing be done through selfish ambition or conceit, but in lowliness of mind let each esteem others better than himself.
Philippians 2:3.

When Harriet Pullen came to Alaska, she had only $7. Her children were living with relatives in another state until she could raise the money to send for them. Harriet was anxious to get a job and start earning some money.

She first worked as a cook in a gold-mining camp. It was hard work, cooking for hungry men. Finally Harriet was able to get together enough money to bring her sons to live with her. Then she raised enough money to send for her horses, which she eventually sold or hired out to pull freight.

Later she opened her home, Pullen House, to boarders. She was so well liked for her kindness and good food that she became known as the mother of the North.

Mrs. Pullen knew a secret of being a hero for God: She took care of people's physical needs in addition to sharing the gospel with them.

Would you be willing to share something in order for someone else to eat? See what you can do today to help take care of someone in need.

COURTESY AND RESPECT

Self-centered or others-centered?

Laban is one of the important characters in the book of Genesis. He helped to arrange Isaac's marriage to Rebekah, and he also arranged Jacob's marriages to Leah and Rachel.

One thing that seems obvious from these stories is that Laban was selfish. Every time he's mentioned, the story shows that Laban was looking out for himself instead of others. When he arranged the marriages, he made sure that he became wealthier. And he tried to cheat his son-in-law, Jacob, many times.

Are you a little bit like Laban? None of us like to think that we are selfish. But we've all been selfish at one time or another. Maybe we didn't want to share, or perhaps we've tried to use people or things to our advantage.

It's never right to use people. It's not a good idea to play with someone's emotions. It only hurts them and leaves you feeling empty. Don't be self-centered, as Laban was. Ask Jesus to help you to be others-centered, as He is.

Let each of us please his neighbor for his good. . . . For even Christ did not please Himself.
Romans 15:2, 3.

COURTESY AND RESPECT

9
MARCH

God is greater than man.
Job 33:12.

A Good Leader

Have you ever heard of George Washington? That's right—he was the first president of the United States. He is also known for being a brave man and a good leader.

Many of the people who lived in America in the 1700s were from England; their ruler was the king of England. Many of them wanted America to be a separate country; they wanted to be free from England. England didn't want to lose America, so there was a war—the Revolutionary War.

Before he became the first president, George Washington was a military leader during this war. His heroic leadership helped the American soldiers to win many battles, and he became one of the most loved men in American history. Even today, hundreds of years later, people respect him for his wise and brave leadership.

God is a far wiser and braver leader than George Washington was. He will help us in our fight against Satan. He is worthy of our respect, and He'll lead us to victory.

COURTESY AND RESPECT

A Respectable Woman

In Deborah's time women were not treated the way they are today. They couldn't hold a position in government; they couldn't go to school. Basically, they weren't allowed to do anything but get married and have babies.

That's what makes Deborah so interesting. You can read about her in Judges 4. Not only was this woman a leader (she was the only woman judge in Israel's history), but she was a prophetess. Deborah was respected by the leaders of the army; in fact, they respected her so much, they wanted her to be with them when they went into battle. They even went into battle when she told them to go.

What was it about her that commanded such respect? The people knew that God was with her, and they wanted her around because she was a good leader.

Deborah had character traits that helped her to be a good leader. But the most important trait she had was that she was willing to let God use her. Will you use the traits God has given you to be a hero for Him?

Now Deborah, a prophetess, the wife of Lapidoth, was judging Israel at that time.

Judges 4:4.

COURTESY AND RESPECT

11
MARCH

We should live soberly, righteously, and godly in the present age.

Titus 2:12.

Hard to Be Different

What if you were really, really good at playing a game, but no one wanted to play with you because of your skin color? How would that make you feel? It wouldn't be fair, would it?

That's what happened to Jackie Robinson. He played football, baseball, and basketball, and he ran track. He was thought to be the best athlete in the United States at that time. However, just because he wasn't White, he wasn't allowed to play in the major leagues. Today that seems silly; people of all different races play in many different sports now. But that's the way it was then.

In 1947 Jackie became the first African-American to play major-league baseball in that century. Everyone was watching to see how he would do. At first many people in the crowds were rude. They called him names, booed him when he came onto the field, and made life hard for him. But people gradually began to realize that he was just like everyone else. He was a good player and a good sport who earned the respect of players and fans.

It's hard to be different. Everyone wants to be liked and have friends. Christians live differently from many people in the world. Other people may tease us or call us names because we are different. But if we ask, God will help us, His heroes, to do our best in the game of life.

COURTESY AND RESPECT

The Little Woman Who Started a War

Harriet Beecher Stowe hated slavery. She wanted to stop it, but she was just one woman. What could she do? She thought about it and decided that since she enjoyed writing, she would write a book. She wrote a story about slavery called *Uncle Tom's Cabin*.

Once the book was printed and people started reading it, they got angry. They weren't angry at Harriett; they were angry about slavery. Her book told the story of a slave and his family and how badly they were treated. Now a lot of people wanted to do something to stop slavery.

But there were others who wanted to keep slavery. They were angry about this talk of taking away their slaves and their way of life. Because of the different opinions in the North and the South, the Civil War started.

When President Lincoln met Mrs. Stowe, he said, "So this is the little woman who started this great war." Although it wasn't the only thing the two sides disagreed on, slavery became a big issue in the Civil War. When the war was finally over, the slaves were freed.

Despite the way other people felt, Mrs. Stowe respected the people who were slaves. People didn't like her for it, but she didn't care.

Are you friendly to only the cool kids or to those who are your friends? Or, as God's hero, do you show courtesy and respect to everyone—even the ones other people don't like?

Accept one another, then, just as Christ accepted you, in order to bring praise to God.
Romans 15:7, NIV.

COURTESY AND RESPECT

Who's Weird?

A man who has friends must himself be friendly.
Proverbs 18:24.

Many people on the crowded dock were crying as the Victoria pulled away. The men on the boat were planning to sail around the world, but everyone knew the earth was flat. Once they reached the edge, the boat would just fall off into space. A few women wailed at the thought that they would never see their loved ones again.

Of course, the world isn't flat. We know now that it is round. But it was the brave Ferdinand Magellan and his men on the *Victoria* who proved it. Eighteen of Magellan's crew of about 260 were the first people to sail all the way around the world. (Magellan died before the trip was complete.)

On their voyage they discovered a new island. They thought the people of the island looked strange because they were very tall, had big feet, and didn't wear clothes. Magellan and his men had never seen such big feet before! So they called the people the Patagones, which meant the big-feeters, and they called the island Patagonia, which meant the land of big feet.

The people of Patagonia thought the Europeans were strange, too. They were so short. And they covered their bodies with such strange things. And their feet were so small. How could they stand?

Even though they were different, Magellan and his men became friends with the Patagonians. They also tried to make friends with the people on other islands that they visited. They learned much from all of their new friends.

Just because you think someone is weird doesn't mean they are weird. You might seem weird to them, too! Everyone is different, and that's OK. Make friends with someone different today, and see what you can learn from them.

COURTESY AND RESPECT

Spared by Kindness

The men came from the hills and asked Nabal for some food. Nabal knew who the men were; they had protected some of his workers. But he didn't want to share, so he told the men no. When they went back to camp and told their leader, David, what had happened, he was angry. During that time it was the custom that any traveler who stopped by should be fed, and Nabal was very rude to tell them no.

David gathered about 400 of his men together, and they started back down the hill to kill Nabal and all the men in his camp because of his rudeness.

The workers that David had protected heard about Nabal's rudeness; they knew David would be angry. They hurried to tell Nabal's wife, Abigail, what had happened. She knew it could cause big problems. Quickly she had the servants load enough food and drink for David's men onto donkeys. Then Abigail and the servants headed off to meet them.

When she met David, he was still angry. She apologized for her husband's actions and asked forgiveness, then gave him the food and drink she had brought for his men. Her courtesy and respect took David by surprise. Because of her kindness he didn't kill Nabal or the men in his camp.

Abigail knew that her husband had been rude to David and his men. He should have at least shown them the courtesy and respect that was the custom of their day. We too should treat everyone we meet with courtesy and respect, regardless of who they are or how they have treated us.

Blessed is the Lord God of Israel, who sent you this day to meet me! And blessed is your advice and blessed are you.
1 Samuel 25:32, 33.

COURTESY AND RESPECT

All Things New

Behold, I make all things new.
Revelation 21:5.

Edgar Helms and his wife started out simply. They collected old, torn clothes from their friends, mended them and made them as good as new, then gave the clothes to the poor.

Soon they had more clothes coming in than they could fix. They had to hire people to help. They decided to hire some of the poor people they were helping. This way they were able to double the help they gave to people—they gave them clothes and a job.

Mr. and Mrs. Helms started what is known today as Goodwill Industries. They made the clothes as good as new so that they could be used again, and they helped the people feel as good as new by giving them jobs.

Goodwill Industries helps thousands of people every year. By making clothes like new again, they help people who might not otherwise be able to afford new clothes.

God promises that when He comes again, He will make all things new. He'll make this old earth beautiful again. But even more important, He'll make you and me new, so that we won't sin again. I think that sounds pretty good. What about you?

COURTESY AND RESPECT

Helped by Helping

*To the righteous,
good shall be
repaid.*

Proverbs 13:21.

Yesterday we read about Mr. and Mrs. Helms and how they helped people by starting Goodwill Industries. Today I want to tell you a true story of how they helped people.

A note was on the secretary's desk to please send someone to clean a room of Grandma M's attic. She was sick and couldn't do it herself.

While the secretary was reading the note, a woman who had a sick husband and no wood for their fire came in. The secretary sent the woman to clean Grandma M's attic; she would be paid with firewood.

No sooner had she left than a man with torn and dirty pants came in. He was offered a new pair if he would chop wood for the woman who was now scrubbing Grandma M's attic. So off he went to chop wood.

Soon another woman came in. Her children couldn't go to school, because it was winter and they didn't have shoes. She was given the job of sewing the pants of the man who was chopping the wood for the woman who was scrubbing the attic of Grandma M.

Later that day a shoemaker came in. He needed to work to support his wife and six children. So he mended shoes for the woman who was sewing the pants for the man who was chopping the wood for the woman who was scrubbing Grandma M's attic.

And on and on it went. Everyone helped each other, and by doing so, they were helped themselves.

If you want to be God's hero, think of some ways you can help others today. You might even be helped by helping.

COURTESY AND RESPECT

17

MARCH

A Thankful Heart

And one of them, when he saw that he was healed, returned, and with a loud voice glorified God, and fell down on his face at His feet, giving Him thanks.

Luke 17:15, 16.

The 10 men didn't dare approach Jesus, so they called to Him from a distance. Because they had leprosy, they were thought to be unclean. They had been ordered to stay away from everyone else. The 10 men asked Jesus to make them clean and heal them from their leprosy.

Jesus told them to go and show themselves to the priest, who could announce that they were clean. That announcement would allow them to go back to their families and jobs. The men, trusting that they would be healed, ran toward the Temple.

As the group ran, one of them stopped. He realized that he'd forgotten to say thank You to Jesus. He wanted the priest to see that he was clean, but he had to say thank You to the Man who had given him his life back.

So while the other nine ran ahead to the Temple, the tenth man ran back to Jesus. The Bible tells us he was so happy he "fell down on his face at His [Jesus'] feet." Jesus was happy that the man had remembered to say thank You.

It makes God happy when we are polite. A hero for God remembers to say "please" and "thank you" and is polite rather than rude and ungrateful.

COURTESY AND RESPECT

Missionary to Her own Country

When she was young, Mary dreamed of becoming a missionary to Africa. But as she got older, she realized that the African-Americans in her own country needed an education and needed to learn about Jesus as much as the people in Africa did.

Mary McLeod Bethune was born to parents who had been slaves before the Civil War. She spent her life trying to make sure that African-Americans had the same freedoms as other Americans.

Mary was one of the few African-Americans of her time who had a formal education, and she believed that education would help other African-Americans have a better life. She worked in Georgia, South Carolina, Florida, and Illinois. She opened schools, visited prisoners, fed the homeless, and worked for equality for all people.

Sometimes God will ask people to travel to faraway countries to be missionaries, but other times He uses people right where they are. Will you let God make a missionary out of you?

Go into all the world and preach the gospel to every creature.

Mark 16:15.

COURTESY AND RESPECT

The Lord God Made Them

So God created man in His own image; in the image of God He created him; male and female He created them.

Genesis 1:27.

James Herriot loved animals. He spent many years working as a veterinarian. He traveled the countryside of England taking care of animals. Horses, cows, dogs, cats—it didn't matter. If there was an animal that needed him, Dr. Herriot came to help. The stories he wrote about his experiences as a vet have helped many people to appreciate animals more too.

Think about all the different kinds of animals God made: giraffes, dogs, squirrels, deer, horses, polar bears, penguins, koalas. He created them large and small, furry and smooth—He definitely used His creativity when He made the animals.

God also used His creativity to make humans. He spoke, and the animals appeared, but He created Adam by forming him with His own hands.

Always remember that whether you are big or small, you are created in God's image and are very special.

COURTESY AND RESPECT

Vaccinated

Polio was a terrible disease that made thousands of people sick every year. Many of the people who got polio either died or became disabled. Everyone was very afraid of polio.

Until Jonas Salk came to the rescue. He worked at the Virus Research Lab at the University of Pittsburgh. After about five years of research he found a vaccine. Dr. Salk was so sure it would work that he tried the vaccine on himself and his family. If he was right, he and his family would not get sick. If he was wrong, they were all at risk of getting the terrible disease.

Thankfully, he was right! None of his family got sick. His discovery was the beginning of the cure for the dreaded disease. Because of Dr. Salk's work, we don't have to be afraid of polio anymore.

Our planet has the disease of sin, but Jesus has offered us the vaccine of salvation. If we take the vaccine, if we accept Jesus as our Savior, we don't have to worry about the lasting effects of sin.

The soul who sins shall die. But if a man is just . . . he shall surely live!
Ezekiel 18:4-9.

COURTESY AND RESPECT

21
MARCH

A Shocking Friendship

For you were bought at a price; therefore glorify God in your body and in your spirit, which are God's.

1 Corinthians 6:20.

Cliff worked as an apprentice with an electrician named Marlin at Ford Motor Company. One day, while they were working on a machine, Cliff got down on his knees to check voltages. They were running tests on the machine to see why it wasn't working. It was routine stuff; they did this all the time.

All of a sudden, Marlin grabbed Cliff and jerked him backwards. At first Cliff wondered what in the world had gotten into Marlin. Why had Marlin interrupted his work? Then he realized that Marlin had just saved his life. Cliff's head had come very close to touching a piece of metal bar that had electricity running through it. If he had touched it, the shock would have killed him instantly.

It is natural for us to try to help when we see someone about to do something dangerous. However, are we as quick to help when we see friends doing something they shouldn't? Perhaps we tell ourselves that it isn't a big deal.

It is a big deal. If you are a true friend, you will help your friends avoid all things that are bad for them. You will do what you can to keep them from making bad decisions about smoking, drinking, and doing drugs.

Ask God to help you make good decisions and to help your friends make good choices too.

COURTESY AND RESPECT

First Lady of Families

And this commandment we have from Him: that he who loves God must love his brother also.

1 John 4:21.

Do you know what a first lady is? No, I'm not talking about Eve, although she was actually the very first lady. A first lady is the wife of a president. Often when people talk of the first lady, they mean the wife of the president of the United States. As I'm writing this, the first lady is Laura Bush. She is the wife of President George W. Bush.

Mrs. Bush has worked with children for many years as a teacher and librarian, and she knows how important it is for kids to learn to read and go to school. She works hard to make sure that all kids get that chance.

Mrs. Bush also works hard to help people understand the importance of families. She hopes that families will spend time doing fun things together. She hopes that families will teach their children that everyone should be treated with kindness and respect.

Heroes for God love their families and treat everyone they meet with kindness and respect. Can you think of something fun to do with your family this week? Ask your parents to help you plan it; then go have fun!

COURTESY AND RESPECT

23
MARCH

Granted Mercy

Therefore be merciful, just as your Father also is merciful.
Luke 6:36.

The Civil War had been long and terrible. For four long years the North and the South had fought—sometimes brother fought against brother, friend against friend. Many thousands of brave men had died on both sides, and the country was tired. Everyone wanted the war to be over.

General Ulysses S. Grant and General Robert E. Lee were both respected army men. General Grant was the leader of the Northern Army, and General Lee was the leader for the South. They had faced each other in battle before, but finally Grant's army had Lee's army trapped.

General Grant wrote on a piece of paper that General Lee and his men were free to go if they gave up. They wouldn't even have to go to jail for betraying their country. On April 9, 1865, at Appomattox Court House in Virginia, General Lee surrendered. The war was finally over, and the United States were united again.

Grant could have demanded that Lee and his men be tried for treason and even executed, but he showed mercy to them.

God shows us mercy when we accept Jesus into our hearts. We won't have to pay the penalty for our sins. We can live in heaven with God and our family and friends who have accepted Him.

Because we have been shown mercy, God expects us to show mercy to others too. Will you accept His terms of surrender?

COURTESY AND RESPECT

A Member in God's Gang

When he was growing up, Jose was part of a gang. His own brother was killed by a gang when Jose was young.

Jose came from a bad neighborhood, but he didn't know it. He had a hard family life, but he didn't let it hold him down. Everything around him influenced him, but it didn't force him to behave a certain way.

Jose fell in love with Jesus and let Him lead. That decision changed his life. When he met Jesus, he didn't want to be part of a gang anymore.

Jose still loves to work with young people, and he tells them how much God loves them.

Jesus was from a bad neighborhood too. People judged Him because of where He was from. They didn't think anyone good could come from the town where He lived.

Even though Jesus was from a bad neighborhood, He was perfect. We should never judge anyone by where they live. God has heroes from everywhere, and He loves us all the same, no matter where we're from.

Can anything good come out of Nazareth?
John 1:46.

COURTESY AND RESPECT

93

25
MARCH

We should remember the poor.
Galatians 2:10.

How a Camera Fed a Family

How do you think a camera could help a widow with seven kids get food? Would you like to take a guess?

Dorothea Lange was a famous photographer during a time called the Great Depression. There were few jobs and even less money. Almost everyone was very poor.

Dorothea took her camera to a field in California. The people working in the field were called migrant workers; they moved from place to place to find work. The workers were so very poor that Dorothea wished she could help. She was just a photographer. What could she do?

She started taking pictures. She took pictures of the people as they worked and tried to survive.

One of her photos was called *Migrant Mother*. It was a picture of a widow working on the farm trying to feed her seven children. The picture was published in a San Francisco newspaper, and when people saw it, they wanted to help. Money and food were sent to the farm where the woman and her children were staying.

Even though Dorothea worried that she was just a photographer, she helped however she could.

Look for creative ways to help those around you. There's always something you can do.

COURTESY AND RESPECT

What I Like About You

Is there someone you really don't like? Maybe a bully at school, or a grumpy neighbor, or someone who goes to your church? What about in your family? Or are you one of those children who never fight with your brothers and sisters?

George Vandeman knew that sometimes adults don't like each other and get into arguments, just as kids do. It made George sad to see people argue over their differences, so he created a new television program called *What I Like About . . .*

Usually people from different religious groups focus on their differences. In this program Pastor Vandeman helped people see what they had in common so they wouldn't fight as much. If they got along, they could work together to help tell people about Jesus.

There will always be people who are hard to get along with, but God's heroes will do their best to focus on the positive instead of the negative. Who knows—you might even find something you like about them!

A servant of the Lord must not quarrel but be gentle to all.
2 Timothy 2:24.

COURTESY AND RESPECT

27
MARCH

*For there is
no distinction
between Jew
and Greek.
For "whoever
calls on the name
of the Lord shall
be saved."*
Romans 10:12, 13.

Justice for All

Almost 200 years ago, when Susan B. Anthony was young, women had few rights. They couldn't vote, go to college, own property, or be doctors or lawyers. Men could do all of those things, but women were not allowed to. And that's not all—at the jobs women were allowed to do, they earned only a quarter for every dollar a man was paid.

As Susan grew up, she saw that things weren't fair. She wanted to fix them. But because she was a woman and had no rights to start with, it was very hard.

Many people didn't want things to change. They argued with her, threw things at her, attacked her, and even had her thrown in jail—just for wanting to be treated like a human being and a child of God.

But she kept trying. And because of Susan B. Anthony and people like her, today women in the United States of America have the same rights as men do.

In God's eyes it doesn't matter whether you are a boy or girl, skinny or fat, popular or unpopular. It doesn't matter where you live or what your house looks like. He loves us all the same. We're all His children, and He asks us to treat one another with respect.

COURTESY AND RESPECT

God's Team

S am Walton was just a guy from the South who liked working with people. He owned several stores, and the people who worked for him liked him a lot. Sam believed it was important to give his customers what they wanted and needed and to make it cost as little as possible. His businesses started to grow.

Sam took those two things—happy employees and happy customers—and combined them with the way he ran his businesses. And that made him one of the richest men in the world. What's the name of his store? You may have heard of it before: Wal-Mart.

Sam knew the importance of treating people right. One of his favorite sayings was "Individuals don't win; teams do." You may be able to accomplish some things by yourself, but if you work with others as a team and ask God to guide you, you'll go much further. Will you be a player on God's team today?

Now whatever you request of me, I will do for you.
2 Samuel 19:38.

Sharing His Gifts

*Freely ye
have received,
freely give.*
Matthew 10:8.

Barry Black grew up in a poor family in Baltimore, Maryland, with seven brothers and sisters. His dad wasn't around much, but the people in his church were good role models. His church friends liked to help, and because of their generosity, Barry and his siblings were able to go to academy and college.

After receiving his first college degree, Barry went back for five more. Many people never get even one degree, but Barry knew that it was important to learn as much as he could, and he did his best for God.

When Barry got out of college, he joined the Navy. He wasn't a sailor, though; he became a chaplain. He worked on boats helping sailors with their problems and teaching them about Jesus.

Through the years he was promoted to become the head chaplain of the entire U.S. Navy. Then, in 2003, he became chaplain to the U.S. Senate in Washington, D.C. He is the first African-American and the first Seventh-day Adventist to have that job.

Because of the help that was given to him by his church when he was young, Barry now uses his talents and money to help young people.

God is very generous with us. He wakes us up in the morning, gives us sunshine, air, homes, families, pets, toys—the list goes on and on. God loves to give us good things. He asks us to share the good things He's given us by being generous with others too.

COURTESY AND RESPECT

cotton-pickin' Machine

Picking cotton was hard work. For many years slaves were put to work in the cotton fields to pull the fluffy white stuff from the plants. They spent their days bent over in the hot sun, dragging heavy bags of cotton behind them as they went down the rows.

Once the cotton was gathered, the slaves had to sit and pick the seeds out of it. The process was long and slow.

Eli Whitney thought there must be a better way to pick the seeds out of cotton. After thinking about it for a while, he invented a machine called the cotton gin. Eli's machine picked the seeds out of cotton so quickly that in one hour it could do the same work that several slaves could do in a whole day.

The Holy Spirit works in the same way as Eli's cotton gin. If we allow Him to comb through our lives, He'll pick out all the bad stuff and leave a clean, pure life behind.

The fruit of the Spirit is love, joy, peace, longsuffering, kindness, goodness, faithfulness, gentleness, self-control. Against such there is no law.
Galatians 5:22, 23.

COURTESY AND RESPECT

In Need of a friend

Let brotherly love continue.

Hebrews 13:1.

Tito has autism. Children with autism have trouble learning, in addition to other problems. Because his autism is so severe, Tito can barely talk, but he loves to write. Even though he can't communicate by speaking, Tito writes beautiful poetry. His poems have been published in books, and he's been on television.

Doctors used to think that people like Tito weren't smart, because they couldn't talk and they were so different. But Tito has showed them that that isn't true. He has said in his writing that he hopes one day people will just be people. He hopes for a world in which people aren't thought of as being normal or weird—a world in which everyone is just a person who needs a friend.

That's the way Jesus treated people when He was on earth. No matter who they were, He treated each person the same. He was a friend to everyone and showed love to everyone equally.

Do you know someone who is different? Be a hero for God today and treat that person the same way you treat everyone else.

COURTESY AND RESPECT

Missing You

Have you ever missed someone? Maybe a friend moved away or one of your parents had to go on a business trip. It's hard to be separated from people you love, isn't it? Even if you get to talk to them on the phone or send them an e-mail, it's not the same as hugging them in person.

Did you know that Jesus misses you? We can talk with Him in prayer anytime, but it's not the same as it will be to hug Him in person when we get to heaven.

When Jesus went to heaven, He told the disciples that He was going to prepare a place for the people who love Him. And He promised that He'd come back. It's been a long time since Jesus made that promise, and I believe it won't be very much longer until He comes to take us to heaven with Him. Do you ever wonder what's taking so long?

Sometimes when we see bad things going on, it's hard to understand why God lets them happen. Why doesn't He just come and get us right now?

God will wait until He knows that every single person has decided whether or not to follow Him. And before He comes, He also wants us to see just how bad sin and Satan are so that we know for sure that God's way is better.

Even though He loves us, wants to be with us, and has the power to wipe out sin, He is waiting for us to make our own choices. Now, that's patience.

The Lord is not slow in keeping his promise, as some understand slowness. He is patient with you, not wanting anyone to perish, but everyone to come to repentance.
2 Peter 3:9, NIV.

PATIENCE AND PERSEVERANCE

The Man Who Wouldn't Give Up

I can do everything through him who gives me strength.
Philippians 4:13, NIV.

No one thought William Eustis would live long enough to grow up. Back in those days the doctors in his little town didn't know how to treat tuberculosis of the hip, and his family was too poor to pay for treatment even if they had. The disease left him unable to walk, and for five years he lay with nothing to do but look out the window at the other children playing. It made him sad to think that he couldn't play with them and that he might never be well enough to get a job.

Even though he was sick, William wanted to go to school. Eventually he was able to get out of bed, and his father gave him permission to go to school. William took his crutches and clothes and set out for college. He not only made it through college at Wesleyan University; he also finished a law degree at Columbia Law School. Eventually he became a lawyer with John R. Putnam, who had been impressed by William's ability to work his way through school.

No one thought this boy would live long enough to grow up, yet he outlived most of his college classmates. He felt that his biggest achievement was saving up enough money to fulfill his life's dream: He donated $1.5 million and 65 acres of land in the suburbs of Minneapolis, Minnesota, to build a school and hospital for children with disabilities like his. There was enough money so that both places could be run without any cost to the public. He said, "There is no greater service than helping those who cannot help in return, and I am glad that I can do my bit of service in brightening the lives of helpless children."

Despite his disability, Mr. Eustis accomplished great things with patience, perseverance, and God's help. We can too.

PATIENCE AND PERSEVERANCE

Why Me?

Job had it all: wealth, family, possessions. Then, in a very short time, he lost it all. His oxen, donkeys, and camels were stolen, his children died in a freak accident, and Job found himself covered from head to toe in painful sores. He didn't understand why all this was happening to him, but he still trusted God.

Job's wife and friends weren't very helpful. His wife told him to curse God and die. His friends told him that he was being punished for something he did wrong. Job knew that wasn't the case, although he couldn't figure out why all this was happening.

Job never did find out the answers to all his questions. But he did learn that God is in charge. Eventually Job got his health back. He and his wife had more children. And Job became even more wealthy than before.

We may not understand why things happen to us or our loved ones, but we don't have to. We just need to trust that God is in control and, through faith, persevere with God's help.

Though He slay me, yet will I trust Him.
Job 13:15.

PATIENCE AND PERSEVERANCE

103

old Discoverer

I am . . . the Bright and Morning Star.
Revelation 22:16.

Galileo loved experimenting. Whenever he had a new idea about science, he would set about proving it with an experiment.

His greatest discovery came in 1609. Galileo heard that an eyeglass maker's assistant had discovered that if you hold one glass lens in front of another and look through them, things appear larger. He tried it and saw that it worked. Before long he had fashioned two larger lenses into the first telescope. Soon he was making telescopes to sell. He made one for himself and called it "Old Discoverer." It made things appear to be 33 times nearer.

One great night Galileo turned his telescope to the sky. He was amazed at what he saw! Instead of seeing a handful of stars, he saw thousands and thousands of them. He saw that the Milky Way was actually a huge band of stars and that Jupiter had moons moving around it, just as our moon moves around the earth. He felt very small.

Since that night hundreds of years ago, we have learned that the universe is much, much bigger than anyone, even Galileo, ever imagined.

The Bible is like a telescope. The more we read the Bible, the closer it brings us to God. It can reveal a God much bigger and more exciting than we have ever imagined!

PATIENCE AND PERSEVERANCE

Patience Pays

Love is patient.
1 Corinthians 13:4,
NIV.

When Ann agreed to teach the children's Sabbath school at her church, she didn't know what she was in for! In her class were twin boys with a lot of energy. Every Sabbath it was a different challenge: they didn't pay attention, they wouldn't sit still, they got into things without permission, and they kept the other children from listening. These boys were so active that some weeks they would crawl under the pews in the sanctuary and have rolling races, bumping into people's legs and generally disturbing the service.

However, Ann was gentle, kind, and patient with the boys. She never gave up. Each week she greeted them with a smile, and eventually her patience paid off. The lessons she taught them in Sabbath school stuck with them, and now they both are adults who love Jesus.

There may be people in our lives who seem hopeless, but we should never give up on them. In much the same way, Jesus is patient with us, even though we do things we shouldn't. He loves us no matter what.

PATIENCE AND PERSEVERANCE

6
APRIL

A Happy Man

et's try an experiment. Try to pick up this book without using your hands. It's hard, isn't it? Now try to carry it across the room without using your feet to walk on. Impossible? Not for Michael Dowling.

Michael lost both hands and both feet to frostbite in a blizzard when he was a teenager. Yet he became a bank president, the president of the Yellowstone Trail Association, and a famous public speaker. He was also a husband and father, a hunter and a hiker. He even learned to roller-skate!

Michael said, "I knew that if I treated myself as if I were different from other people, the world would follow my example." So he decided that he would do everything that everyone else could do. He went to school and became a teacher, often walking to school in the snow on his artificial legs. Later in life he became a school principal, then a superintendent of schools.

Michael proved that disabilities are more a state of mind than of body. Many people who don't have any physical disabilities cannot—or will not—do many of the things he did. It is your mind that counts. It's your brain and your willingness to let God use you that will help you make a difference.

Michael may not have had a whole body, but what he had was strong and healthy, and he used it as best he could. That's all God asks of us—to do what we can with whatever we have. If we give our lives and hearts to Him, He'll take care of the rest!

PATIENCE AND PERSEVERANCE

Skating Around the Truth

Everything is possible for him who believes.
Mark 9:23, NIV.

Tenley Albright wanted to do two things in her life: become a surgeon, like her father, and win a gold medal in figure skating. People told her just to go to medical school and not worry about skating, but she really wanted to do both. And she did both in a surprisingly short time.

Tenley became the first American woman to win the figure-skating world championship. She also was the first person ever to win the triple crown—the world, United States, and North American championships (all in the same year).

A few months later she entered college. Even though she had a very busy schedule of classes, practice, and homework, she graduated after just three years. Then she went on to Harvard Medical School, where she was one of only six women in her class of 130 people.

While practicing for the Olympics, Tenley had a bad fall. Her left skate cut deeply into her right ankle. She had to have surgery, and she suffered from quite a bit of pain. But in spite of this she skated beautifully, and she became the first American woman to win the gold medal for figure skating.

Her hard work paid off. Tenley was able to achieve both of her goals.

Do you have any goals you want to reach in your life? Don't let people tell you it can't be done. Pray that God will lead and guide you; with His help, you can do anything!

PATIENCE AND PERSEVERANCE

8
APRIL

*Whatever your
hand finds
to do, do it
with your might.*

Ecclesiastes 9:10.

Reach for the Stars

Since she was the youngest of three children, Mae Jemison got picked on a lot. Her siblings loved to tease her. So Mae learned to put up with teasing without getting angry. She learned never to give up and to do her best at whatever she was doing, no matter what others were saying or doing. Those things would come in handy later in her life.

As an adult Mae went to school and became a doctor. She traveled to other countries to help the people there and to search for ways to stop diseases. When she came back to the United States, she worked hard as a doctor, but her real dream was to be an astronaut. She wanted to go into space.

Mae's first application to NASA was denied. She was so disappointed! Two years later she tried again, and this time NASA accepted her application. She was going to live her dream of being an astronaut in space.

Mae could have given up when her first application to NASA wasn't accepted; however, because she didn't, she became the first African-American female astronaut. She had a dream and she worked toward it, even though other people didn't think she could reach it.

The Bible tells us to do whatever we find to do with all of our heart. Don't give up. If you have a dream, go for it. Work toward it with all your heart, and ask God to help you reach for the stars.

PATIENCE AND PERSEVERANCE

The Long-ago Prayer

During the Great Depression in the 1930s most families had very little money; sometimes they couldn't even afford to buy food. Wayne's family was no exception. Wayne left home when he was very young and took whatever odd jobs he could find. He worked for his meals and for a place to stay. Life was hard, and he learned to rely on no one but himself.

As he grew older, Wayne was able to find better jobs, and soon he was supporting a family. His wife, Harriett, was a Christian, and she took their three children to church every week.

Harriett and the children prayed for Wayne. Through the years he would go to church now and then for special occasions. His family was always so glad when he came to church, and they prayed for him every day, but he never made a public decision for God. Until many years later.

One Sabbath morning, after his children were grown up with families and homes of their own, Wayne announced that he wanted to be baptized. He was 87 years old, and he wanted to show that he had chosen Jesus as his Savior.

It was a beautiful day, both inside the church and out, when Wayne was baptized. Harriett, all three of their children, and most of their grandchildren came to help him celebrate the special day. At the age of 87 Wayne was starting a brand-new life as a Christian.

God is patient with us, and will give us every possible chance to make a decision for Him. He is always listening to our prayers, even if we don't see immediate results.

For the eyes of the Lord are on the righteous and his ears are attentive to their prayer.
1 Peter 3:12, NIV.

PATIENCE AND PERSEVERANCE

The Girl Who Couldn't Walk

Let us run with perseverance the race marked out for us.
Hebrews 12:1, NIV.

Although Wilma Rudolph was tiny when she was born, weighing only about four pounds, she was born into a huge family. She was the twentieth of 22 children. As a girl she suffered from many illnesses, including polio, and she wasn't able to walk until she was 8 years old. Even then, she was able to walk only with the help of a leg brace.

When she was 11, she traded in her brace for corrective shoes. But she started taking the shoes off to play basketball barefoot with her family. By the time she was in high school, she was good at both basketball and track. And at age 16 she qualified for the 1956 Olympic team, where she won a bronze medal for running.

After the 1956 Olympics Wilma went to Tennessee State College. She qualified for the Olympics again in 1960, where she won gold medals and set world records for running.

The girl who couldn't walk until she was 8 became an Olympic gold medal winner and world record breaker through patience and perseverance. She didn't just start running one day. She practiced and worked hard at it day by day until she had achieved her goals.

Our lives can be the same way. We may not be the best at something right away, but if we keep at it, with God's help we can win the race of life!

PATIENCE AND PERSEVERANCE

Lazy Lynn

Whatever you do, do it heartily, as to the Lord and not to men.
Colossians 3:23.

Lynn had a bad habit. Oh, she was a pretty nice person, but her habit was bad. She procrastinated; she put things off. She'd done it all her life.

When Lynn was a girl, she put off doing her chores. In school, she put off her homework until the last minute. Then, in a rush, she'd pull something sloppy together and turn it in. She could have done better work if she had tried.

Lynn meant well; she wanted to do better. But then she would get sidetracked playing with her friends, watching TV, or working on another project. She had a hard time being disciplined and getting things done.

As God's heroes, we should always do everything to the best of our ability—as if we were doing it for God Himself. If there is a big project we have to do, we should pace ourselves and do it one step at a time in order to finish what we started.

Don't be a procrastinator like Lynn. Putting things off is much harder in the long run. And it causes more stress than sticking to a plan and doing things over time. Be a hero for God instead and do your best in everything you do.

PATIENCE AND PERSEVERANCE

12
APRIL

So stand fast in the Lord, beloved.

Philippians 4:1.

failproof

Osama bin Laden hated the United States because the people who live there enjoy so many freedoms. He said that God is not a God of freedom, but is harsh and unforgiving. He told his followers that they were allowed to kill people who are different. We know that he was wrong; that is not God's way. God loves everyone the same—no matter what their religion or where they live.

President George W. Bush knew that Osama bin Laden was wrong, and he promised to punish the terrorists for the bad things they did. President Bush promised the world, "We will not tire, we will not falter, we will not fail." The people fighting the war on terror promised that they wouldn't give up, no matter how hard it became, until Osama bin Laden and other men like him were stopped.

God's heroes don't give up either. Keep your eyes on Jesus and stand for what's right no matter what. With His help, you will not fail.

PATIENCE AND PERSEVERANCE

Strong Legs

*Hold on
to what
you have
until I come.*
Revelation 2:25, NIV.

Raymond Ewry spent a lot of time exercising his legs. Because he had had polio, he had to use a wheelchair. However, day by day his legs became a little stronger because of the exercises. Eventually he was able to walk.

Then he started jumping to continue building up the strength in his legs. His legs became so strong that he became the greatest competitor ever in the standing jump event at the Olympics.

Raymond won a record 10 Olympic gold medals in his events. Three of those medals were won in one day. The boy who had been stuck in a wheelchair became one of the greatest track and field competitors of his day.

Raymond's legs became stronger because he worked hard at exercising them. He didn't give up when he got tired or when his muscles ached or when it got boring.

As heroes for God we should exercise our faith muscles every day so that they will become strong. Don't give up when things get hard, and with God's help you can stand strong on your faith.

The Wizard of Menlo Park

Patience is better than pride.
Ecclesiastes 7:8, NIV.

Do you know what electric lights, video cameras, vote-recording machines, and rubber have in common? If you guessed Thomas Edison, you're right! Although Mr. Edison didn't invent everything on that list, he played a part in making them what we know today.

Thomas was born in 1847 and had only three months of formal schooling. His mother taught him many things, though, and he really liked to learn. As a young man he held many jobs, but eventually he used all of his time to experiment. He was a hard worker and practically lived in his laboratory. When an experiment was almost finished, he would sometimes spend two to three days at a time in his lab.

People thought he was a genius because of his many inventions. They called him the Wizard of Menlo Park—that's where he lived. He wasn't so sure he was a genius, though. He said, "Genius is 1 percent inspiration and 99 percent perspiration." He meant that his discoveries took an amazing amount of plain hard work. It wasn't because he was smart or well educated that he was able to accomplish the things that he did; it was because he worked hard to make it happen.

Most of the important things that have been accomplished through the years have taken a lot of hard work. People like Thomas Edison try thousands of different experiments before they discover the right one, and in the process they learn many things.

Do you have a great idea? Is there something you'd like to do? Don't just sit around and hope that it will happen. Work hard for your dream to come true, and don't give up!

PATIENCE AND PERSEVERANCE

Johnny Appleseed

When John Chapman was young, his father gave him and his brother a Bible. They spent many hours studying it together. John wanted to share what he knew and help people live better lives, so he began to travel. Wherever he went, he took apple seeds and his Bible. He became known as Johnny Appleseed.

Johnny planted more apple trees up and down the East Coast of the United States than you can count. But even more important, he planted the Word of God into an untold number of people's minds. He planted the seed of God's love and let God take care of growing the crop.

In time, seeds produce a crop. Apple seeds grow into apple trees; watermelon seeds grow into watermelon plants. Apple seeds don't grow into watermelon plants, and watermelon plants don't grow into apple trees.

The same is true of the seeds we allow to be planted in our minds. If we allow bad things into our minds, we can't expect kind, loving, and patient actions to come out. We can't be mean to the people around us and expect them to be nice to us. What kind of seeds are you planting today?

But the seed on good soil stands for those with a noble and good heart, who hear the word, retain it, and by persevering produce a crop.

Luke 8:15, NIV.

PATIENCE AND PERSEVERANCE

16
APRIL

*If you have faith
as a mustard
seed, . . . nothing
will be impossible
for you.*
Matthew 17:20.

Against All odds

Condoleezza Rice was born in Alabama at a time when African-Americans weren't treated fairly in most of the country. She didn't have many of the things most kids have, but she worked hard and did her best at everything.

Because of her perseverance and hard work, and because she has always done her best, Condoleezza has achieved many things in her life. Among other things, she became the first female national security adviser—a very important job helping the president of the United States. She was chosen to give the president advice on how to keep our country safe.

Condoleezza started out as just another kid from the South, but she used the gifts God gave her to make a difference.

God has given each of us gifts, too, and He wants us to use them for Him. With God it doesn't matter what the odds are. He will help any heroes who ask to use their gifts for Him.

PATIENCE AND PERSEVERANCE

The Running Man

It [love] . . . always perseveres.
1 Corinthians 13:7, NIV.

Glenn Cunningham was badly burned in an explosion when he was six years old. After the accident he spent several weeks in bed before he was able to walk on crutches. Eventually he was able to get rid of the crutches, but he said later, "It hurt like thunder to walk, but it didn't hurt at all when I ran. So for five or six years about all I did was run."

In high school Glenn ran in track meets and set speed records for his running. Even though he needed long warm-up periods because of problems caused by his accident, he kept running and setting records for his speed.

In addition to being a good runner, Glenn was a good student. He earned a master's degree from the University of Iowa and a doctorate from New York University. Six years after he retired from running in competitions, he and his wife opened the Glenn Cunningham Youth Ranch in Kansas. There they helped raise thousands of underprivileged children.

Glenn could have felt sorry for himself after his accident. He could have moped around and accepted that he would barely be able to walk. But he didn't. He worked hard and eventually was able to regain the use of his legs. Not only that—he went to college and dedicated his life to helping kids.

It is tempting for all of us to feel sorry for ourselves sometimes. It's easy to think that one person can't make much of a difference. But Glenn Cunningham is a shining example of the difference one person can make in thousands of lives, no matter the circumstances.

PATIENCE AND PERSEVERANCE

18
APRIL

Wait on the Lord; be of good courage, and He shall strengthen your heart; wait, I say, on the Lord!

Psalm 27:14.

I Can Do It Myself

Jacob was a mama's boy. His mother favored him over his twin brother, Esau. But his father favored Esau over Jacob. Before the twins were born, God had told their mother that Jacob would be greater than Esau.

Esau was the older twin, so he had the right to be the leader of the family someday—this was called the birthright. But when they were older, Jacob tricked Esau into giving up his birthright. Then Jacob lied to his blind father and tricked him into blessing him instead of Esau. Jacob didn't always make good decisions.

Because Esau was so angry with him for stealing the birthright, Jacob ran away. On his journey he had a dream that God would be with him, and it changed his life. Jacob made many foolish mistakes in his life, but he finally learned to ask God for wisdom and direction.

God had promised that Jacob would be the leader of the family, but he became impatient and took matters into his own hands. As it almost always does, that caused a lot of unnecessary problems. It would have been better if he had waited for God to work it out for him.

Is there a decision that you're having trouble with? Is it is hard to be patient about something? Ask God to take care of it for you; then have patience and trust that He'll do it.

PATIENCE AND PERSEVERANCE

Talking Wires

He just knew it could be done—if only he could figure out how. Alexander Graham Bell spent many years teaching people who couldn't hear or speak. Because of his work in this area, he got the idea that, somehow, sound could be made to travel across a wire. He spent hours experimenting, never becoming impatient or discouraged. He believed in his idea and knew that it could be accomplished. All he had to do was figure out how.

Finally, on March 10, 1876, Mr. Bell was in one room with his latest invention, and his friend, Thomas Watson, was in another room at the other end of the wire. Suddenly Mr. Watson heard Mr. Bell's voice say, "Mr. Watson, please come here. I want you." And with that, the telephone was discovered. Mr. Bell's idea had become a reality.

He could have become discouraged when people told him his invention was useless or impossible, but he believed in his dream. Because he believed and kept working, he changed the world.

Doing something worthwhile takes a lot of patience and hard work, but don't give up! With God's help, you can do great things.

And in every work that he began . . . , he did it with all his heart. So he prospered.
2 Chronicles 31:21.

PATIENCE AND PERSEVERANCE

20
APRIL

Man does not live on bread alone but on every word that comes from the mouth of the Lord.

Deuteronomy 8:3, NIV.

A Slave for God

At the age of 17 Charles Tindley could read and write only one word: cat. By the end of his life he could read and write Greek and Hebrew, he had preached to thousands of people weekly, and he had written hymns that are still sung today.

Charles was born to a slave family in Maryland. His mother died when he was 5, and shortly after that he was separated from his father. After slavery was abolished, he worked odd jobs and dreamed of becoming a minister. After much hard work, he finished second in his class and began preaching in his own church. His enthusiasm was contagious; before long his church had to move to a bigger building to hold all the people that came!

Near the beginning of his ministry Charles was the pastor of a church in New Jersey. It was winter, and a blizzard was howling outside. There was nothing to eat but stale bread, which he and his wife dipped in water to feed the two children. At breakfasttime Charles asked his wife to set the table as usual. She said, "But Charles, we have nothing to eat!" Again he asked her to set the table. She did, and they all sat there in front of their empty plates while Charles prayed. The prayer was interrupted by a bundled-up man, his arms full of groceries. He said he was sorry he was so late, but the snow was really heavy! God had provided for them when they needed it most.

God will provide for us in our times of need too. All we have to do is ask. Sometimes He will be the one providing for us. Other times He will use us to help Him provide for other people. He is always watching out for us and will always take care of us.

120

PATIENCE AND PERSEVERANCE

Handyman

Judge Quentin Corley knew that attitude determines whether a person succeeds or fails. Although he didn't have either of his hands, he believed that he was not helpless unless he allowed himself to be. He knew that even though he was physically challenged, he had a strong mind, and he could use that to succeed.

Even without hands Judge Corley was able to invent several things that helped him be independent. With the help of his machines, he could do everything he wanted to. He could start a fire, shave, dress himself, write, comb his hair, and eat with a knife and fork. He could even work in the garden, go bowling, and drive a car!

Although his hands had been lost in an accident that could have been prevented, Judge Corley never wasted time wondering about what might have been. He was happy for the blessings in his life and proud of his accomplishments and independence. He realized that the things he had in his life were more important than what he had lost.

Judge Corley knew that anyone who is willing to stick with something will succeed. No one is helpless unless they allow themselves to be helpless.

As God's heroes we have unlimited resources and power on our side. God is always willing to help us through any situation we might face. We never have to feel helpless, because God is always ready to help.

God is our refuge and strength, an ever-present help in trouble.
Psalm 46:1, NIV.

PATIENCE AND PERSEVERANCE

Wait on the Lord

Sarai was tired of waiting. God had promised her and her husband, Abram, a son, but it was taking so long, and they were getting so old. She was impatient.

Sarai decided that God must want them to have a son through her servant Hagar. But the problems really started after Hagar got pregnant and Ishmael was born. Hagar bragged about her son and teased Sarai because she didn't have a son of her own. Sarai became jealous of Hagar and the baby. The whole family was upset. It would have been so much better if Sarai had just been patient!

The trouble started when Sarai took matters into her own hands. She and Abram both had trouble believing God's promise and decided they should help Him out. Their lack of faith caused a lot of problems for many people.

It can be hard to wait for something we really want, but if we pray that God will lead us in His time, He will give us what is best.

PATIENCE AND PERSEVERANCE

Try-on

Doctors had come and gone from the little town of Tryon, Nebraska, so no one expected Dr. Harriet McGraw to stay. After all, she was a woman. There was no electricity, no paved roads, and no other doctor for many miles. But she did stay. She took the name of the town as a challenge: to "try on." She helped everyone who needed her, regardless of whether or not they could pay.

In her first year in Tryon, she braved the worst winter they'd had in years, delivered many babies, and didn't lose a single patient. Each patient she helped became a friend, and she soon won the respect and admiration of the whole county. They knew that she could be depended on to help, no matter what.

She wasn't in it for the money, because she didn't make much. She wasn't in it for the easy hours, because she was always on call and had to take care of patients day and night. She was in it because the people needed her, and she wanted to help.

Who needs you today? There may be problems, people, or situations in your life that seem impossible to you, but with God's help you can "try on" and succeed.

Let us not grow weary while doing good, for in due season we shall reap if we do not lose heart.
Galatians 6:9.

PATIENCE AND PERSEVERANCE

Love Is Patient

Love is patient.
1 Corinthians 13:4,
NIV.

Jacob and Rachel loved each other very much and wanted to be married. Jacob spoke to Rachel's father, Laban, and asked if he could marry his daughter. Laban agreed, but he told Jacob he would have to work for him for seven years before he could marry Rachel. Jacob loved her so much that he agreed. The Bible says that the seven years "seemed only a few days to him because of the love he had for her" (Genesis 29:20).

When the seven years were finished, and it was time for Rachel and Jacob to be married, they were so happy and excited!

But Laban came up with a plan to trick Jacob. Rachel's older sister, Leah, wasn't married yet. It was the custom of their country that the older sister had to be married before the younger sister could get married. Instead of giving Rachel to Jacob, Laban put a veil on Leah and sent her to the wedding instead. Jacob was angry when he found out that he'd been tricked, but he agreed to work another seven years for Rachel.

Jacob worked 14 years to marry Rachel! Sometimes we may wonder if working a long time for something is worth it, but important goals are worth working and waiting for.

It is easy to get the impression from TV and movies that we can solve our problems or get what we want quickly. After all, everything in a TV show takes only about an hour to take care of. That's not the way it is in real life, though. Patience is usually hardest to find when we need it the most, but it's important to be patient if we want to reach our goals.

PATIENCE AND PERSEVERANCE

Never Give Up

England needed Winston Churchill during World War II. The Germans, after conquering other countries, had decided to try to take over England by force. The German war planes bombed London, England's capital, day and night for many, many days. Imagine living with that fear day after day. The people never knew when the next bomb would come; they had to always be ready to run to the basement every time they heard the warning sirens.

Winston Churchill was a politician known for being as stubborn as a bulldog. He didn't give up. He wasn't very successful in the early years of his political career, but when his country was in terrible trouble during World War II, he became a great leader.

He gave many speeches encouraging the English people. In one of his most famous speeches, he told the people of his country, "Never, never, never, never" give up. His encouragement helped them to get through the difficult days of the war.

There may be times in our lives when we are facing bad or scary things, but we must remember that God is always with us. He has written letters of encouragement in the Bible and has promised that He will be with us. Never give up!

Do not be afraid nor dismayed because . . . the battle is not yours, but God's.
2 Chronicles 20:15.

PATIENCE AND PERSEVERANCE

26
APRIL

*Be glad
and rejoice:
for the Lord will
do great things.*
Joel 2:21, KJV.

Superman

Christopher Reeve played Superman in the movies. Nothing was impossible for him. He was young and strong, and in the movies he was always able to save the day.

In his free time Christopher loved to ride horses. One day in May 1995 his horse stopped suddenly in front of a jump, and Christopher was thrown off. The fall hurt him badly; since then he has not been able to move. Superman was not able to save the day this time. Now the actor who played Superman needs help from a machine to breathe.

But he didn't give up. Christopher Reeve, even though he can't move, works very hard for charities that help others with spinal cord injuries. Even though he can't play Superman anymore, he's doing what he can to be a real live superman.

Sometimes a hero is someone who does something great or brave to help others, and sometimes a hero is an ordinary person who perseveres no matter what obstacles are in their path. If we trust in God and allow Him to use our lives, He'll help us to be superboys and supergirls for Him.

PATIENCE AND PERSEVERANCE

A Lasting Influence

Joyce was a good nurse and a good teacher. Part of her job as a nurse was to teach student nurses how to become good nurses. Some days her job was easy, other days it was hard, but she never lost her temper. She was always patient, even when she had to show the student nurses again and again what to do.

The student nurses who spent their days with her learned more than just the job. They learned other important things, such as how to be patient and kind with the people they took care of, even when it wasn't easy.

The students who learned from Joyce were thankful for her patience and kindness in teaching them to be good nurses. Because of her good teaching, many nurses are able to take good care of their patients' needs. Because of her good example, many nurses learned to be better at their job and in their lives, too.

It can be easy to lose our tempers and be impatient with people. Remember that God is always patient with us, and His patient kindness will help us to be better people. Our influence will reach further than we may ever know.

The Lord is gracious and full of compassion, slow to anger and great in mercy.
Psalm 145:8.

PATIENCE AND PERSEVERANCE

28
APRIL

Been There, Done That

For in that He Himself has suffered, being tempted, He is able to aid those who are tempted.

Hebrews 2:18.

Have you ever stubbed your toe? It hurts! When a friend stubs their toe, you can empathize—you understand what it feels like, because you've done it before too.

Grace Noll Crowell went through a lot in her life. She was in and out of hospitals and was almost always very sick. The poems she wrote about her life and the things she went through helped many people. The people who read her poems felt as though she empathized with them. She knew what it was like to go through bad things and make it through. Her poems helped people to know that someone else understood what they were going through. It gave them hope that they could get through difficult things all right.

Jesus can empathize with our problems. No matter what is happening in our life, He understands, because He lived here on earth and went through the same kinds of things. If you have a problem, take it to Jesus. He understands!

PATIENCE AND PERSEVERANCE

Irritations

Be . . . patient in tribulation.
Romans 12:10-12.

How do you react when something bothers you? What do you do if a friend says something mean or if your brother tells a lie about you? How do you feel? You probably feel irritated.

When an oyster has a problem, it does something interesting. Let's say a piece of sand gets inside an oyster. The sand is irritating. It bothers the oyster. But the oyster doesn't get upset or angry. God designed the oyster so it can make a special covering for the problem. The oyster puts layer after layer of a special film called nacre around its problem until it turns into a pearl. What was once a problem is now a beautiful jewel.

How do you react when something bothers you? Do you let yourself get upset and angry? Or do you ask God to help you make something better from it? Let's say a prayer that God will help us react more like an oyster: *Dear God, sometimes things happen that really bother me. Rather than getting angry, please help me, as Your hero, to be more like the oyster and find a way to benefit from these things. Thank You for loving me. Amen.*

PATIENCE AND PERSEVERANCE

A Great Adventure

Come, and let us go up to the mountain of the Lord. . . . He will teach us His ways, and we shall walk in His paths.

Micah 4:2.

Look around the room where you are right now. What do you see? Furniture? Toys? People? Maybe you can see outside through a window.

Could you find your way through the room without hurting yourself if your eyes were closed? Could you walk through the rest of the house without peeking? It would be hard, wouldn't it? Now imagine climbing a mountain without being able to see. Impossible?

Not for Erik Weihenmayer. Erik became blind at age 13 from a rare eye disease. But he has lived a more adventurous life than many people who can see. In high school he was a wrestler and athlete. He became a teacher after college.

Then he started climbing mountains. Erik has climbed the Seven Summits—that's the nickname for the seven highest mountains in the world. That includes Mount Everest. Mount Everest is so tall that only one climber out of every 10 who try is able to reach the top. Erik is living the life he wants to live without letting his blindness get in the way.

Sometimes sin can blind us to what God really wants for our lives. But God will help His heroes to see clearly and live a life of adventure with Him.

PATIENCE AND PERSEVERANCE

Loyal God

Do you know what loyalty means? Loyal people are faithful—they will stick with someone or something. Loyalty can be good (such as when you are loyal to your family or God) or bad (such as when you choose to be loyal to something more than you are loyal to God).

Our first loyalty should be to God. Nothing should ever change that. We should also be loyal to our family and friends as long as they don't ask us to do something that goes against God.

Jesus showed His loyalty to us by coming to earth and dying on the cross for our sins. He didn't have to leave His home in heaven, but He chose to do so because we are part of His family and He loves us. Does the way you live your life show your loyalty to your family and to God?

I have set the Lord always before me; because He is at my right hand I shall not be moved.
Psalm 16:8.

LOYALTY AND COMMITMENT

Family Ties

For wherever you go, I will go; and wherever you lodge, I will lodge; your people shall be my people, and your God, my God.
Ruth 1:16.

Ruth loved the family she had married into. Her husband's family had come to her country because there had been a famine in Israel. They settled in nicely. Then tragedy struck: her husband's father died. They were all so sad! Soon after, Ruth's husband and his brother died too. The three women were now all widows.

Ruth's mother-in-law, Naomi, made up her mind to go back to her relatives in Israel. Naomi told Ruth and her sister-in-law to go back to their families too, since their husbands had died. After many tears Ruth's sister-in-law left, but Ruth didn't want to go. She loved Naomi and her God, and she wanted to stay with her. Ruth told Naomi that no matter what happened, she would stay with her, and that nothing would ever separate them. And that's what happened. You can read their story in the book of Ruth in the Old Testament. It has a very happy ending.

God made families to stick together and help each other. When we are tempted to fight and argue with our family, we should remember Ruth's loyalty to Naomi. We can honor God's faithfulness and loyalty to us by being faithful and loyal to our family as well.

LOYALTY AND COMMITMENT

An Unlikely Hero

Priscilla wasn't an average pig. She loved people. She had been fed from a bottle when she was a tiny piglet, and she lived in a playpen on the porch. Priscilla didn't want to eat with the other pigs or play in the mud with them. She was a funny pig. She didn't like to get dirty.

But oh, how she loved to swim! One day she was swimming in a lake near her Texas home. Her friend, Carol, held on to her leash, and Carol's son, Anthony, watched from the shore. Anthony couldn't swim, so he played on the bank and laughed at Priscilla playing in the water.

All of a sudden, Priscilla heard a shout from Carol. Anthony was up to his waist in the water and headed their way. He didn't realize he was in any danger, but within minutes he walked into a deep spot and disappeared under the water. Carol immediately dropped Priscilla's leash and began swimming toward the spot where Anthony had gone under. But she was so far away! The water churned up as Anthony struggled to the surface.

Priscilla also took off toward where Anthony had disappeared. Because she was smaller, Priscilla was able to swim faster than Carol. Her little legs churned, and she snorted piggy noises as she charged toward Anthony. When she reached him, he grabbed her and pulled her under too. Struggling free, little Priscilla headed toward the surface. This time when Anthony surfaced, he grabbed the leash. Both of them were exhausted, but Priscilla headed stubbornly for shore, not stopping until Anthony could touch the bottom again.

The little pig saved a life because of her loyalty to the people who cared for her. Her story is proof that God can use anyone to be a hero. And sometimes heroes come in unlikely packages.

Whatever is commanded by the God of heaven, let it diligently be done.
Ezra 7:23.

LOYALTY AND COMMITMENT

4
MAY

Best Friends

He who loves father or mother more than Me is not worthy of Me. And he who loves son or daughter more than Me is not worthy of Me.

Matthew 10:37.

David and Jonathan had an unusual friendship. Jonathan, as King Saul's son, was next in line to be the king of Israel. However, God had chosen David to be king instead. Jonathan could have been jealous, but David was his friend, and he trusted that God knew what was best.

It got even more complicated because Jonathan's father, Saul, hated David and wanted him dead. It must have been difficult for Jonathan to remain loyal both to his father, the king, and to his best friend, David, who was going to take his place as king. If he had been loyal only to his father, he couldn't have been friends with David. But if he had been loyal only to his friend, he couldn't have been loyal to his father, the king, who hated David. It must have been stressful for Jonathan.

But Jonathan's first loyalty was to God. He knew that if he stayed loyal to God, the rest would work out. And it did. Jonathan's first loyalty was to God, and that made his other choices clearer.

What about you? Who has your greatest loyalty?

134

LOYALTY AND COMMITMENT

freedom Worth fighting for

Benjamin Franklin is famous for being an author, printer, diplomat, philosopher, and scientist. He worked to help the United States become a country during the American Revolution, and afterwards he helped set up the new government.

Perhaps the thing for which he is best remembered is as one of the signers of the Declaration of Independence. America was a colony of England, and it was subject to English rule. The men who declared their independence from England could have been sentenced to death if the Revolution hadn't worked. It took a lot of courage and commitment for them to sign their names on the Declaration. Benjamin Franklin told them, "We must all hang together, or assuredly we shall all hang separately." They knew that they could be signing their death warrants, but they believed that freedom for America was the right thing to do, and they were willing to fight for it.

We live in a great country that was founded on freedom. We can be proud of what it stands for. Being a hero for God includes being a good citizen—voting, showing respect for our flag, and defending our country when necessary. Freedom isn't free; we have to work to keep it. Freedom is God's way, and it is worth standing up for.

Where the Spirit of the Lord is, there is liberty.
2 Corinthians 3:17.

LOYALTY AND COMMITMENT

6
MAY

Lord, what do You want me to do?

Acts 9:6.

Seeing the Light

Saul was on his way to Damascus to kill Christians. As a good Pharisee he thought that anyone who believed in Christ was wrong and should be killed.

Saul and his men were riding their horses along the road when all of a sudden they saw a blinding light. Saul fell from his horse and heard a voice say, "Saul, Saul, why do you persecute Me?" It was Jesus! Jesus Himself had come to talk to Saul.

Saul was afraid, and so were the men with him. They could hear the voice, but they didn't see anyone. Saul realized that he had been very, very wrong about Jesus and the Christians. Jesus told him to go to Damascus and wait. And then He was gone.

Saul tried to look around him, but the bright light had blinded him. His men took his arms and led him into the city. He was blind for three days before his sight came back.

Saul's experience on the Damascus road changed his life for good. He went from being Saul, the killer of Christians, to Paul, the preacher for Jesus.

Paul was a hero for Jesus because he was willing to give everything to do what was right. He had to change his way of thinking after God showed him that he was wrong. He lost his job, and probably many of his friends and family did not understand, but Paul was willing to put Jesus first.

There is nothing worth more than a relationship with Jesus. Like Paul, we should turn our whole lives over to Jesus and commit ourselves to doing what is right.

LOYALTY AND COMMITMENT

Dr. Rabbit

Eric B. Hare was a wonderful storyteller. He spent much of his life working as a missionary in Burma (now Myanmar). The people in Burma were suspicious of Dr. Hare at first. He was different from them, and they didn't know if they could trust him or not.

There is an animal called a hare that looks a lot like a rabbit. Because his name was Dr. Hare, they started calling him Dr. Rabbit. As he patiently worked among them, his kind, gentle ways helped them to learn to love him.

When he lived in Burma, he would tell the children stories from the Bible. His stories helped them learn about Jesus and His love for them. When he left Burma, the stories he told of his time there and the people he knew have helped many other children around the world to learn more about Jesus.

Because Dr. Hare was committed to sharing Jesus with others, his stories have helped many people to know God better and live better lives. Each of us tells a story by the way we live our lives. What will your story say?

And this gospel of the kingdom will be preached in all the world as a witness to all the nations.
Matthew 24:14.

LOYALTY AND COMMITMENT

8
MAY

The Prayed-for Boy

*For this child
I prayed . . . .
Therefore I also
have lent him
to the Lord;
as long as he lives
he shall be lent
to the Lord.*

1 Samuel 1:27, 28.

Every year Hannah and her husband, Elkanah, went to the Temple. There Hannah would see mothers with their babies, and it made her sad that she and Elkanah didn't have any children. She prayed to God that she could have a baby. She prayed so hard that the priest, Eli, thought she was drunk! Hannah told God that if He would give her a son, she would give that son back to God to work for Him.

The next year when they came to the Temple, Hannah and Elkanah weren't sad anymore. There were still plenty of mothers with babies, but this year Hannah and Elkanah had a baby of their own—Samuel. God had heard Hannah's prayer and had given them a baby son.

When Samuel was 3 years old, Hannah brought him back to the Temple so he could begin his training to work with Priest Eli. It was hard for her to leave him; she loved him so much. But she knew she had to follow through on her promise to God. Because she did, God used Samuel to be a great spiritual leader of his country.

Sometimes it is hard to follow through with what we have promised, but we should always do what we say we will. God will honor our commitment, as He honored Hannah's.

LOYALTY AND COMMITMENT

Lifesaver

Ever since he was a child, John wanted to work in a job that helped people. After graduating from high school, he decided to go to school to become an EMT (emergency medical technician). Then he could drive an ambulance and help paramedics care for people in emergencies. After finishing EMT training, he went back to school to become a paramedic so that he could do even more to help people.

One day John's ambulance was called to the scene of a car accident. When they arrived, John ran to the accident and found a 7-year-old girl who had stopped breathing and whose heart was not beating. Because of his training, John knew what to do. He quickly began CPR and gave her the medicines needed to save her life. John's commitment to learning his job well had helped to save the girl's life. He didn't have to think about what to do; he knew his job so well that it came naturally when he needed it.

When Adam and Eve sinned, our world became an accident scene. Jesus raced to the scene and did what was necessary to save our lives. No matter what we do in our lives, we should do our very best. We never know how we may help others by what we do well.

You do faithfully whatever you do for the brethren and for strangers.
3 John 5.

LOYALTY AND COMMITMENT

10
MAY

You have forgiven the iniquity of Your people; You have covered all their sin.
Psalm 85:2.

oil for the Soul

The only thing William Crawford Gorgas ever wanted to be was a soldier. He saw his father in his uniform with the shiny buttons and crisp fabric, and he was so proud that his father was a soldier. More than anything, William wanted to be a soldier himself.

When he was old enough, William applied to the military academy at West Point. He was so disappointed when they told him he didn't meet the requirements needed to be a soldier. But he made up his mind that he would be in the Army anyway. If he couldn't be a soldier, he'd train to become an Army doctor.

Yellow fever was a big problem in William's day, and many people died from this disease. William came down with it, but fortunately he recovered. Because he'd had the disease once, he was now immune to it, so the Army sent him to Cuba to take care of the many people there who were sick with it.

While he was there he studied yellow fever to figure out what caused it, but he couldn't find the cause. An old Cuban doctor thought it was caused by a certain type of mosquito. Finally a group of four doctors found out that the old doctor was right. Then William and his coworkers waged war on the insects by pouring oil on water puddles, where the mosquitoes laid their eggs. The oil covered the top of the water and smothered the mosquitoes. This helped control the spread of yellow fever.

Sin can easily infect us, as yellow fever infected the people in Cuba—unless we let God, like the oil on the puddles, cover our lives and get rid of that old pest, Satan.

LOYALTY AND COMMITMENT

Salty

Stand firm. Let nothing move you.
1 Corinthians 15:58, NIV.

Salty spent most of his time lying under Omar Rivera's desk on the seventy-first floor of the World Trade Center. Omar, who had been blind since he was 14, relied on Salty, his yellow Labrador retriever guide dog. They were always together, and they were together on the morning of September 11, 2001, when an airplane crashed into their building.

When the first explosion rocked the tower, Omar was sitting on his desk. He heard many noises: people scrambling around, the crunching of broken glass, and the sound of his computer falling off his desk. Omar said a quick prayer and called Salty to guide him. Salty was nervous, but he came when he was called. Omar held on to Salty's harness with one hand and a friend's arm with the other, and they began to make their way out of the building. Because the elevators were out of service, they had to walk down 71 flights of stairs.

It took an hour and 15 minutes for them to reach the ground floor, but Salty refused to leave Omar, even when someone else tried to take his leash. He guided his friend to safety; his loyalty and commitment, even when things got scary, helped save Omar's life.

Salty didn't have to stay with Omar. He could have run away and tried to make it out of the building more quickly. But because of his training and loyalty, he did what he knew was right and stayed by his friend, helping him to safety.

We receive training every day. The things we say and do, what we watch, and how we spend our time—all these things are training us either for good or for evil. Is your training teaching you to stand strong for God?

LOYALTY AND COMMITMENT

Anita's Stand

Watch, stand fast in the faith, be brave, be strong.
1 Corinthians 16:13.

The news was totally unexpected: In a blinding snowstorm, Anita's brother had been in a car accident that killed one of his daughters and badly injured the other. The family was devastated. The terrible news shook Anita and made her think.

Anita decided that she wanted her family to go to church together. She and her husband, Cliff, had a happy family with five children. But they didn't attend church because she and Cliff had different beliefs. Now they knew that something had to change. They needed to go to church together.

When Anita talked to Cliff about it, the only church he would go to was the one he'd been raised in—the Seventh-day Adventist Church. They called the local pastor for Bible studies, and soon they were going to church together as a family on Sabbaths.

This didn't make Anita's parents, siblings, and friends very happy. They thought her new beliefs were silly and strange. They teased her and her family for going to church on what they said was the wrong day. Anita and her family stood for what they believed in spite of it all.

Sometimes it can be hard to stand for what is right, especially if our family and friends don't agree. God tells us in the Bible that we should stand strong for the right, even when it isn't the popular thing to do. Making a stand for God and the Bible may cause some people to make fun of us or tease us, but in the end choosing God and His way is always the right decision.

LOYALTY AND COMMITMENT

Zorro

Guard what has been entrusted to your care.

1 Timothy 6:20, NIV.

Mark Cooper and his dog Zorro were hiking with friends through the Sierras on a bright, cool day in November. Mark and Zorro were ahead of their friends on a steep trail when suddenly Mark lost his footing. Bouncing over boulders and sharp rocks, he fell 85 feet down a cliff. When he hit the bottom, he lay facedown in the river, so badly injured he couldn't move.

Zorro, who was the only one to see Mark fall, scrambled down after his master. Racing down the steep cliff, he threw himself into the cold river and made his way to Mark. Inch by inch he closed in, finally getting close enough to grab Mark's backpack. With a mighty struggle Zorro made his way to the shore, pulled Mark onto the riverbank, and began to howl. At the top of the trail, Mark's friends heard Zorro, but the cliff was too steep for them to climb down. They called down that they would go for help. And then they disappeared.

At the bottom of the canyon Zorro and Mark lay cold and shivering as night fell. Zorro lay down across Mark's body, his own body heat protecting Mark from the freezing cold. He stayed there through the long dark night.

When morning finally came, a team of rescue workers was able to airlift Mark from the canyon by helicopter. As the ground crew left the scene in a jeep, they called for Zorro to follow them out. He ran beside them for a while, but soon he left them and went back to the river—the last place he'd seen Mark. Several days later he was rescued there, still lying by Mark's backpack.

Sin is like that cliff. We may not realize the trouble we're in before it's too late. But God is even more loyal to us than Zorro was to Mark. He will rescue any of His heroes who call to Him.

LOYALTY AND COMMITMENT

The Town That old Clothes Built

Eustace and Mary Sloop had always dreamed of being missionaries. As they sat on their horses high above the North Carolina valley, they knew they didn't have to go to Africa or China or some faraway place. They could be missionaries right here.

They knew it wouldn't be a good idea just to barge into the town of Crossnore and declare themselves missionaries. The people wouldn't know them or trust them. So they set out to be missionaries in the way they lived. They built a home and became teachers of a class at their church every week.

At that time in Crossnore, girls married when they were about 13 or 14. Mrs. Sloop knew this was too young; she wanted the girls to go to school. That took money, though, and the girls needed clothes to wear to school. Mrs. Sloop wrote to some of her relatives, asking them to send any clothes they could. She forgot that her relatives were in mourning; someone had died, so all of them were wearing black. Therefore, all the clothes they sent were black! The Sloops sold the black clothes to buy different clothes that the girls could wear to school.

Soon people from all over were sending the Sloops clothes; they opened a store to sell them. The money went to build a school, then a hospital. Everything they received they used to help their town. The people of Crossnore were able to become better educated and healthier in body and soul.

If the Sloops had tried to push their religion on people, they wouldn't have gotten nearly as far. Because the people were impressed by how the Sloops lived their lives, their influence was far-reaching. People notice how we live our lives. How will you use your influence?

LOYALTY AND COMMITMENT

Practice Makes Perfect

It seemed as if Ignace Paderewski always had music running through his head. Every chance he got he'd scribble some notes on whatever scrap of paper was nearby. He could hardly wait to grow up and write music for other people to play.

In the meantime he took piano lessons. He was able to have only one lesson a month, but he did his best to study hard and practice well between his lessons. He knew that in order to write music well, he had to play music well, so he spent as much time as he could in practice. Eventually his hard work paid off, and he became a famous composer and musician whose music is known worldwide.

Doing your best can take hard work, but it is always worth it in the end. As God's hero, try to do even better tomorrow than you did today. Do your best at the things God has given you to do.

You shall rejoice in all to which you have put your hand, . . . in which the Lord your God has blessed you.
Deuteronomy 12:7.

LOYALTY AND COMMITMENT

Plant Wizard

A good tree cannot bear bad fruit, nor can a bad tree bear good fruit. . . . Therefore by their fruits you will know them.

Matthew 7:18-20.

Luther Burbank was really interested in plants. He liked to put seeds in the ground and watch for the little green shoots to poke out of the dirt. He always took good care of his plants, and he tried to think of ways to help them grow better.

When he planted, he followed the principle of selection—that meant he used seeds from only the best plants to grow new plants. By experimenting this way, he figured out how to grow a better potato. From one seed more than 500 million bushels of potatoes were produced.

Luther was always making things better. He found ways to sweeten up fruit that had always been sour. He worked with plants that had tasteless berries until he was able to turn them into something edible. He made people's lives better by developing better plants, and he did it by being sincere and modest. He had a mission and a desire to do it well.

With God's help we can use the principle of selection in our lives too. Ask God today to use the best parts of your life to help make life better for others.

LOYALTY AND COMMITMENT

The Most Important Race

Ion Falconer was a champion bicycle racer back when bicycles were a new invention. With their tall front wheel and small rear wheel, the old-fashioned bicycles were harder to balance than today's bikes, but Ion was a champion. He loved the speed and challenge of racing. He'd race anyone at any time, and eventually he became a world-champion bicycle racer, winning a lot of prize money.

You might think he would have used that money to buy a better bicycle, but instead he spent all of it to go as a missionary. His friends thought he was crazy. But even more than he loved racing bicycles, Ion loved to share Jesus with people.

While he was a missionary Ion learned the language of the area, helped to build schools, taught about the Bible, built a hospital, and was always ready to help any way he could. He worked even harder to share Jesus and make people's lives better than he did at the bicycle racing he loved so much. And Ion won the greatest race of all—the race for salvation. The best part of this race is that we can all be winners!

You will receive the crown of glory that will never fade away.
1 Peter 5:4, NIV.

LOYALTY AND COMMITMENT

Called to Serve

*Who then
is willing to
consecrate himself
this day to
the Lord?*

1 Chronicles 29:5.

Narcissa's friends were worried about her. She was a science teacher, and she had this crazy idea that she should go across the country to teach the Indians. Her friends asked Marcus Whitman to talk her out of it. He agreed that it was outrageous—who ever heard of a woman traveling west by herself, by covered wagon no less, to teach Indians? He had never met Narcissa in person, but he was willing to do a good deed and try to discourage her from such a silly idea.

Instead, she persuaded him to go with her! They fell in love and were married. Then they did what everyone thought was crazy—they traveled west to spend their lives working with the Flathead Indians.

Jesus can use each of us in different ways, and He has a special job for each of us. Like the Whitmans, we should be committed to following God's calling in our lives. We should be willing to go where He asks us to, no matter what others think.

LOYALTY AND COMMITMENT

Trusting Son

Isaac and his dad were close. Since he was Sarah and Abraham's only child, there was nothing they loved more than him. Or was there?

One day God spoke to Isaac's dad, Abraham. He told Abraham to take Isaac to Mount Moriah and offer him as a sacrifice. God didn't really want Isaac to die; He wanted Abraham to show that he loved God more than anything—including Isaac.

Abraham must have been very sad. He loved his son, and he didn't understand why God would ask him to do such a thing. But He trusted that God was in control, and he obeyed. Abraham and Isaac went with some servants to Mount Moriah.

Once there, Abraham told the servants to stay behind. He and Isaac took some wood and headed up the mountain. Isaac asked his father where the lamb was that they were going to sacrifice. Poor Abraham. He couldn't bring himself to say that Isaac was to be the sacrifice, so he said, "The Lord will provide."

When they reached the top, Abraham explained to Isaac what God had told him to do. Neither of them understood it, but they trusted God to do what was best.

Just as Abraham raised the knife to kill his son, God spoke to him again, and told him not to kill Isaac. They must have been so relieved and thankful!

Isaac trusted his father, Abraham, to do the right thing. He was willing to be sacrificed if that was what God wanted. Jesus, too, trusted His Father's will and gave Himself as a sacrifice for all of our sins.

Children, obey your parents in the Lord, for this is right.
Ephesians 6:1.

LOYALTY AND COMMITMENT

Bad Timing

Do not be overcome by evil, but overcome evil with good.
Romans 12:21.

The villagers were in a state of shock when Elizabeth Thompson arrived as a missionary. The village had been attacked and all the men had been killed, leaving the women and children terrified and helpless. None of them knew how to do anything that the men had always done. The whole village was falling apart. There was no one who knew how to chop wood, fix houses, or do the hunting, fishing, and farming.

Elizabeth set to work educating the women and sharing Jesus with them. She taught them to do the farming and other "men's work" so that life in the village could continue, despite the bad things that had happened to them. Although everyone was still sad and upset, they slowly set to work rebuilding their lives and their village.

There may be bad things that happen in our lives too, but those things don't have to determine who we are. We can ask God to use the bad things for good, and He will help us move on to become a better person.

LOYALTY AND COMMITMENT

Humble Scholar

Have you seen a movie or read a book so many times that you know it by memory? Because you've seen it so many times, you remember what it's about and you know what's going to happen next, don't you?

The Bible sometimes uses the words "write it on your heart" as another way to say "memorize." They are beautiful words for a beautiful idea. Whatever you memorize becomes a part of who you are; you can always remember it, even if it isn't written down in front of you.

Norman has much of the Bible memorized. By just looking at him, you might not guess it. He doesn't dress very nicely, and sometimes his clothes are all wrinkly. Even though he can't drive, he's always at church, singing a measure behind everyone else during the song service, at the top of his voice.

But Norman knows and loves Jesus. You can ask him any question about the Bible, and he can answer it for you. He can quote Scripture from memory and has read the Bible through many times. Jesus is his personal friend.

By reading the Bible, we too can come to know Jesus as a personal friend. Knowing Jesus is even more important than being smart. Knowing our Bibles well will help us to stand up for what is right no matter what is happening around us.

I will put My laws in their mind and write them on their hearts.
Hebrews 8:10.

LOYALTY AND COMMITMENT

A Man After God's own Heart

I have found David the son of Jesse, a man after My own heart, who will do all My will.

Acts 13:22.

David's life had many ups and downs. He was a shepherd, king, poet, and giant killer, but he was also a liar, murderer, and thief. In spite of all of the "down" times, God still called David "a man after My own heart." This does not mean that God does bad things, as David did; God meant that He loved David very much despite his problems.

Throughout his life David believed in the faithfulness and goodness of God. He also learned, from personal experience, the importance of God's forgiveness. Even though David did bad things, he learned from his mistakes, asked for forgiveness, and turned away from his sin. He knew that he was forgiven, even when he had to suffer the consequences of his sin.

God will always forgive us when we ask Him to, but there may still be consequences to that sin. God is always willing to forgive us if we honestly admit our mistakes and turn away from the sin. Are there any changes you need to make in your life? Is God able to call you a hero after His own heart?

LOYALTY AND COMMITMENT

Led Singer

You shall be witnesses to Me . . . to the end of the earth.
Acts 1:8.

Chris Rice had a good career in Christian music, but he felt that God was calling him to do more. Before he had begun giving concerts and recording music, he had worked with young people. He remembered how God had used people in his life when he was young to help build his faith. Those people made more of a difference in his faith than any of the music he listened to. He knew that music is important and can help people, too, but he felt that God was calling him to take a break.

So, just as he was becoming famous, going on tour, and living the life that many people dream about, he stopped. Chris knew that doing what God wants you to do will bring the greatest happiness and satisfaction, as well as do the most good for eternity. He quit recording music and giving concerts for a while and went back to working with young people. Now he does both, but he makes sure that the music doesn't squeeze out the people.

Just because we may be good at something doesn't necessarily mean that is what God wants us to do. Pray today that God will show you what He wants you to do and where you can do the most good for Him. Maybe there's someone you know whom you can help toward heaven by being a friend.

LOYALTY AND COMMITMENT

24
MAY

Blood Bank

Christ . . . by his own blood . . . obtained eternal redemption for us.
Hebrews 9:11, 12, KJV.

Charles Drew probably saved more lives than we can count. He wasn't a firefighter, a police officer, or even a superhero. He was a doctor who helped develop the idea of a blood bank. Whole blood had to be refrigerated, and certain people could be given only certain types of blood. However, when people needed blood, sometimes they could be given just part of the blood—the blood plasma—instead of whole blood. Plasma could be taken anywhere and used by anyone.

Dr. Drew developed a system to separate the plasma out of the blood. Dr. Drew's work saved thousands of lives during World War II. Because of his research with blood plasma, medics were able to take care of many soldiers who needed help right away on the battlefield. People who would have died otherwise were saved.

Jesus has a special blood bank. The blood He offers us will wash away all our sins. All we have to do is tell Him that we accept His gift of salvation and want to live for Him, and we, who would die otherwise, will be saved.

LOYALTY AND COMMITMENT

Good Neighbors

When Jane Addams was a child, she lived in a big house. One day as she was walking with her father, they came to a section of town where the people lived in very small houses. She asked her father why anyone would want to live in a small house, and he explained that sometimes people don't have a choice. Jane told him that when she grew up, she would live in a big house, but it would be in the middle of small houses like those.

Her prediction came true. When Jane grew up, she wanted to become a doctor, so she started medical school. However, she had to drop out of school because she got sick. Then she traveled through Europe. She saw many beautiful things there, but she also saw people suffering and starving because they were poor. She wanted to help.

When Jane came back to the United States, she and a friend bought a big house called Hull House in Chicago. Just as she'd said when she was a young girl, the big house had small houses all around it. Jane made friends with her neighbors. Soon her one house was being used for 13 different purposes: kindergarten, day care, meeting rooms, and other things that were needed. Because Jane was such a good neighbor, the whole neighborhood started to improve. Everyone wanted to make their neighborhood, and even their whole city, a better place to live.

Hull House wasn't just for certain types of people, either. Everyone—young and old—was welcome, and everyone was Jane's friend.

What is your neighborhood like? Do you know your neighbors? Are you everyone's friend? What can you, as God's hero, do to make your neighborhood a better place?

LOYALTY AND COMMITMENT

Rescued by Love

For the Lord your God is He who goes with you, . . . to save you.

Deuteronomy 20:4.

The day was bright and sunny, and Woodie was happy to be on a walk with her two favorite people—Rae Ann and Ray. The big, shaggy dog was known for being friendly and obedient, so when Ray ran ahead to take a picture, Rae Ann was surprised that Woodie jerked loose and ran too. What Rae Ann didn't know was that Woodie had seen Ray fall over an 80-foot cliff. (That's about the height of two houses stacked on top of each other.) Woodie took one look at Ray lying facedown in the shallow water at the bottom of the cliff, and she knew she had to help. Without thinking of her own safety, she threw herself off the cliff with a mighty "Woof!"

The rocky canyon bottom made for a hard landing, and the fall broke Woodie's hips, and her back legs wouldn't work. She knew she had to get to Ray. Because he was only semiconscious and facedown in the water, he was drowning. Woodie pulled herself to Ray with her front legs. She gently moved his head out of the water so he could breathe. When she heard him coughing, she lay down beside him and stayed there until help arrived. Only then did Woodie let Rae Ann take care of her and her own injuries.

If it hadn't been for Woodie's selfless heroism, Ray would have drowned before help got to him. Thanks to her, he lived and got better. Oh yes, Woodie got better too.

Jesus saw our world in trouble and rushed to help. If not for His selfless sacrifice on the cross, we would have all drowned in sin. Thanks to Him, though, we can get better. Ask God to help you be a hero for Him; perhaps you can help Him rescue someone who is drowning in sin.

LOYALTY AND COMMITMENT

Tough as Granite

John Quincy Adams knew what it was like to be president even before he was elected, because his father had been president. John Quincy Adams and George W. Bush are the only presidents in American history whose fathers were also president.

Everyone knew that President Adams was as tough as a rock. He wouldn't give in to peer pressure, even from his friends. And he always stuck to what he felt was right. Some people liked him for that and some people didn't, but he didn't care. He only cared about what God thought. He wanted to do what was right in God's sight.

It can be hard to stand up for what is right when you are being pushed to do something else by the people around you—especially when it is friends and family who are doing the pushing. Remember, you are God's hero! Ask Him today to help you to stand up for what is right and to plant your feet on the rock that really matters—Jesus.

The Lord is my rock . . . ; the God of my strength, in whom I will trust.
2 Samuel 22:2, 3.

LOYALTY AND COMMITMENT

28
MAY

Trust in God, Not Men

We trust in the living God, who is the Savior of all men.

1 Timothy 4:10.

More than 700 years ago the power of the Roman Catholic Church was very great. The pope, who was the head of the church, told everyone that they had to pay him taxes and that he was the boss, even of the king. He said he had the power to forgive sins, but he would do it only if he was paid. We know that only God can forgive sins, but most people in those days had never even seen a Bible. If they had, it wasn't in their language, and they probably couldn't read it anyway. The pope didn't want the people to have Bibles. He made it illegal for anyone who wasn't a leader in the church to have one.

John Wycliffe saw that this was wrong. He believed that Jesus wanted everyone to have access to Him and to salvation. John could read the Bible, and he knew that only God could forgive sins.

He and some friends started to translate the Bible into English. It was slow, hard work because they didn't have printing presses, as we do today. Every word had to be translated from Latin into English and written down by hand. The leaders in the Roman Catholic Church were very angry with John. They didn't want people to have Bibles or to think that the church wasn't in control.

John Wycliffe knew it was more important to follow God than to follow men. Because of his hard work, anyone who wants one can have a Bible today. He was a hero for God who knew that no one and nothing has authority over the Bible. The Bible is God's Word; if anyone tells us something that goes against what the Bible says, we should always stay true to the Bible.

LOYALTY AND COMMITMENT

Study for Yourself

Joe Crews wanted to tell everyone about Jesus. However, he knew that some people wouldn't be interested in his radio program. He wondered how to make it interesting to everyone. Then he had an idea.

He began to look high and low for interesting facts to use in his radio programs. For every program he did research—not just in the Bible, but also in the world of science, history, or nature. He found an amazing fact for each program; then he applied it to Scripture and his message. At the end of each program he offered a Bible study. Joe didn't want people to take his word for things. He wanted them to study the Bible and find things out for themselves.

Joe's love for Jesus shone out of his programs. All kinds of people loved listening to him and studying the Bible for themselves. Because of Joe and his amazing facts, many people who might not have listened otherwise have come to know Jesus.

Since you're God's hero, don't just take someone's word for it. Study for yourself and find out about Jesus on your own. You can't be a hero for someone you don't know!

Study to shew thyself approved unto God, . . . rightly dividing the word of truth.
2 Timothy 2:15, KJV.

LOYALTY AND COMMITMENT

30
MAY

I will give you a new heart.
Ezekiel 36:26.

A New Heart

Louis Washkansky needed a new heart. Without it, he would die. His weak, diseased heart didn't work very well, and it was just a matter of time before it stopped working completely.

Dr. Christiaan Barnard wanted to try to give Louis a new heart. But it was something that had never been done before. Was it possible to give someone a different heart? It would be a long and risky surgery.

The surgery was going fine, but everyone held their breath as Dr. Barnard removed Louis's old, weak heart and put the new one in its place. Would it work? What would happen? The medical team watched closely as the new heart was sewn in. Then the new heart was given a shock to get it to start beating. Their eyes widened and smiles came to their faces when *thump thump, thump thump*, the new heart started beating. Now Louis had a healthy new heart.

Jesus tells us that when we become heroes for Him, He will give us a new heart. Don't worry; you won't have to have surgery! He means that He'll change our thoughts, words, and actions to be more like His. Ask God to give you a new heart—a heart like His—today.

LOYALTY AND COMMITMENT

The Master's Voice

Sheba strutted around her cage, bobbing her green parrot head on her yellow parrot neck and talking to herself. She whispered and mumbled, laughed and chattered. When she heard the telephone ring, she'd say, "Hello? Oh, hi!" Then she'd make funny parrot noises while her people talked. Sheba could tell when they were almost done talking, and she'd squawk, "Well, Goodbye! Goodbye!" just before they hung up.

She sang "Oh, How I Love Jesus" from her cage in her funny parrot voice, and she loved to hang upside down on people's hands and swing back and forth. She'd yell, "Wheee! Wheee!"

One of Sheba's favorite things was to call the dog. Sheba had learned to imitate her owner's voice very well. She would call, "Nikki! Wanna go out?" Then the dog would come zooming down the stairs to sit, wagging her tail, by the door. Sheba would pace back and forth in her cage, laughing to herself while the confused dog tried to figure out why no one was opening the door.

Jesus said that the people who love Him know His voice and follow Him. There are a lot of imitators in the world who try to sound like Jesus. By reading the Bible and praying, we will learn to know our Master's voice so we don't get tricked.

My sheep hear My voice, and I know them, and they follow Me.
John 10:27.

LOYALTY AND COMMITMENT

1
JUNE

True Strength

Take my yoke upon you and learn from Me, for I am gentle and humble in heart, and you will find rest for your souls.
Matthew 11:29.

Sometimes we think that being gentle and humble means being weak, but Jesus is both strong and gentle.

For many years Jesus helped His earthly dad, Joseph, in a carpenter shop. Have you ever seen a carpenter? They're usually pretty strong. My guess is that Jesus and Joseph were even stronger than today's carpenters—after all, they didn't have power tools. They had to do everything without the help of electric saws, power drills, and other tools that today's carpenters use. They had a hard job that required them to be very strong.

Jesus was also gentle. All kinds of people loved to be with Him—even little children. Most of us don't like to be around people who are rough, tough, and mean. People in Jesus' time were no different. They came in huge crowds to see Jesus, and they followed Him everywhere He went. Children were often around Jesus too, listening to stories and sitting on His lap.

Is your attitude one that makes people want to be around you? If we show gentleness the way Jesus did, we can become truly strong.

PEACE AND HUMILITY

one Peaceful Hero

Love your enemies and pray for those who persecute you.
Matthew 5:44, NIV.

Squanto had every right not to trust White men. They had kidnapped him from America and taken him to Europe. Then, when Squanto came home, he found that his entire village had been wiped out by a sickness. He was the only one left.

One day, late in 1620, Squanto saw a ship anchor in the bay near his home. White men were coming again. This time the White men had women and children with them. It looked as though they might stay.

Because of his time in Europe, Squanto could speak English well. He learned that the ship was called the *Mayflower* and that the people who sailed on it had come to America to get away from people who had been unkind to them. They had come to live in a place where they could have the freedom to worship God the way they wanted.

These Pilgrims faced many hardships that winter. There was always the danger that other Indians might attack them, but Squanto helped to arrange a treaty with the Indian chief. Because he knew both English and the Indian languages, he was a good interpreter.

In the spring Squanto helped the Pilgrims plant their first seeds. In the fall he was there to help with the harvest. If it hadn't been for Squanto's kindness, the history of the United States could have turned out differently.

One peaceful hero who decides to show kindness rather than hate can make a big difference.

PEACE AND HUMILITY

3

JUNE

Humility and the fear of the Lord bring wealth and honor and life.
Proverbs 22:4, NIV.

Watt an Idea!

Steam fascinated James Watt. As a child he spent hours watching it rise from teakettles, catching and collecting it, and wondering about how it worked. He wanted to figure out why it did the things it did. He spent so much time studying steam that eventually he knew more about it than anyone else. But what good did it do to know how steam works?

So James put his knowledge to work and created a steam engine. His new engine could do the work of up to 5 million men! It became the most powerful engine known, and it was eventually used to power train engines, boats, and all kinds of things.

James knew about more than just steam. He loved to learn, and he spent time learning about all kinds of scientific things. He could talk to anyone about anything. Even though he knew a lot about many different things, he was never proud or rude about it. He never talked down to anyone. James was happy to talk to people about the things that interested them, and he spoke to them on a level that they could understand.

There may be areas in which you excel. But as God's hero, always remember to speak kindly to everyone and never brag. Others may be good at things that you aren't so good at. We can learn from one another if we are humble and willing to learn.

PEACE AND HUMILITY

The Dusty Stranger

Pale (pronounced Pa-lay) was hot and dusty from hiking through the African bush. He had to get to the mission.

Pale lived in a small dirty village where everyone worshipped idols and drank lots of beer. The villagers thought the idols would help them, but the idols never changed anything. No one went to school, the beer made people lazy, and Pale was tired of living that way. He was going to the mission to tell them that he wanted to be a Christian.

When he arrived, the missionaries were surprised to see him. He had walked a long, long way. They talked to him about Jesus and answered all of his questions. Pale told them again how much he wanted to give his life to Jesus. They prayed together, and Pale went back home a happier man.

He and his family walked back to the mission the following Sabbath for church. Soon everyone could see the changes in Pale. His village was still small and dirty. Many people still worshipped idols and drank beer, but Pale and his family knew Jesus and had peace in their hearts.

Peace is God's way. If we ask Jesus to live in our hearts, He will help us to have peace, no matter what is going on around us.

Peace I leave with you; my peace I give you. I do not give to you as the world gives. Do not let your hearts be troubled and do not be afraid. John 14:27.

PEACE AND HUMILITY

The Greatest Genius That Ever Lived

Isaac Newton grew up wondering. He wondered about everything. He wondered how fast the wind blew. He wondered why apples fell down instead of up. He wondered why the moon traveled in a circle around the earth instead of flying off into space. He wondered and wondered.

All of this wondering made Isaac want to learn as much as he could. As he got older, he spent many hours experimenting to find the answers.

Isaac discovered amazing things because of his wondering and experimenting. He discovered that gravity is what makes an apple fall down instead of up, and also what keeps the moon from spinning off into space. He created a whole new kind of math called calculus, and he learned that light is made up of seven colors instead of one. There was always more that Isaac wanted to learn.

Other scientists found out about his discoveries and wanted to learn more. Soon Isaac was very famous. He didn't like being famous very much. He gave his money to people who needed it more than he did. Throughout his life he always stayed humble, never even telling people about some of his discoveries.

There are quiet heroes around us every day—people like Isaac Newton who quietly do what they can to make the world a better place without the need to make a big deal of it. What kind of good things can you do quietly today, without needing to be noticed or praised?

Let another praise you, and not your own mouth; someone else, and not your own lips.

Proverbs 27:2, NIV.

PEACE AND HUMILITY

Washed Clean

Indeed, now I know that there is no God in all the earth, except in Israel.

2 Kings 5:15.

Naaman rubbed his eyes, hoping that he hadn't seen what he thought he'd seen. Surely he, the great Syrian commander, couldn't have leprosy. It was the most feared disease of his time. How could this be?

His whole family was upset when they found out. It would change all of their lives. Naaman's wife cried and cried.

Her servant saw that she was crying and told her that Naaman should go see the prophet Elisha in Israel. He could heal Naaman of the leprosy. Naaman left in a hurry.

Elisha told Naaman to wash in the river Jordan. He told him to dip under the water seven times, and it would make him clean. Naaman was angry. He was an army commander! He didn't want to obey some old man and wash in a dirty old river. He had cleaner rivers in his own country.

Naaman's servants convinced him that he might as well try it; it was such a simple thing. So he swallowed his pride and went down to the river. One, two, three times he went under. Nothing. Four, five, six. Still nothing. He went under one more time, and when he came up, everyone was waiting to see if he had been healed. The leprosy was gone! Naaman was so happy. The God of Israel had healed him.

In order to be healed, Naaman had to listen to God's prophet and do what he was told. We may not always understand them, but God's ways are always best. When we humbly obey Him, God will heal us from the disease of sin, and we will be blessed more than we can imagine.

PEACE AND HUMILITY

The Power of Peace

Blessed are the peacemakers, for they shall be called sons of God.

Matthew 5:9.

Mohandas Gandhi (also known as Mahatma Gandhi) was a lawyer who spent his life working for India's freedom from Britain. He didn't try to fight with violence; he always looked for nonviolent ways to solve problems. Sometimes he would try to get the attention of the British government by holding a hunger strike—he would stop eating. He was so well known and well loved that the British gave in to his hunger strikes several times; they knew there would be an even bigger problem if he died.

Gandhi lived a life of prayer, fasting, and meditation. Earthly possessions weren't important to him. He wore a loincloth and shawl like the poorest Indians. He ate vegetables, fruit juice, and goat's milk. He was arrested many times, but he never fought back. Eventually, in large part because of Gandhi and his leadership, India was declared a free country.

God may not call us to wear a loincloth and drink goat's milk, but we can learn from Gandhi's example. It isn't what you have, but who you are, that will have a lasting impact. Gandhi's peaceful ways changed the world, and our ways can bring changes too.

PEACE AND HUMILITY

Humble Hero!

*Before honor
is humility.*
Proverbs 15:33.

Everyone said it couldn't be done. It was just too far to fly alone from New York City to Paris, France. Charles Lindbergh didn't let that stop him. He carefully mapped out a plan for the 3,600-mile trip. Early on the morning of May 20, 1927, Lindbergh and his plane, *The Spirit of St. Louis,* took off from just outside New York City. Would he ever be seen again?

He flew over Nova Scotia, then Newfoundland. During the night he could see the white icebergs shining through the darkness, but there was no sound other than the hum of the plane's engine.

On and on he flew over the ocean until, finally, he began to see small ships. Before long he saw the coast of Ireland, then England, and finally France. It was about 10:00 p.m. Paris time when Charles circled the Eiffel Tower and landed his plane in a field. He had done the thing that couldn't be done. He had been in the air 33 hours and 30 minutes. About 100,000 people greeted him on the airfield. They were so excited they practically pulled him out of the plane and carried him around the field for a half hour! He was a world-famous hero now, receiving honors wherever he went. Everyone wanted to be near him.

Back home Charles received hundreds of offers to make money from his adventure. His answer was always the same: "Gentleman, I am not for sale." Even though he had done what no one else had ever done, he was always modest and humble. The fame didn't change him. That made him a true hero.

Real heroes for God can be happy about their accomplishments without being boastful. Instead, be like Jesus, the biggest hero of all!

PEACE AND HUMILITY

9
JUNE

The Mother of God

*Let it be
to me
according to
your word.*

Luke 1:38.

God sent an angel to Mary to ask her to do something no one had ever done before. Sure, lots of women had had babies before, but no one had ever had a baby that was God's Son. After listening to the angel, Mary agreed to follow God's plan. It took courage on her part. In those days a woman who was pregnant and wasn't married could have been stoned to death. People would have thought she was crazy if she tried to tell them that her child was God's Son.

Mary trusted that God was in control. With God's help she brought Jesus into the world and raised Him. It would have been easy for her to become proud that God had chosen her to be His Son's earthly mother, but she remained humble. She had the courage to accept the gift that God had given her.

We are proud when we take credit for the gifts God has given or the things He has done for us. We are humble when we accept those gifts and use them for God's honor. Don't deny the gifts God has given you; instead, ask Him to help you humbly use them every day.

170

PEACE AND HUMILITY

friend of Indians

In 1682 William Penn and a group of Quakers set sail from England for America. After a long, hard trip, they landed in what is now Delaware. They were greeted by the English settlers who had gone before them. William had been given the land by the king of England, but he came as a friend to help the settlers, not as a ruler over them. He wanted this new land to be a place of freedom where the people ruled themselves. He wanted to give the settlers freedom to worship as they pleased. This was a big change from the way things were in England.

William wanted this not only for the English settlers but also for the Indians of the area. He treated them with kindness and respect, and they loved him for it. He explained that although their skin colors were different, they were all children of the "Great Spirit," who wanted them to be friends.

Many battles were fought between the White people and Indians, but because of William Penn's kindness, no Quakers were killed by Indians. The Indians knew that he was their friend. They treated William and all of the Quakers with kindness and respect, just as he treated them.

William didn't have to treat the Indians nicely. But as a hero for God, he did what he could to avoid a fight and look for peaceful solutions.

But the meek will inherit the land and enjoy great peace.
Psalm 37:11.

PEACE AND HUMILITY

11
June

He who is greatest among you shall be your servant.
Matthew 23:11.

X-ray Vision

Professor Sklodowska's daughter, Marie, was her father's helper in his laboratory by the time she was 9 years old. She raced to the lab after school. The things she learned there fascinated her.

Marie's love of science never ended. She became very well educated and worked as a scientist. She married Pierre Curie in 1895; together they discovered a thing called radium, which was the basis of X-rays. Because radium was expensive, they weren't able to buy much of it. So they lectured on their discovery and taught, patiently waiting for the time when they could make use of their discovery.

In 1903 the Curies were awarded the Nobel Prize, which they shared with another professor. In 1911, after Pierre's death, Marie was awarded the Nobel Prize again. At that time she was the only person to have received it twice.

Because of her discoveries and awards, Madame Curie became famous. She was asked to give lectures all over the world. Honors came to her from around the globe. She was a quiet, soft-voiced woman who did not brag about the things she'd accomplished. She always kept working to discover other ways to help the world.

God's heroes can be proud of their accomplishments. They work hard and do their best at everything without bragging. And they always look for new ways to make the world a better place.

172

PEACE AND HUMILITY

My Feudiñ' Days Are Through

It all started over a pig. Floyd Hatfield said the pig belonged to him, and Randolph McCoy said it didn't. Finally they had to take it to court, pig and all. Mr. Hatfield got his pig, but the hard feelings continued. They grew and grew until, eventually, violence broke out. It was said that between 30 and 100 people died as a result of this feud. The hatred was passed down through the generations. Hatfields hated McCoys, and McCoys hated Hatfields. That's just the way it was.

Until one day when Old Devil Anse, the leader of the Hatfields, accepted Christ. His two sons had been killed in the feuding. He finally decided to give his heart to Jesus, and it changed his life. He was still a sharpshooter; he could hit pretty much anything he wanted without raising the gun above his waist. But he wouldn't use his gun for violence anymore. After more than 25 years the feud was over.

It took courage for Old Devil Anse to give his life to Christ and change his ways. If we're truly God's heroes, our hearts and lives will be changed when we let Him in our hearts too.

A gentle answer turns away wrath, but a harsh word stirs up anger.
Proverbs 15:1, NIV.

PEACE AND HUMILITY

Robert and the Robber

*You will keep in
perfect peace him
whose mind is
steadfast, because
he trusts in you.*

Isaiah 26:3, NIV.

You can't go there!" the people told him. "He'll kill you!" Everyone tried to warn Robert Moffat not to go to the area of South Africa where Jager Afrikaner lived. Jager was a well-known and much-feared criminal. But Robert had heard that Jager had been converted, and he wanted to see for himself. So off he went.

Soon he was face to face with the famous outlaw. But Jager didn't kill Robert; instead, they shook hands and became friends. It was true—Jager had accepted Jesus as his savior, and was no longer in the outlaw business.

Robert wanted people to know that Jager was a changed man. But Jager was afraid that if he went back to Cape Town with Robert, he would be thrown in jail for the things he had done in the past. Robert pleaded with him, and after three days of prayer Jager decided to go. Even if he was thrown in prison, it was the right thing to do.

Everyone in Cape Town was amazed at the change in Jager, especially the governor. At first he just stared at him. Then the governor was so happy that he gave Jager a letter of pardon and the reward that had been offered for his capture. He was no longer a wanted man!

We don't have to be afraid of judgment if we've accepted Jesus into our hearts. God has given us a letter of pardon too. When Jesus died on the cross, He paid for our sins. We're still wanted, but only because God wants us to be in heaven with Him!

PEACE AND HUMILITY

Mother of the Salvation Army

The Bible verse that hung on her wall summed up everything Catherine Booth believed: "My grace is sufficient for thee." No matter what she faced in her life, she was always peaceful and determined. Her faith was strong.

She was sick most of her life, but she still managed to get married and have eight children. Despite her bad health, Catherine's first priority was to help people come to know Jesus. Her husband, William, was an evangelist, and she did everything she could to help him in his ministry. Together they started the Salvation Army, which has helped thousands of people through the years.

Catherine allowed God to use her in spite of her sickness. God can use anyone—young or old, healthy or sick, big or small, short or tall—if they will let Him. Will you allow Him to use you to do good for Him today?

My grace is sufficient for you, for my power is made perfect in weakness.
2 Corinthians 12:9, NIV.

PEACE AND HUMILITY

175

I Have a Dream

Seek peace and pursue it.
Psalm 34:14.

Martin Luther King, Jr., saw things happen around him that weren't fair—things that made many people angry. Instead of fighting, as some of the angry people suggested, King taught that we should solve our problems by talking about them. He wanted people to think of nonviolent solutions.

In one of his most famous speeches, King said that he had a dream that one day people of all colors and religions would be able to be friends. He helped our country begin to solve many problems.

When problems come up in our lives, our first reaction many times is to fight with our friends, siblings, or almost anyone else. But heroes for God will talk through their problems instead of fighting about them. Heroes find other ways to solve their problems.

Ask God today to help you make good decisions and to think of good ways to solve problems.

PEACE AND HUMILITY

Singh a New Song

Sundar Singh's family was unhappy that he had decided to become a Christian. His family was Hindu, and it was hard for them to understand why he would turn his back on their religion. At first they were just sad, but then they became angry. They decided they would make him change his mind.

They made him live in the barn and eat with the servants. They treated him as if he were no longer part of the family. They even had him thrown into a pit, as Joseph was, and they left him there for three days. After he was rescued, he kept right on preaching.

One day an uncle of Sundar's thought he'd found the sure way to change his nephew's mind. He took Sundar to a room and showed him all the wealth he could imagine. There was enough money for him to buy anything he could ever want. His uncle told him that all he had to do to make all of it his was to renounce Christ. If he would just say the word, it could all be his. He'd never have to worry about paying bills or not having enough money.

But Sundar knew that stuff isn't what makes you really happy. He knew that what he already had was more important than all the money in that room. Sundar turned down his uncle's offer.

Throughout our lives there will be many temptations to deny Christ for what may seem to be good reasons—wealth, school, friends, family. But nothing will give us peace like knowing Jesus and asking Him to live in our hearts. He's the greatest gift of all!

Delight yourself in the Lord and he will give you the desires of your heart.
Psalm 37:4, NIV.

PEACE AND HUMILITY

17

Chief Gwamña

A good man . . .
will guide his
affairs with
discretion.
Psalm 112:5.

Gwamna was an orphan living with his uncle's family. His uncle and cousins teased him because he believed in Jesus. They beat him, kept food from him, and made him do extra work.

Eventually Gwamna and a friend were sent to a government school for training to become teachers. While he was there, Gwamna also enjoyed studying the Bible, praying, and sharing Jesus with others. He learned much while he was there and became a preacher as well as a teacher.

When it was time for Gwamna's tribe to elect a new chief, his name was one of three being considered. Many people didn't want Gwamna to be the chief because he was a Christian, and they had never had a Christian as a chief before. But when the people voted, Gwamna was elected.

Being chief was a great honor, but for the remainder of his life, Gwamna was humble and committed. He kept preaching in addition to his other duties, and he started every day with prayer.

If we are truly heroes for God, we will be humble no matter what position we find ourselves in. God needs us to be honest, truthful, and humble heroes for Him.

PEACE AND HUMILITY

A True Christian

Rich Mullins was a very rich man. But he didn't act like it. He lived in an average house and got by on an average salary. He didn't trust himself to use his money wisely, so he asked someone to manage his money for him. He used the rest of his money to help people. When he heard that a person needed help, he did what he could. Once he even gave someone the shirt off his back.

Everyone who knew him could see that he didn't just say he was a Christian—he lived his faith. He could have spent all his money on himself, but instead he used it to help other people and lived on only what he needed.

Rich knew that the things of earth aren't what are most important. He knew that whatever he had on earth wouldn't last. He knew that the most important thing was to know Jesus and have his treasure stored up in heaven.

The Bible tells us that wherever our treasure is, our heart will be there too. Where is your heart today?

Where your treasure is, there your heart will be also.
Luke 12:34.

PEACE AND HUMILITY

179

19
JUNE

Admirable Admiral

To God, alone wise, be glory through Jesus Christ forever.
Romans 16:27.

David Robinson's basketball teammates nicknamed him the Admiral because he had served in the Navy. In a game in which many players have big egos, he was known for his quiet humility. He donated much of his salary to charity, and in interviews he would often give thanks to God for the talents he had. David knew that any good things he could do were gifts from God, not something he could take credit for or brag about.

David Robinson is good at basketball, but he is also a good person. His influence on the basketball court helped others to know that he is a Christian. Can people tell that you're a Christian by the way you live? What gifts has God given to you? How can you use these gifts for His honor and glory today?

PEACE AND HUMILITY

The Man Who Loved Freedom

I will walk at liberty, for I seek Your precepts.
Psalm 119:45.

Thomas Jefferson was interested in a lot of things. He loved to think, teach, learn, experiment, build, invent, farm, write, and play music. But most of all he loved freedom. He spent most of his adult life helping to build a country in which the people were free.

Mr. Jefferson wrote the Declaration of Independence, one of the most important documents in our country's history. He was also the third president of the United States. His whole life was devoted to making sure that people would be able to think, work, and worship the way they believed was right. He worked hard to make sure the United States of America was that kind of place.

In the country that Mr. Jefferson helped to build, there is the freedom to choose. We can choose what church to attend, we can choose where we want to live, and we can say what we want to say. People who live in the United States have more freedom than those in many other countries in the world.

God's way is freedom. He won't force us to do anything, but He will always give us a choice. Will you choose to live your life in God's freedom?

PEACE AND HUMILITY

A Different Kind of Weapon

Always be prepared to give an answer to everyone who asks you to give the reason for the hope that you have. But do this with gentleness and respect.

1 Peter 3:15, NIV.

The other soldiers didn't like Desmond Doss. Because he believed he should obey the Ten Commandments, Desmond didn't want to kill anyone. He trained to work as a medic to take care of the wounded soldiers instead. He worked extra hours to make up for not working on Sabbath, but the other soldiers teased him and were mean to him because he was a Christian. One man even told Desmond that he'd kill him himself when they went into battle.

In spite of everything, Desmond stood strong and never did anything he felt was wrong. Even though the others teased him, he kept reading his Bible and saying his prayers.

When they went into battle, Desmond kept praying. The other soldiers noticed that even though they had teased him, he still showed love and compassion to each of them when he took care of them. The others saw that he was really living what he believed, and they stopped picking on him quite as much.

In one battle alone Desmond saved at least 75 lives. Because of his brave service, many lives were saved and many friends were made.

It may seem that we have to give up our beliefs to be friends with some people. But if you want to be a true hero for God, don't give up what you believe. True friends won't ask you to do that. Ask God to help you show peace, kindness, and love to everyone—even those who aren't nice to you.

PEACE AND HUMILITY

Peacemaker Pocahontas

Have peace with one another.
Mark 9:50.

The men with the pale skin brought many new things to Pocahontas's world. She had never seen men who had such light skin or who wore so many clothes. They said they came from a faraway place called England. Pocahontas had never heard of England before, but she decided to make friends with the strange White men.

That's just what she did, too. Even when the White men were at war with her people, she still worked hard to keep peace between the White men and her people. Years later an Englishman named Captain John Smith said that without Pocahontas's help the colony at Jamestown, Virginia, would never have survived. She was a true friend.

Have you ever been the new kid? Did you feel that everyone looked at you as if you were from another planet? It is hard when that happens. Just remember what Pocahontas did. If you're the new kid or if there's a new kid in your school, church, or neighborhood, be a peacemaker and make a new friend.

PEACE AND HUMILITY

23
JUNE

Peacekeeper or Warmaker?

Let the peace of God rule in your hearts.

Colossians 3:15.

In New York City there are many really tall buildings. Some buildings are so tall you have to stop walking, crane your neck, and look up until you almost bend over backwards before you can see the top!

One of these tall buildings is called the United Nations Building. A man named Kofi Annan works in that tall, tall building. Mr. Annan works with all the countries of the world to try to help them solve their problems and keep peace. He has traveled all over the globe to try to help people of many countries solve their problems.

Sometimes it works, and sometimes it doesn't, but Mr. Annan and his workers always try to help keep the peace. They know that peace and happiness go together; when they help people to make peace, they help them to be happy, too.

Do you help keep peace or make war in your home? Peace in the world starts in your home and mine. Today, ask God to help you be a peacekeeper instead of a warmaker.

PEACE AND HUMILITY

The Better Way

What do you want to be when you grow up? A firefighter, a doctor, or maybe a teacher?

When Colin Powell grew up, he became the secretary of state for the United States. The secretary of state works for the president. Part of the job is to help smooth over problems and promote understanding with other countries.

During the time that Mr. Powell was secretary of state, a lot of things, both good and bad, happened in the United States and the world. He was secretary of state in 2001, during the September 11 terrorist attacks. That was also a time when much progress was made to help people who were sick with HIV/AIDS.

Mr. Powell tries to help people build better governments in countries that don't have freedom. He once said that he wanted to help everyone in the world live in democracy and freedom if they wanted to. In many places people aren't free to worship as they choose, travel where they want, or do many of the things we sometimes take for granted in the United States. Mr. Powell wants to help everyone in the world who wants to live a better life.

As God's hero you can help others to live a better life. You can help by obeying the law, by being kind, and also by helping them to know Jesus. When you pray today, ask God to help you live the best life you can and to help others do the same.

Be an example to the believers in word, in conduct, in love, in spirit, in faith, in purity.
1 Timothy 4:12.

PEACE AND HUMILITY

Life's Adventure

For the ways of the Lord are right; the righteous walk in them.

Hosea 14:9.

Daniel Boone was born at a time when very little land in America was settled. Most of the new country was wilderness—woods and streams, forests and prairies. Kentucky, which we now think of as being in the East, was thought of as the far West. Today our country goes west all the way to California, Oregon, Washington, Alaska, and even Hawaii. In Daniel's time, though, Kentucky was as far west as settlers went.

Daniel loved to explore and be in nature. He spent most of his life helping people get to Kentucky. Along the way there was always the chance they might meet danger or have to fight wild animals. But Daniel brought many people safely to Kentucky and helped them build houses and towns in the wilderness.

Daniel's adventures traveling west were sometimes very hard, and our life on this earth may be hard at times too. But if we trust and follow Jesus as our guide, our adventures will lead to a better place than we can ever imagine. Along the way, invite friends to travel with you on our great adventure to heaven.

PEACE AND HUMILITY

Just Doing His Job

Alvin York did not want to fight. He knew that killing people was wrong, and he didn't want to be a part of war. But he was drafted into the Army and sent to France to fight in World War I.

In a battle on October 8, 1918, in Argonne, France, Alvin and his company of 17 soldiers captured 132 enemy soldiers all by themselves. Even though there were almost eight enemy prisoners to every one American soldier, they managed to lead all of the prisoners to the American side. Later Alvin said he wasn't a hero. He said he had just done his job and wanted to go home.

God has given each of His heroes a job to do. You may have the chance to help your parents around the house without complaining, do something kind for a neighbor, or make a new friend at church or school. Pray that He will show you what job He has for you to do today. Then do it well so we can go home to heaven soon.

And now, Israel, what does the Lord your God require of you, but to fear the Lord your God, to walk in all His ways and to love Him, to serve the Lord your God with all your heart and with all your soul.

Deuteronomy 10:12.

PEACE AND HUMILITY

27
JUNE

Teachable Teacher

Blessed are the pure in heart, for they shall see God.

Matthew 5:8.

I don't remember ever seeing Karen Minner without a smile on her face. And in all the years I knew her, I don't remember hearing anyone say anything bad about her. Everyone loved Karen, and Karen loved everyone. She was a peacemaker and always tried to help people be friends instead of fighting.

Karen didn't just love people; she loved God with all her heart, and she wanted to work for Him. Her love for God took her to Pohnpei, Micronesia, as a student missionary for a year. It was a hard year for her. She didn't like being away from her friends and family. But she made many friends in Micronesia, and she kept in touch with her new friends even after she came back to the United States.

Karen especially loved children. She had just started a job teaching elementary school when she suddenly got sick. The doctors didn't know why Karen was sick, and even though they tried very hard to help Karen get well, she died in 2001. She was only 23 years old.

Everyone was surprised when hundreds of people came to her funeral. Even though her life was short, her sweet, kind, peaceful spirit had a huge impact on everyone she met. Her family and friends were so sad that Karen died, but they know that she loved God very much and that they will see her again someday soon in heaven.

It doesn't matter how young or old we are—our actions always impact others, whether we know it or not. Ask God to help you have a pure heart so that you can see Him in heaven. And say hi to Karen when you get there!

PEACE AND HUMILITY

God's Engine

So we, being many, are one body in Christ.

Romans 12:5.

The little missionary boat *Portal* was being used by the British in World War II when it broke down in a lagoon. The British had to leave, but the boat wouldn't budge. Rather than risk having the boat fall into enemy hands, they dumped gasoline on the deck and set the little ship on fire. Then they sailed away in another boat.

The Christians in the area didn't want God's little missionary boat to burn, so they prayed that He would save it. Almost immediately the fire went out, and the little boat rocked quietly on the waves. The people praised God for saving the *Portal;* then they swam or took small boats out to where it sat. They pushed it to the mouth of a little creek that was almost covered by trees, and hid it there.

Then the people began to take the engine apart piece by piece. Some pieces were buried; others were hung in trees or became part of a necklace. Each person was put in charge of knowing where one part of the engine was hidden.

When the missionary returned, he was surprised to see the *Portal.* He'd been told by the British that it had been destroyed. He gladly went on board, but was sad to discover that the boat didn't have an engine. What good was a boat without an engine?

Word spread that the pastor who had been at the mission was back. Pieces of the boat engine started coming in—dug up, pulled out of trees, and taken off necks. Everyone brought in their piece of the engine, until all the pieces were all there. For weeks they worked to put it all back together, until one day they pushed the button, and the *Portal* roared back to life.

Think of the church as being God's engine. It needs all of its parts to run too. What part do you play in God's engine? Together, if we all do our part, we can do great things for God!

PEACE AND HUMILITY

Brought Together by Kindness

When a man's ways please the Lord, he makes even his enemies to be at peace with him.

Proverbs 16:7.

The sun beat down on the little airplane as it made its way through the desert from Cairo, Egypt, to Baghdad, Iraq. The two Spanish men on board talked about how bad it would be to get stuck in that desert with nothing but sand as far as you could see. They flew for a long way with no trouble, but then their plane ran out of gas, and they were forced to land the airplane in the sand.

After several days their food and water ran out, and the men decided to start walking. If help couldn't get to them, they hoped they would be able to get to help.

Meanwhile, the men's friends in Cairo were worried. They knew the men had not arrived in Baghdad. On the third day after they disappeared, the British Royal Air Force in Egypt sent out eight airplanes to look for them.

Finally, on the sixth day, the British pilots saw a dot in the sand. Twenty-five miles from the downed airplane they picked up one of the men. Hot and tired, he was awfully glad to see his British rescuers. He told them the pilot had gone ahead to find help, so they went on. Later that day, 45 miles away from his airplane, the pilot was rescued from the hot sand.

When word reached Spain of the kindness of the British pilots, the people of Spain sent thousands of thank-you notes to the British. In the middle of a war, two countries were brought together by kindness.

Kindness and peace go hand in hand. Where there is one, there is almost always the other. Can you think of something that you can do today to spread peace?

PEACE AND HUMILITY

Brave Hannah

When Hannah was 3 years old, she was afraid of going to sleep. She thought big, mean dinosaurs (she called them "dina-sorns") would come and get her as she lay in bed in her dark room. For a while she was even afraid that giant rabbits would come in her room.

"I'm scared," she told her parents. She wanted her mommy to sleep with her so she wouldn't be afraid.

To comfort Hannah and help her fall asleep, her mommy and daddy played soft lullaby music and rubbed her back for three songs. Mommy and Daddy reminded her every night that her guardian angel was in her room to protect her. They also prayed to ask Jesus to place angels at every door and window of their house to guard Hannah and their family from harm.

Hannah's parents reminded her that Jesus promised in the Bible that He would never leave us alone. She learned to pray, "Dear Jesus, please keep me safe tonight." She learned to talk to Jesus about feeling afraid and to lie quietly so she would fall asleep.

Now when Hannah goes to sleep at night she says, "Good night, Mama—sweet dreams!" and falls asleep knowing that Jesus and the angels will watch over her.

There's nothing to be afraid of when you're God's hero. He's bigger than everything, and we can sleep in peace knowing that He'll send His angels to watch over us.

I will both lie down in peace, and sleep; for You alone, O Lord, make me dwell in safety.
Psalm 4:8.

PEACE AND HUMILITY

Integrity

Man looks at the outward appearance, but the Lord looks at the heart.

1 Samuel 16:7.

Integrity is a big word that people don't use as often as they used to. If people have integrity, it means that they do what is right, no matter what is happening around them or who is watching.

There are a lot of people in the world today who don't have integrity. They may look nice on the outside, but that's not what matters to God. He looks at our hearts. God knows what we're really like deep down.

It's more important to Him that we have a clean heart and mind than if we dress in fancy clothes, live in a nice house, or ride in an expensive car. God wants us to love Him and others, and to show it by living lives of integrity.

Jesus has integrity. Do you?

HONESTY AND INTEGRITY

Daniel and His Lyin' Friends

The new law said that people could pray to only the king for 30 days—anyone who disobeyed would be thrown into the lions' den. The king's sneaky advisers wrote the law as a trap for Daniel. They knew that Daniel prayed to his God three times a day. They were jealous that Daniel had been given the best job, and they wanted to get rid of him. The king was honored by this new law, and he put his wax seal on it, meaning it could not be changed.

Near Daniel's home the sneaky advisers waited. Right on schedule Daniel opened his windows and knelt down to pray to his God. The advisers ran off to tell on him.

The king was upset when he heard the news about Daniel. He knew he'd been tricked. But he also knew that he had no choice, and Daniel was thrown into the lions' den. All night the king worried about his friend. As soon as it was morning he ran to the den and called down, "Daniel, . . . has your God, whom you serve continually, been able to rescue you from the lions?" (Daniel 6:20).

He was happy to hear Daniel answer, "O king, live forever! My God sent his angel, and he shut the mouths of the lions. They have not hurt me" (verses 21, 22). The king ordered his guards to get Daniel out, and there wasn't a scratch on him! He had spent all night in a den of lions, but God had protected him.

Daniel didn't have to pray to God during those 30 days. He could have chosen to close his windows so that no one could see him. However, Daniel knew the importance of doing what is right, and God honored his integrity by protecting him from the lions.

The could find no corruption in him, because he was trustworthy and neither corrupt nor negligent.

Daniel 6:4, NIV.

HONESTY AND INTEGRITY

3

JULY

Accept one another, then, just as Christ accepted you, in order to bring praise to God.

Romans 15:7, NIV.

This Seat's Taken

Rosa Parks of Montgomery, Alabama, was tired after a hard day of work. Her feet ached, and she was so thankful to be able to sit down. The bus she was riding was getting full, and soon they would be on their way. But before they could get going, they ran out of seats. The bus driver told Ms. Parks to get up and give her seat to a man. He said she had to do it because her skin was black and the man's skin was white. Does that sound fair? I don't think so. Ms. Parks didn't think so either. She was tired, and she had just as much right to sit in that seat as anyone else. And she told the bus driver so.

What do you think happened? The bus driver had her arrested because she wouldn't give up her seat. But Ms. Parks was brave enough to refuse to go along with something that was wrong, even though it meant getting arrested. In the long run her simple act of courage led to the United States Supreme Court outlawing segregation on city buses. People could no longer be forced to go to the back of the bus because of the color of their skin. Ms. Parks continued to work for freedom and equality for all Americans.

It may seem silly to us today that people of different skin colors had to sit on separate bus seats, but that's the way it was. Do you think a hero for God would treat people differently just because they had a different color of skin? I don't think so. God loves each of us the same, and wants us to have the courage to stand up for each other and for what is right.

HONESTY AND INTEGRITY

194

Honest Abe

Have you ever been dishonest? Perhaps you've told one of those little white lies that is sort of the truth. I think most of us probably have.

Does the fact that it is partially true make it better than a "real" lie? No, it doesn't. A half truth is a whole lie.

In the 1800s the United States had a president who was known for being honest. His name was Abraham Lincoln, and he did many good things for our country. He was president during the Civil War, a very difficult time in our nation's history. Even though it wasn't always the easy thing to do, President Lincoln tried to be honest and do the right thing. In fact, he was so well known for his honesty that people started calling him "Honest Abe."

Whether you realize it or not, people around you notice what kind of person you are. Younger siblings look up to you as a role model—you might even be their hero. Your friends' actions may be affected by you, too—at home, church, and school.

What kind of role model do you think a hero for God would be? Do people know by your everyday actions and attitude that you are a hero for God?

You shall not give false testimony against your neighbor.
Exodus 20:16, NIV.

HONESTY AND INTEGRITY

5
JULY

Look, Lord, I give half of my goods to the poor; and if I have taken anything from anyone by false accusation, I restore fourfold.

Luke 19:8.

Short Man, Long Rewards

Zacchaeus was a Jew who collected taxes for the Romans. The other Jews hated him and called him a traitor. He was known for being greedy, and he'd gotten rich by cheating them.

When Zacchaeus heard that Jesus was coming to town, he wanted to see Him. He was short and couldn't see over the crowd, so he ran down the street and climbed a tree that Jesus would most likely pass under. He wanted to see this Man that everyone was talking about.

Soon he saw Jesus coming. His faced looked kind. Zacchaeus wondered if He could really be the Messiah.

As Jesus made His way down the street, He stopped under the tree where Zacchaeus was sitting. He looked up and told Zacchaeus to come down from the tree—He wanted to stay at his house. Zacchaeus was so excited. Jesus wanted to stay with him! He realized that Jesus loved him even when everyone else hated him.

The short time they spent together changed Zacchaeus. He promised Jesus that he would pay back everything he had stolen from others.

Zacchaeus' change of heart was shown by his actions. It's not enough just to follow Jesus in our hearts. If we really love Him, it will change our whole lives, including the way we treat others.

HONESTY AND INTEGRITY

A Trusted Friend

For whom the Lord loves He corrects, just as a father the son in whom he delights.

Proverbs 3:12.

Nathan had a hard job. He was a prophet, and God had given him a hard assignment. God wanted Nathan to tell King David the truth when David didn't want to hear it. King David could order his guards to kill Nathan for saying something he didn't like. But Nathan knew that telling the truth was important.

King David had taken another man's wife; he had sent that man to a war, knowing he would be killed. Nathan told the king a story to help him see the wrong in his actions. David repented of his sins. He knew that he wouldn't have liked it if someone had done that to him. He was sorry for what he had done.

Nathan knew the importance of being honest. He told King David what was right, instead of telling him what he wanted to hear. That's what a true friend does.

It's hard, sometimes, to tell someone the truth in love, but with God's help we can always be honest and help others to be honest too.

HONESTY AND INTEGRITY

The official Lifeguard of Newport Beach

*Well done,
good and
faithful servant.*
Matthew 25:23.

Pluto, the big, shaggy 150-pound Saint Bernard, had already saved four children from drowning at Newport Beach, California. He somehow seemed to know the difference between a child who was just playing in the water and one who was in trouble.

One cloudy morning Pluto saw that little George was playing tag with the waves, daring them to catch him, while his father fished nearby. Only Pluto saw when the waves did catch George. Immediately the child was pulled out to sea. When he opened his mouth to yell for help, a wave filled it with cold, salty water.

In a flash Pluto leaped into the ocean. The strong current tried to pull him under, but he fought to swim toward the little boy. Pluto struggled to keep his head above the waves as he slowly made his way out to sea. Finally the big dog was able to swim behind George and grab his swimming trunks. Then the tired pair headed for shore.

They finally made it, shivering and dripping. Little George had been hanging on so tightly that his father had to pry his fingers out of Pluto's fur.

Pluto had saved his fifth child, and he was given the title "Official Lifeguard of Newport Beach." The people of Newport Beach knew that they could count on Prince Pluto. Even though he didn't have any special training, they trusted him to help people when he saw a need, and he always did.

It's important that God's heroes can be trusted. We should be honest and truthful in our words, and we should always do what we say we will or what we are asked to do.

HONESTY AND INTEGRITY

The Man Who Did His Best

May integrity and uprightness protect [us].
Psalm 25:21, NIV.

Booker T. Washington was born to a slave mother. He didn't have an opportunity to go to school until after President Lincoln freed the slaves. Even then, he had to walk a long way and life was hard. But in everything he did, Booker was honest and faithful, and he did very well in his studies.

As an adult Booker wanted to build a school where other children could go to learn. He dreamed of the day when Black people would be treated the same as White people, and he spoke to many groups of people about it. He met with presidents, queens, and many other important people, but was always humble and kind to everyone.

One time Booker found out that someone had been saying ugly things about him. He said that he had decided that, no matter who was mean to him, he wouldn't hate him. He asked God to help him not to have any bad feelings toward others, no matter what. He knew that hate would only hurt him and was against God's will.

Booker eventually started Tuskegee Institute in Alabama—a school that became known for its excellence. Many people learned many things at Tuskegee Institute, and it helped thousands to live better lives.

Although Booker started out as the son of a slave, he became known for his patience, thoroughness, dignity, humility, and service to others. At his funeral it was said, "He loved all men and all men loved him."

When we live our lives as heroes for God, we will be an honest, hard worker, and we will show kindness and love toward everyone we meet.

HONESTY AND INTEGRITY

The Devil Made Me Do It

There is a way that seems right to a man, but its end is the way of death.

Proverbs 14:12.

Adam and Eve lived a perfect life in a perfect world. The temperature was just right, there was no pollution, and the animals were not afraid of them. They even walked and talked with God. He was their personal friend.

Satan didn't like the new perfect world or God's new friends. He used to be God's friend, but he had become proud and rejected God and His friendship. Now he was jealous; he wanted to take God's new friends away from Him.

One day Satan talked to Eve by the tree of knowledge. He asked her why God didn't want them to eat the fruit from it. Then he convinced her that God was just trying to keep good things from her and that nothing bad would happen if she ate from it. Unfortunately, Eve listened to Satan instead of God. She ate the fruit, then took some to Adam, and he ate it too.

Satan was delighted, but God was heartbroken. He had given Adam and Eve everything, and just asked them to not do one little thing, but they had disobeyed. When God came to visit them that evening, He asked them what had happened. Adam blamed Eve; Eve blamed Satan. Neither wanted to admit that they had done anything wrong. It was easier to blame someone else.

It's easy for us to try to excuse our sins by blaming other people. But God knows the truth and holds us responsible for our actions. We should admit it when we are wrong, and we should apologize instead of trying to blame someone else. We shouldn't make excuses; it's better to accept responsibility for our actions and admit the truth. And always trust what God says. His way is always best!

HONESTY AND INTEGRITY

A Professional Good Example

*J*esse loved to run. He was good at it, too. Over the years he won many, many races and set several world records.

Perhaps what Jesse Owens is most remembered for is competing in the 1936 Olympics in Berlin, Germany. Jesse was an African-American, and the leader of Germany at that time, Adolf Hitler, thought that only White people were any good. God's heroes know that that isn't true, but that's what Hitler thought.

Do you know what happened at those Olympics? Right there in front of Adolf Hitler, Jesse, the African-American, broke or tied Olympic records nine times and won four gold medals. Jesse Owens proved that he was just as good as anyone else there—even Adolf Hitler. It was an embarrassment for Hitler and a triumph for Jesse and the United States. One journalist called Jesse a "professional good example."

Are you a professional good example? Do you try your best at everything, no matter what other people say? Do your best today at everything you try, and with God's help be a professional good example like Jesse.

In everything set them an example by doing what is good.
Titus 2:7, NIV.

HONESTY AND INTEGRITY

A Dishonest Deal

Ananias and his wife, Sapphira, sold a piece of land. Ananias brought part of the money to Peter and told him that this was all the money they had been paid. Peter knew that was a lie, and he asked him about it. Ananias was so surprised, and so upset, that he fell down and died right there in front of Peter.

Several hours later Sapphira showed up. She told Peter the same story her husband had told. Peter asked her about it, and told her what had happened to her husband. She was just as surprised as Ananias had been—and she also fell down and died.

Ananias and Sapphira had listened to Satan instead of God. When they lied to Peter, they were also lying to God. They told Him that they were giving Him everything when they really weren't.

Satan was working hard in Bible days to trick Christians, and he's still working at it today. Ask God to help you each day to avoid Satan's traps. Ask Him to help you always tell the truth to the people in your life and also to Him. Give God your all today and see what great things you can do together.

HONESTY AND INTEGRITY

Peculiar Uncle Bob

*Do not . . .
share in other
people's sins;
keep yourself pure.*
1 Timothy 5:22.

Bob Sheffey made no apologies for who he was. A lot of people called him crazy, but these same people knew he loved them. They knew Bob would do anything he could for them, and they knew he loved the Lord.

Uncle Bob, as people called him, wasn't a good public speaker, but he sure could pray! He loved to pour out his heart to God, and he would tell Him everything on his mind. And God answered many of his prayers—sometimes almost immediately, and many times in miraculous ways.

Uncle Bob didn't care what other people thought about him. He did what he thought was right, and he didn't change just because people thought he was weird.

Although people sometimes were frustrated with him, Uncle Bob knew that it was OK to be different. He was happy to be who God made him to be, rather than who others wanted him to be. Who are you?

HONESTY AND INTEGRITY

No Joking Matter

Lot and his family lived in a very wicked city. They claimed to follow God, but they were content to mind their own business and not tell others about Him.

One evening two angels came to Sodom. Lot, not knowing that they were angels, invited them to stay at his house for the night. When they got there, the angels told him to take his family out of the city because God had sent them to destroy it. Lot believed them, and went to tell his family. But his family thought he was joking, and they didn't want to leave.

Lot had minded his own business for so long that he was no longer a believable witness for God.

What about you? Are you a reliable witness for God, or do you blend in with the crowd? Lot had tried to fit in, and now no one believed him when he stood up for God. As heroes for God, we don't have to be weird, but people should see the difference in our lives and know that we are Christians.

HONESTY AND INTEGRITY

What's in a Name?

Let everyone who names the name of Christ depart from iniquity.
2 Timothy 2:19.

Washington Irving's parents named him after General George Washington. They hoped he would become a great and honorable man like George Washington. When he was young, Washington met the man he was named after, and he was impressed with his dignity and kindness. He wanted to be like him too.

Washington hadn't tried very hard in school, and he had been a fairly poor student. Because he hadn't learned his lessons well in school, he had to work harder in life. He always wished that he would have studied harder.

But Washington loved to write. He wrote many books, including one on George Washington, and he became one of the first famous American authors.

Washington Irving wanted to honor the name of the man he was named after. We are Christians—we're named after Jesus Christ. Do you bring honor to the One you're named after?

HONESTY AND INTEGRITY

Pillar of Salt

No one can serve
two masters.

Matthew 6:24.

The angels had warned them to leave the city early in the morning, so they got up before the sun and ran. Lot, his wife, and his two daughters were the only ones who escaped alive because they were the only ones who had listened to the warning of the angels. As they entered a city called Zoar, fire came down from heaven and destroyed the cities of Sodom and Gomorrah, including the plains around them and the plants that grew on the ground. There was nothing left but ashes and smoke.

The angels had told them that they must not look back when the cities were destroyed. If they looked back, they would be destroyed too. The temptation was too much for Lot's wife, though, and she disobeyed. She turned to look at the city where she had lived so many years and raised a family. And she turned into a pillar of salt.

Lot's wife wasn't willing to follow the angels' instructions. Instead of turning her back on her longtime home, she took one last look.

We can't continue to look back at sin and at the same time move ahead in our relationship with God. He tells us in today's Bible verse that we cannot serve two masters. Who will be master of your life today—sin or God?

HONESTY AND INTEGRITY

Quiet Heroes

Whenever they saw a need, Carol and Danny were there to help. When a friend was going through hard times, they lent her a car and a shoulder to cry on. When people were lonely, Carol and Danny would drop in for a visit or invite them over for dinner. If they knew of someone who didn't have enough money, they'd quietly help however they could.

Sometimes the people they were helping never even knew about it. Carol and Danny just quietly went about the business of being good friends. They didn't care if people knew about it or not. In fact, they preferred that people didn't know about it. They just wanted to do the right thing.

Do you do good only when you think other people are watching, or do you do it because that is what God's heroes should do?

When you do a charitable deed, do not let your left hand know what your right hand is doing, that your charitable deed may be in secret; and your Father who sees in secret will Himself reward you openly.

Matthew 6:3.

HONESTY AND INTEGRITY

A Stubborn King

Repent, and turn from all your transgressions, so that iniquity will not be your ruin.

Ezekiel 18:30.

King Asa started out being a good king. For many years he and the Israelites worshipped God, but then he got off track.

Asa had an enemy named Baasha. Rather than working things out with Baasha, Asa bribed another king to help him defeat his enemy. The plan worked, but it wasn't God's way.

One of God's prophets came to tell King Asa that he wasn't following God's plan. Asa got very angry and had the prophet thrown in jail. He wouldn't listen to the prophet or anyone else, and he wouldn't admit that he had been wrong.

The king thought that, as long as he got his way, it didn't matter how. But a hero for God would have asked God for guidance. A hero would have done it the right way instead of doing whatever it took to get his own way.

It can be hard to admit when we are wrong. Rather than sticking up for your mistakes, it's better to admit that you goofed, learn from it, and move on. Don't be like stubborn King Asa and miss out on the blessings God has for your life.

HONESTY AND INTEGRITY

The Importance of a Promise

Dwight's mother taught him the importance of keeping a promise, whether it was a promise to take out the garbage or a promise to help a neighbor. She wouldn't ask him, "Can you do it?" She would ask, "Did you say you would?"

One winter he worked for a neighbor for room and board while he was in school. He got frustrated and went home. He wanted to quit because for 19 meals in a row all they'd given him to eat was cornmeal, milk, and hard bread crusts. He felt as if he were being fed like a chicken! When he complained to his mother, she asked him if he was going hungry. He had to admit that he wasn't, so she sent him back to keep his agreement.

Dwight Moody, one of the great Christian preachers of the nineteenth century, learned from his mother the importance of keeping a promise. God will keep His promises to us. We too should be careful about making promises, and do what we can to keep any promise we make.

My covenant I will not break, nor alter the word that has gone out of My lips.
Psalm 89:34.

HONESTY AND INTEGRITY

The Boy Who Did Things Differently

We are His workmanship, created in Christ Jesus for good works.
Ephesians 2:10.

John Wanamaker was different from the other kids. He usually got hurt when he played sports, but he enjoyed reading and exploring in nature. He knew that when he grew up he wanted a job in which he would use his brains instead of doing hard physical work.

John was honest and always did his best. He worked hard and eventually owned stores in New York and Philadelphia. One of his stores covered 45 acres!

The key to John's success was treating everyone with kindness and respect. He was always thinking of ways to make his stores better for customers. He tried to think of things that no one else had done before. For instance, his stores were the first ones to offer free public restrooms to customers. He was always trying to think of new, interesting, and different ways to be helpful to the people who visited his stores.

It's OK to do things differently. Just do your best. God made you to be who you are, with special talents, thoughts, and ideas. There's no one else on earth quite like you.

HONESTY AND INTEGRITY

A New Kind of Champion

You are . . .
known and read
by all men.
2 Corinthians 3:2.

Althea Gibson was a pioneer in her sport. Many women had played tennis before, but she was the first African-American woman to be a world champion in tennis.

Althea played tennis during a time when many African-Americans were treated unfairly in the United States. She was always a good sport, though, and she played so well that people couldn't help respecting her. Althea behaved with politeness and courtesy both on and off the tennis court. She became known for being a good athlete and a good person.

We all notice how people act. God's heroes will act like Jesus no matter where they are or what is happening around them. Can people tell that you are a Christian by the way you act?

HONESTY AND INTEGRITY

21

An Inside Look

For the word of God is living and powerful, and sharper than any two-edged sword.

Hebrews 4:12.

Dr. Paul Lauterbur and Dr. Peter Mansfield wanted to find a better way to see the inside of a person. They wanted something that showed more than an X-ray showed. They wanted to find a way to look inside without having to do surgery. After a great deal of studying and thinking, they came up with a plan, and they set to work putting it together.

Their work was the beginning of what we know today as MRI, or magnetic resonance imaging. This process helps doctors see problems faster. An MRI gives a detailed picture of the inside of whatever part of the body they need to see. Because of the hard work of Drs. Lauterbur and Mansfield, the MRI has helped many people get better medical care, and many lives have been saved.

Reading the Bible can be like an MRI. The Bible helps us to see what is wrong with our lives and what we can do to make things better. It might even save your life!

HONESTY AND INTEGRITY

God's Way to Fight

Have you ever gotten into a fight because someone said something about you that wasn't true? Andrew did. He was in many fights because he got angry about something that someone said. Once he even killed a man who said something ugly about his wife.

Does that sound like someone who is a hero for God? I don't think so. When Jesus lived on earth, many people said unkind and untrue things about Him. But He didn't get into fights or kill anyone over it. He let them say what they wanted and just kept on loving them.

That's hard to do, but that's what God asks His heroes to do. Don't bother with getting into fights whenever someone says something mean or untrue about you. Stand up for what is right, but always do it with kindness and love.

To him who strikes you on the one cheek, offer the other also.

Luke 6:29.

HONESTY AND INTEGRITY

Job Versus Conscience

The righteous man walks in his integrity.

Proverbs 20:7.

William Jennings Bryan wouldn't budge when he believed in something. It didn't matter what other people thought of him or what the consequences were. If he believed something was wrong, he wouldn't go along with it.

Once that cost him his job. He was working for President Woodrow Wilson in 1913, helping to keep peace between different countries in the world. One day President Wilson asked him to sign a piece of paper that said something Mr. Bryan didn't agree with. Rather than signing it, which would have meant keeping his job, he quit. Standing up for what he believed in was more important than his job.

It can be easy to talk yourself into doing something you know isn't right "just this once." However, God's heroes know it's better to make the right choice. Stand up for what you believe—every time, even when it's hard.

HONESTY AND INTEGRITY

The Hasel Family

The Hasel family lived in Germany when World War II broke out. Mr. Hasel was drafted to serve in Hitler's army. He knew that the things Hitler said were not true. He did not want to fight for Hitler's army, but he had no choice. When Mr. Hasel asked to be excused from working on Sabbaths, it made his commanding officer very angry. But he was determined to follow God.

God blessed the Hasel family for staying true to Him even when things got hard. Their family was kept safe through the whole war. Buildings all around them were bombed and looted, but their home was never touched. They trusted in God to take care of them and to follow through with the things that He promised in the Bible, and He did.

No matter what is going on around us, God is always in control. God can be trusted to keep His promises.

A thousand may fall at your side, and ten thousand at your right hand; but it shall not come near you.
Psalm 91:7.

HONESTY AND INTEGRITY

25

optical Illusions

Blessed is he who reads and . . . [keeps] those things which are written in [the book of Revelation]; for the time is near.
Revelation 1:3.

Have you ever seen a real live elephant? They're really, really big. It would be hard to miss an elephant in your living room. Of course, an elephant is so big, it couldn't even fit through your front door. And even if it did, your mom probably wouldn't be very happy about an elephant sitting on your couch.

Harry Houdini could make an elephant disappear. Well, he didn't really make the elephant disappear. It was a magic trick. Harry was famous for the tricks he performed. His tricks were called optical illusions—he tricked your eyes and your brain so that you thought you were seeing something you really didn't see. He built a career out of performing these kinds of tricks.

Harry's tricks never hurt anyone, but there were other people who created optical illusions that were mean. They tricked people into thinking that loved ones had come back from the dead. Many lonely people paid a lot of money to see these optical illusions, and they believed they were true. In order to keep people from being tricked, Harry worked to reveal the way these kinds of optical illusions were performed. He wanted to show that you can't always believe what you see.

There are all kinds of things in the world today that look good at first, but they are optical illusions. Things we see on TV or in movies, read about in books, or hear about on the radio aren't always as good as they seem. God's way is the only true way. Follow Him, and you won't get tricked!

HONESTY AND INTEGRITY

A Captain's Search for Treasure

Joseph Bates spent many years looking for lost treasure. Not the kind that's found in a treasure chest or on a pirate's map—the treasure he was looking for was truth. He was the captain of a ship, and everyone knew he was honest. Once he even turned his ship around to return money to someone who had overpaid him. Honesty and truth were very important to him.

Joseph wasn't the only one on the ship to be honest. He expected his sailors to be honest too. He made all of them promise not to drink alcohol while they were working for him. He knew that drinking alcohol didn't help people to be honest.

Joseph searched for honesty and truth in all parts of his life, including religion. He wanted to be part of a church that taught only the truth from the Bible. He looked and looked for that kind of church, but couldn't find one. So, together with some friends, Joseph Bates became one of the first Seventh-day Adventists.

When he gave his heart to God, Joseph said he'd found "the pearl of great price which was . . . worth more than all the vessels and cargoes I have ever commanded." He spent the rest of his life working for God and sharing truth with anyone who would listen.

God's heroes are on a treasure hunt for truth too, and it can be found in the Bible. Start digging and see what truths you can uncover.

The kingdom of heaven is like a merchant seeking beautiful pearls, who, when he had found one pearl of great price, went and sold all that he had and bought it.

Matthew 13:45, 46.

HONESTY AND INTEGRITY

27
JULY

An Angel Inside

The Lord does not see as man sees; for man looks at the outward appearance, but the Lord looks at the heart.

1 Samuel 16:7.

The huge rough lump of marble was about to be thrown away. Everyone thought that it was useless and that nothing good could be made out of it. It was to be hauled away so that a beautiful, useful piece of marble could take its place.

Before it could be thrown away, the great sculptor Michelangelo saw the rough marble. He asked to have the big ugly rock sent to his studio. When it arrived, he carefully chipped and polished, cut and carved, until a beautiful sculpture was created out of the ugly old rock. When asked why he chose the ugly rock instead of a more beautiful one, Michelangelo said, "I saw the angel in the marble and carved until I set him free." He'd made something beautiful out of something everyone else thought was useless, because he wasn't looking at the outside.

Jesus loves to use people others think are useless. Moses, Matthew, Mary Magdalene. There are many stories in the Bible. God sees more than what everyone else sees. We look at the outside, but He sees our hearts. God asks us to look past the rough outside to see the angel inside of others.

HONESTY AND INTEGRITY

Telling a Marco Polo

Heaven and earth will pass away, but My words will by no means pass away.
Matthew 24:35.

The people of Venice thought that their city was the best, richest, and most beautiful city in the whole world. They believed that no city could be as wonderful as Venice. Marco Polo heard everyone say this as he was growing up in Venice. But he loved to hear the stories the sailors told of places they visited and things they saw.

Marco's father and uncle were sailors and had seen other parts of the world. They knew there were places as beautiful as Venice; they had seen things the people of Venice couldn't imagine. They took young Marco with them on a journey to Asia to see for himself.

The trip took them more than three long years by boat. When they finally arrived at the Chandu palace, the emperor, Kublai Khan, welcomed them. He treated them with kindness, and he and Marco became good friends. Marco spent most of the next 20 years exploring for Kublai Khan. He saw many wonderful things that no European had ever seen and went places no European had ever been.

When he finally went back to Venice many years later, no one believed the stories he told. In fact, people were so sure that Marco was lying that they would say that someone had "told a Marco Polo" instead of saying they'd lied. They still thought that nothing could be as wonderful as their Venice.

Many people in the world today don't believe the Bible. They think the stories are too far-fetched to be true. They believe that nothing could be as beautiful as this world. Don't be like the people of Venice and miss out on an adventure just because of your own stubbornness. Let Jesus into your heart, and you'll get to go on the best adventure ever—to heaven!

HONESTY AND INTEGRITY

The Seeing Eye

*Enter by the
narrow gate;
for wide is the
gate and broad is
the way that leads
to destruction, . . .
narrow is the gate
and difficult is
the way which
leads to life.*

Matthew 7:13, 14.

Morris Frank lost his sight at the age of 16. Despite not being able to see, he finished high school and college, paying his expenses by working as an insurance salesman.

One day he heard of a place in Europe that trained dogs to help blind war veterans. Interested, he went, alone, to check it out. He came home with Buddy, his new guide dog. She safely led him across crowded streets and helped him to find his way around easily. Morris and Buddy became a familiar sight on the streets of Nashville, Tennessee.

Interest in Morris and Buddy led to the beginning of The Seeing Eye, an organization that trains dogs to help blind people. Each dog is given special training to learn how to be a guide. The dogs learn many commands and ways to help their new masters. Today guide dogs help many physically challenged people to live more independent lives. All this happened because Morris Frank didn't keep looking at his blindness as a disadvantage; instead, he looked for ways to overcome it.

If you see someone with a guide dog, please remember not to distract the dog. You would be taking the "eyes" of the blind master away while the dog is distracted. When guide dogs are working, they should not be bothered.

When we choose not to follow Jesus, we are like blind people without their Seeing Eye dogs. We stumble off the road to heaven and get lost in sin. But if we follow Jesus, He will open our eyes to truth and help us to stay on His road to heaven.

HONESTY AND INTEGRITY

Almost Home

Ahoming pigeon isn't just any old pigeon. Even though they look like regular pigeons, they are special. They love to be at home. No matter how far away they are, they always fly toward home. They have an amazing sense of direction and can fly home from wherever they are released.

In wartimes people used to use homing pigeons to carry messages. The pigeons would be carried to the battlefield. When the soldiers needed to send a message, they would tie a note to the pigeon's leg and let it out of its cage. The pigeons would always fly for home, where its owner read the message and did whatever needed to be done to help whoever sent it.

Nothing can distract a good homing pigeon from going home. It doesn't matter what the weather is like, or if there is anything in the way. The pigeons just want to go home.

Heaven is our home and where our thoughts should be focused. Like the homing pigeon, we should always keep in mind where we're headed and not get distracted on our journey. I just want to go home. What about you?

For where your treasure is, there your heart will be also.
Matthew 6:21.

HONESTY AND INTEGRITY

An obedient Hero

Pick up the dog!" Caitlin only had time to scoop her Jack Russell terrier, Penny, into her arms before a solid white blur knocked them to the ground.

Caitlin had spent a fun afternoon with her Pathfinder group hiking at Sweetwater Creek. They were tired after a long walk and a nature scavenger hunt. They were sitting on a fence to rest when Caitlin heard her pastor yell to pick up Penny. Without question she yanked Penny's leash and grabbed her in her arms just as a white pit bull charged them and knocked them off the fence. The big dog had broken free from its leash and was after Penny. Caitlin hadn't seen the other dog coming, but thankfully her pastor had.

The angry dog stood over Caitlin, trying to get to Penny, who had been knocked out of Caitlin's arms in the fall and had just enough room to stay out of reach of the pit bull's snapping jaws. Quickly an adult ran to help, pulling the angry dog off Caitlin. Everyone was so thankful that Caitlin's angel had protected them and that both she and Penny were OK.

Caitlin knew that even though most dogs are friendly, she should never approach a strange dog until she knew for sure. She also knew that she shouldn't run and scream if she was chased. Because she stayed still and covered her head and face with her arms when she was knocked down, the dog didn't hurt her. And because she obeyed quickly, Penny was saved too.

Obeying your parents and God is important. They don't give you orders just to make life hard; they want what is best for you and are trying to protect you. Be like Caitlin today, and be a hero for God!

HONESTY AND INTEGRITY

Who's in charge?

When Jesus was on earth, He talked to His heavenly Father every day. They had a strong connection. Jesus loved His disciples and friends, but God always came first. No matter what was happening in His life, Jesus depended on His connection with God to help Him make the right choices.

At the end of His life Jesus knew that Judas would betray Him and the soldiers would soon be there to lead Him to His execution. Jesus didn't want to die—especially not on a cross. He knew that people would make fun of Him. He knew that it would be hard on the people He loved the most. But He trusted that God knew what He was doing.

It made God sad that Jesus had to die, but He knew that our sins had to be paid for, and this was the only way. And there's good news! On the Sunday after He was crucified, Jesus rose from the dead. His death on the cross meant that our sins have been paid for, and since He's alive again we can go to heaven to live with Him forever.

Jesus could have decided the cost was too high. He could have said that it wasn't worth it to die on the cross just to save a bunch of sinners. He showed self-control by trusting God rather than taking the easy way out.

Do you trust God to work in your life, or do you do your own thing? Imagine what would have happened if Jesus had done that. Trust God today and ask Him to do what is best for your life.

Nevertheless, not as I will, but as You will.
Matthew 26:39.

SELF-CONTROL

2
AUGUST

Runaway

The Angel of the Lord said to her, "Return to your mistress, and submit yourself under her hand."

Genesis 16:9.

Hagar was Sarai's servant. They had a good friendship and worked well together, until Hagar became pregnant with Abram's son. Then Hagar became proud, and she was rude to Sarai. Sarai complained to her husband, Abram, about it, and decided to have a talk with Hagar about her attitude.

Hagar was upset when Sarai spoke with her. Instead of trying to fix her relationship with her master, she ran away. God spoke to her at a well and told her to go back, and she obeyed.

How do you handle trouble in your life? Do you face it, or do you run away? Hagar ran away from her problems. When we have troubles, it's tempting to try to run away from them, but that's only a temporary solution.

God is patient with us, even when we try to run away. But it would be better if we faced our problems with His help. No problem is too complicated for Him. Are there problems in your life that you've been running away from? Ask God today to help you to face them.

SELF-CONTROL

Bratty Benjy

Benjy didn't get along with his two sisters. When Mom wasn't looking, he would make faces at them. If she wasn't in the room, he would say mean things and sometimes even hit or kick them. Benjy was a brat. It seemed that he was always stirring up trouble of some kind. Does that sound like someone who is a hero for God?

One day after a particularly loud fight with the girls, Benjy was called into the other room for a talk. "Benjy," Mom said, "you must try to control yourself. You've got to stop being so mean. Instead of being nasty, why don't you try to think of how you can make others happy?" Although it was a tough assignment, Benjy promised to give it a try.

The next day when he came home from school, instead of teasing Hannah and Emily, he tiptoed up behind them and surprised them each with a piece of candy. He ran into the kitchen, leaving the girls wide-eyed in surprise. He noticed some dirty dishes in the sink and began to put them in the dishwasher. Mom came into the kitchen when he was almost done, and she couldn't believe her eyes.

Benjy noticed that the whole family was much happier when he was kind than when he was a brat. He began to try, every day on his way home from school, to think of ways to be nice to his family.

Today's Bible verse tells us that we should do everything we can to live in peace with the people around us. We can use self-control to help us treat other people the way we should.

If it is possible, as far as it depends on you, live at peace with everyone.
Romans 12:18.

SELF-CONTROL

225

4
AUGUST

A man's heart plans his way, but the Lord directs his steps.

Proverbs 16:9.

A Deep Hunger

Esau had been out hunting, and he was very hungry. When he came back to the camp, his twin brother, Jacob, was cooking a stew that smelled great. He asked Jacob for some, but Jacob wanted something in return: Esau's birthright. A birthright was very important. It gave a special blessing to the firstborn son. Esau was so hungry that he told Jacob he could have the birthright. He felt as if he would die if he didn't get food right then, and if he died, the birthright wouldn't be any good to him.

Esau lived to regret that hasty decision. He traded the lasting benefits of his birthright for the immediate pleasure of food. He acted without thinking about the long-term results of his decision. He made his decision based only on what he felt he needed right away.

We sometimes do the same thing. We make decisions based on what we want right now rather than thinking things through. When you make an important decision, ask God to help you to think about the long-term consequences so that you can make better decisions than Esau did.

226

SELF-CONTROL

Wild Child

Behold, I am with you and will keep you wherever you go.
Genesis 28:15.

Helen Keller was a wild child. Because she couldn't hear or see, she wasn't able to communicate with anyone. Her life was one big temper tantrum after another. No one could help her.

Then Anne Sullivan came to teach her. Anne worked patiently with Helen until she taught her to understand words by finger-spelling letters in Helen's hand. The first word Helen learned was "water," and learning about words changed her life. Rather than being wild, she learned to communicate and be civil.

Helen was very intelligent. When she grew up, she spent her life traveling and speaking to people about overcoming difficulties. Her constant companion was Anne Sullivan, who had helped her to live a more normal life.

God is our constant companion. If we listen to what He has to teach us, He will help us to live a better life too.

SELF-CONTROL

6
AUGUST

*A new
commandment
I give to you,
that you love one
another; as I have
loved you.*

John 13:34.

Anyone
but Him!

Ananias loved and obeyed the Lord, but this time he didn't want to do what he'd been told. God had spoken to him in a dream, telling him to go to Straight Street in Damascus and ask for Saul. Then God wanted Ananias to put his hands on Saul, and God would use him to restore Saul's sight.

This was the same Saul who had been looking for Christians so he could kill them. Ananias wanted to run away from him, not go visit him! But he trusted God and started out, even though he was afraid.

All the way down Straight Street he must have been wondering if this was really a good idea. There was still time to run. Instead he asked God for courage as he put his hand on the door. It opened with a creak, and there, in the dim light, he saw Saul. He laid his hand on Saul as God had told him. When Ananias said a prayer, something like scales fell from Saul's eyes. He could see again!

Ananias treated Saul with respect and love even though he was afraid of him. It can be hard to show love to people who are mean to us or whom we are afraid of, but we should be like Ananias and treat people with the same love and respect that Jesus would.

SELF-CONTROL

Winning the Good Fight

*I have fought
the good fight, . . .
I have kept
the faith.*
2 Timothy 4:7.

George Foreman learned everything he knew about boxing from Sonny Liston, one of the biggest names in boxing of that time. He learned how to throw a punch and how to avoid punches. He learned how to take a hit and how to be tough, mean, unfriendly, and rude. Sonny was his hero.

Then one day George realized that Sonny acted the way he did to cover up something he was embarrassed about. Sonny couldn't read. He acted tough and mean so that people wouldn't find out that he couldn't read. George began to realize that there was something more to life than fighting.

In his hotel room one night after a fight, George gave his heart to Jesus. The change was complete and immediate. Everyone could tell that something had changed. And ever since, George has been a different man. He's still big, but the eyes that once held so much hatred in the boxing ring now shine with love and kindness. His wife and family of 10 kids are the most important thing to him now, next to God. At the church he pastors, George tells others how Jesus changes lives. Everyone who knows him likes him and talks about how nice he is.

George Foreman, a former heavyweight champion of the world, won the most important fight of all when he gave his heart to Jesus, the champion of the universe. You don't have to prove anything to anyone by fighting. Just do your best and trust God, who has won the fight against Satan for us.

SELF-CONTROL

8
AUGUST

The Wise Fool

The fear of the Lord is the beginning of wisdom; a good understanding have all those who do His commandments.
Psalm 111:10.

Wisdom doesn't do you any good if you don't act on it. Early in his reign, Solomon asked God for wisdom. As Israel's third king, he knew he needed God's help. God answered his prayer and made him the wisest man who ever lived.

Even though God had given Solomon wisdom, Solomon still had choices to make. Unfortunately, not all of the choices he made were good ones. He built the Temple, which was good, and he made many wise rulings as a judge. But he married more than one woman—he had hundreds of wives—and that certainly wasn't wise. Even worse, many of these women didn't worship the true God. Slowly but surely he gave in to their ways of believing, until he walked away from God. Even though he was wise, he made some foolish choices.

Solomon didn't walk away from God all at once, but little by little, step by step. One bad decision led to another. Having wisdom isn't enough. We have to choose to act wisely. Don't be a wise fool, as Solomon was. Ask God to help you make wise choices.

SELF-CONTROL

Hot Dog

Buster woke up slowly, sleepily shaking his shaggy brown head and realizing that something was wrong. Next to him was his friend, Fluffy the cat. A year before, Buster had saved Fluffy's life after she had become caught in a trap. Buster had carried her, trap and all, back home to get help.

Now, as smoke crept into the room, Buster realized that their lives were in danger a second time. Buster was up in a flash, racing to his owner's bedroom, pressing his nose to her face and licking her cheek. Sleepily she pushed him away, so he jumped up on the bed and began to whine. Still she did not respond. Finally, not knowing what else to do, Buster barked and bit her arm. That got her attention! She woke with a start and realized what was happening. Buster raced to the door and began flinging his body against it.

But after she opened the door, Buster didn't run immediately to safety. Instead he ran down the hallway of their apartment building, throwing himself, again and again, at each door until someone came to answer it. By doing this, he saved 35 lives. Not one person in the building died because of the late-night fire, even though the building was destroyed. In fact, when Buster got outside and realized that Fluffy the cat wasn't out, he raced back into the burning building, found his friend, and carried her out to fresh air and safety as well.

Buster knew that the fire was dangerous. He could have run to safety. Instead, he put his own well-being aside and did everything he could to help save his neighbors. As heroes for God we too should help our neighbors whenever and however we can.

The entire law is summed up in a single command: "Love your neighbor as yourself."
Galatians 5:14, NIV.

SELF-CONTROL

10
AUGUST

But Daniel purposed in his heart that he would not defile himself.
Daniel 1:8.

Pure Inside and out

Daniel and his three friends lived in Jerusalem with their families until the terrible day that they were taken captive and marched to Babylon. It was a long, hot, and dusty trip. They were tired and frightened when they got there.

The king of Babylon decided that some of the new captives should be taught the ways of their new country. Daniel and his friends were chosen to be in that group. They were told that they would be taught many things and that they would be eating the same food as the king ate. They were glad to learn, but they knew that the food the king ate wasn't healthful. Daniel and his friends asked if they could eat the foods they were used to—vegetables, bread, and water.

The kings' servant knew he would get in trouble if the king saw that these boys weren't as strong as the others. At first he refused; he worried that if they didn't eat the king's food they would be weak. But he finally agreed to let them try it for 10 days.

When the king's servant checked Daniel and his friends at the end of the 10 days, he found them to be stronger and smarter than the boys who were eating the king's food! So they were allowed to continue eating the good food.

God's heroes keep themselves pure, not only by eating well and taking care of their bodies but also by guarding the things they allow into their minds. When we follow God's way, we will be stronger and healthier, just as Daniel and his friends were.

SELF-CONTROL

A Strong Will

Yet not my will,
but yours be done.
Luke 22:42, NIV.

Trouble burst onto the scene the day Molly, the Australian shepherd, went to live with her owner. Molly had a strong will. When she set her mind to something, she had a hard time listening to anyone else. She thought her way was the only way.

After several years of destruction and wildness, Molly's owner was ready to take her to the pound. Molly had chewed up a plant stand, the corner of a couch, a football, some new curtains, and a down comforter. Whenever someone rang the doorbell, Molly went crazy, barking and jumping. Despite her owner's attempts to train her, Molly wouldn't learn to behave.

But somehow her owner just couldn't bring herself to get rid of the fuzzy little dog. Molly was affectionate and very loyal. Despite her bad points, her owner still loved her. Gradually Molly began to calm down, and eventually she turned into a pretty good dog. She still had her silly days, but she was much better.

Sometimes we too think that our way is the only way. Fortunately God, our heavenly owner, will always love us in spite of our bad choices. We should always be working toward becoming a better person. And we should always be kind and loving to the people around us, in spite of their bad choices.

12
AUGUST

Jailhouse Song

But at midnight Paul and Silas were praying and singing hymns to God, and the prisoners were listening to them.

Acts 16:25.

Paul and Silas had been beaten and jailed because they had cast a demon out of a girl. She had made her masters rich by telling fortunes with the demon's help. The masters were angry that she couldn't work for them anymore. Instead of being thankful that the girl didn't have the demon, they were selfish and upset because she wouldn't make them any more money.

Paul and Silas had been beaten with rods and put in chains in the cold prison. Their bodies ached from the beatings. The heavy metal chains scraped on their wounds, and the stone floor was cold and damp. They could have felt sorry for themselves, but instead the Bible tells us that they were praying and singing hymns to God. The other prisoners were listening in amazement.

Even though they were in a bad situation, Paul and Silas were still praising God. Later that night God released them by opening the prison doors with an earthquake. Because of their witness, the jailer and his whole family became Christians. You can read the story in Acts 16:16-34.

It's easy to feel sorry for ourselves when things aren't going our way. It is better always to look for the good, rather than the bad, and praise God in all things, as Paul and Silas did.

SELF-CONTROL

A New Story

Shi Kwei-Piao made his living telling stories. He told stories on street corners, at parties, and wherever anyone would listen. Then one day a friend told him a story. It was a story about someone named Jesus, and it changed his life forever. Instead of telling just any stories, Shi Kwei-Piao began to tell stories about Jesus. His new stories made some people angry, but he didn't stop. He wanted people to know about his new friend.

Shi Kwei-Paio had some bad habits in his life that he wanted to get rid of once he knew Jesus. He was addicted to drugs, gambling, and drinking. He knew those were not habits that a hero for God would have, but they were very hard habits to give up. His favorite Bible verse when he was giving up his bad habits was the one that goes with today's story. He knew that with God's help he could overcome his addictions, and he did.

Giving up bad habits can be very hard. It's much easier never to start them in the first place. Avoid such bad things as drugs, drinking, gambling, and smoking, and keep your body pure for God.

But God is faithful, who will not allow you to be tempted beyond what you are able, but with the temptation will also make the way of escape, that you may be able to bear it.

1 Corinthians 10:13.

SELF-CONTROL

14
AUGUST

My Brother's Keeper

My dear brothers,
take note of this:
Everyone should
be quick to listen,
slow to speak and
slow to become
angry, for man's
anger does not
bring about the
righteous life that
God desires.

James 1:19, 20, NIV.

Cain was angry. He had brought his best fruits and vegetables to give to the Lord, but his offering wasn't accepted. He had worked hard to grow them, and was upset that God didn't accept his offering. His brother Abel had brought the best from his flocks, as God had told them to do, and had given them as an offering to the Lord. Abel's offering was accepted. It made Cain angry that God had accepted Abel's offering and not his.

Cain asked Abel to come out to a field with him, and Abel went. When they got there, Cain's anger bubbled over, and he killed his own brother. Cain let his feelings get the best of him, and he committed the first murder. His actions hurt not only his brother but also his whole family, God, and even himself.

It's up to us to keep our feelings under control, rather than letting them control us. Let's ask God to help us keep our feelings under control today.

SELF-CONTROL

Lifesavers

Trixie and Duke were as unlikely a pair as you'll ever find. Trixie was a small white fox terrier with black ears and a black spot around one eye. Duke was a tall, lanky hound dog. Trixie could run circles underneath Duke.

One day Trixie's and Duke's master, Mr. Hobright, was fishing in a creek. The current was very strong as he stood in the creek to cast his line. Duke and Trixie watched from the bank as he slowly made his way across the creek to where he thought the fish might be biting better. As he walked, his ankle twisted on some rocks on the bottom, and he tripped. With a yell, he fell and hit his head on a large rock.

The two dogs looked up just in time to see their master fall, unconcious, facedown in the water. Because his boots were filled with water, he didn't float away. But he didn't wake up, either. Duke threw himself into the icy water and swam toward his master while Trixie ran up and down the bank, barking. Mr. Hobright was too heavy for Duke to pull to shore, but he was able to pull his face out of the water. Duke didn't know what else to do, so he just kept paddling there, holding his master.

Trixie knew that if Duke couldn't pull their master out, she couldn't either. So she ran up the steep hillside to the road. There her barking got the attention of a hiker, and he came down to help. Together the hiker and Duke were able to pull Mr. Hobright out of the water.

If it hadn't been for the quick thinking and teamwork of his dogs, Mr. Hobright would have drowned. By themselves, neither Trixie nor Duke could have saved him. But because they worked together, their master was rescued. We can accomplish a lot more when we work together too. Be a hero today and work with, instead of against, others.

Finally, all of you be of one mind, having compassion for one another.
1 Peter 3:8.

SELF-CONTROL

16
AUGUST

Rise Above It

Do not be conformed to this world, but be transformed by the renewing of your mind, that you may prove what is that good and acceptable and perfect will of God.

Romans 12:2.

Ishmael was born into a troubled family. His mother, Hagar, and her master, Sarah, were jealous of each other, and things were tense. He was treated as an honored son, though, and life was good for him. But then Isaac was born. Isaac was Sarah and Abraham's son, and Ishmael's half brother. When Sarah caught Ishmael teasing Isaac, Ishmael and his mother were thrown out of the camp.

Although many of the things that happened in Ishmael's life weren't his fault, his own actions didn't help. He chose to let his situation rule him, rather than living above it.

Like Ishmael, all of us have to make choices. There are some things in our lives that we have no control over—the family we are born into, our name, the color of our skin. However, we can always control our own decisions and should try to change the things we can change.

God can help. He doesn't want to force us, but He'd like to help us live a better life. Our life can be changed when we ask forgiveness and change our attitude toward Him and others. Don't be like Ishmael and let your circumstances rule you. Rise above them and, with God's help, be the person He wants you to be today.

SELF-CONTROL

Strikeout

The Israelites were whining again, and Moses was frustrated. They were in the desert, and there was no water. They blamed Moses and Aaron for bringing them out into the desert. They wanted to be back in Egypt. They had been slaves there, but at least they'd had enough to eat and drink!

Moses and Aaron asked God what to do. He told them to take Moses' staff and gather the people together. Then He told Moses to speak to the rock, and water would come out of it. Moses almost got it right. He took his staff and gathered the people together, but he was angry with them for complaining. Instead of speaking to the rock as God had told him, he hit it twice with his staff.

Water came out of the rock, and the people had enough to drink, but Moses hadn't followed God's instructions. Because he didn't follow God's instructions, Moses wasn't allowed to lead the Israelites into the Promised Land. God used Joshua to do that instead.

Our actions always have consequences. But when you make a mistake, God still loves you, just as He still loved Moses. He can still use you for good, even when you don't make good decisions.

Because you did not trust in me enough to honor me as holy in the sight of the Israelites, you will not bring this community into the land I give them.

Numbers 20:12, NIV.

SELF-CONTROL

18
AUGUST

Little children, keep yourselves from idols.

1 John 5:21.

The Tower of Babel

The people who lived after the Flood all spoke the same language. They thought it would be a good idea to build a tall, tall tower in their city so that everyone would see how great they were. They made plans, made bricks, and began building.

God saw that the people were building the tall tower so they could become famous. He was sad that they were building monuments to themselves rather than loving Him. He knew a way to stop them. He "[confused] their language" (Genesis 11:7). God mixed things up so that the people would speak different languages. They had to stop building the tower because they couldn't understand one another. They gathered in groups that could understand each other, and the different groups moved to different areas of the earth.

The Tower of Babel was a monument to self—the people were building it to prove how great they were. We can have monuments to self in our lives, too—clothes, toys, friends, or anything that takes the place of God in our lives. Those things aren't bad, but when we use them as the source of our self-worth, they can take God's place. Are there any towers that you need to stop building?

SELF-CONTROL

Fight for Truth

Sojourner Truth had been a slave. She knew what it was like to be worked too hard, fed too little, and treated unkindly. She knew that slavery was wrong and had to be stopped.

Sojourner talked a lot about slavery. She said that slavery was against what God teaches in the Bible. Some people listened, and others didn't. Some people liked slavery because it meant they didn't have to work as hard, and they didn't want it to stop.

One man was tired of hearing her talk about slavery. He said to her, "Old woman, do you think your talk about slavery does any good? I don't care any more for your talk than I do for the bite of a flea." Sojourner answered him, "Perhaps not, but, the Lord willing, I'll keep you scratching."

Sojourner could have been discouraged by the man's words, but she knew that what she was fighting for was right. And she promised to keep talking about it until everyone listened.

How easily do you give up? When something gets hard, do you walk away from it? God's heroes, like Sojourner, stick to what is right, even when it gets hard. Even when it seems as if other people don't care.

Let us hold fast the . . . hope without wavering, for He who promised is faithful.
Hebrews 10:23.

SELF-CONTROL

241

20
AUGUST

Meeting the Need

Whether you eat or drink, or whatever you do, do all to the glory of God.

1 Corinthians 10:31.

When the Civil War broke out, Clara Barton volunteered to help. She collected bandages, socks, and medical supplies to help the wounded soldiers. She did such a good job that she was given permission to deliver the supplies directly to the front lines. She did that for two years; then she became superintendent of the Union nurses. After the war was over, she wrote letters to try to help find missing soldiers.

In the 1880s Clara became the first president of the American Red Cross, and she worked tirelessly to help those in need. In addition to helping the soldiers during the Civil War, she helped people who had gone through natural disasters, such as famines, floods, and earthquakes. The work she started so long ago is still being carried on by the Red Cross.

When asked about her work, Clara said, "You must never so much as think whether you like it or not, whether it is bearable or not; you must never think of anything except the need, and how to meet it."

Today you may be faced with a job you don't like—cleaning your room, doing your homework, or being nice to someone you might not like very much. If so, remember Clara's words, and, with God's help, work to meet the need.

SELF-CONTROL

The Boss

Lance Armstrong is one of the most recognized names in professional bike racing. He started racing when he was very young, but he lost his first professional race. He says he might have quit that day if it hadn't been for the encouragement of his mom, who is his biggest hero even today. With her encouragement he kept trying, and three years later he won the very race he'd lost on his first try. He learned never to quit, despite the odds.

The lesson Lance learned from that race was useful a few years later when he was diagnosed with cancer. Lance was scared, but went through the treatments and had several surgeries. He was very sick, but the love of his family and friends, his strong body and mind, and the strong medicines and surgeries helped him to get better. The doctors had given him less than a 50/50 chance of living, but he didn't give up, and he beat the odds.

Lance was even able to come back to racing within five months of his diagnosis. He came back strongly, too. He became one of only a handful of riders to win the top bicycle race in the world—the Tour de France—five times.

It's natural to want to give up when things get hard—whether it's with homework or friendships or something else. But with God's help we can, like Lance, push on and win, despite the odds.

Do you not know that those who run in a race all run, but one receives the prize? Run in such a way that you may obtain it.
1 Corinthians 9:24.

SELF-CONTROL

243

22
AUGUST

Death and life are in the power of the tongue.
Proverbs 18:21.

Hold Your Tongue

Everyone likes to be around Dr. Cetta. He works in an emergency room, where it can be very stressful. It is easy to get upset and snap at people in such a stressed-out place, but Dr. Cetta is always kind and friendly. He takes good care of the people who come to his hospital. People like to work with him because of the way he treats others.

When we are having a bad day, it's easy to snap at people and say unkind things. But as heroes for God, we should always be careful with what we say. Instead of being unkind and mean when you have a bad day, try instead to be kind and friendly like Dr. Cetta.

People would much rather spend time with someone who is like Dr. Cetta than with someone who spreads a bad mood. Which do you do?

SELF-CONTROL

Corps of Discovery

Meriwether Lewis and William Clark are two of the most famous explorers in our nation's history. President Thomas Jefferson sent them and their helpers, called the Corps of Discovery, on a mission to find the Northwest Passage. People believed that there had to be a river connecting the Atlantic and Pacific oceans. Lewis and Clark were going to find it—or so they thought.

They never did find it (because it isn't there), but during the three years they were looking they did find many other things. They walked and canoed for thousands of miles. They discovered new plants and animals, charted new territory, and explored much of what would someday be part of the United States.

During their trip they went through many hard times, from bad weather to sickness to unfriendly natives, but always they pressed on. If they had given up, much of our nation's history and borders might be different today.

Because Lewis and Clark didn't give up when things got hard, they changed the course of history. Ask God to help you not to give up when things get hard, and see what He can do with your life.

Commit your way to the Lord, trust also in Him, and He shall bring it to pass.
Psalm 37:5.

SELF-CONTROL

24
AUGUST

*He shall bruise
your head, and
you shall bruise
His heel.*

Genesis 3:15.

Leo the Lion-hearted

The jeep roared down the road with Leo, the big white poodle, grinning into the hot wind. He was going to the river with his family.

As soon as the jeep stopped, the children piled out and began looking for sticks to throw. Time after time they tossed sticks into the water, laughing as Leo splashed in after them.

Nearby, in the roots of a big tree, a huge rattlesnake lay, waiting out the heat of the day. Its forked tongue flicked in and out. Sean, one of the children from Leo's family, was hunting for more sticks to throw when he knelt down in front of the tree. He screamed as he saw the snake, coiled and about to strike.

Leo heard Sean's scream and, bounding out of the water, raced to him. Jumping in front of Sean, he barked angrily and lunged at the five-foot-long snake. It struck, sinking its long, hollow teeth into Leo's skull. Leo stumbled back, then threw himself at the snake again and again until Sean had time to get to safety. Finally, the snake slithered off as Leo lay on the ground, paralyzed by the venom.

Leo's owner hurried over to him and scooped him up, then dashed toward the jeep. They sped off to the vet, where they were told he might not live. There was no doubt that if the snake had bitten Sean instead, he would not have survived.

Miraculously, Leo did survive, and he was soon back to his old jeep-riding, grinning self again, with no side effects from his tangle with the rattler.

There's an old snake named Satan slithering around our planet, but Jesus took the venom that was meant for us. When Jesus comes again, Satan and all sin will be destroyed.

SELF-CONTROL

free to Choose

John F. Kennedy was the youngest man to be elected United States president. He had to make many hard decisions during his time in office. At that time Russia and Cuba were trying to convince the world that their type of government, Communism, was best. President Kennedy worked hard to convince the world that America's way, democracy, was best.

President Kennedy said in a speech that he was trying to help create a "world of law and free choice."

Did you read that? Law and free choice. They go together. Freedom doesn't mean that we can do whatever we want. As long as we live on this sinful earth, bad things will sometimes happen. But following the laws of our country and God's laws will keep us happy and help to make the world a better place.

You shall therefore keep . . . His commandments . . . , that it may go well with you.
Deuteronomy 4:40.

SELF-CONTROL

26
AUGUST

Do you not know that you are the temple of God and that the Spirit of God dwells in you?

1 Corinthians 3:16.

Ironman

A.C. Green's nickname is "Ironman" because he played more than 1,000 basketball games without missing a single one. He has played for several different teams, but three things never change: he plays, he plays well, and he has a good attitude.

A.C. is liked by teammates, coaches, and even the men he plays against. A.C. is a winner both on and off the basketball court. When he's not playing basketball, he works with young people and encourages them to make good decisions in their lives. He shows them the importance of good decisions in dealing with other people and in taking care of their bodies.

If you are a hero for God, you can be counted on to make good decisions in the game of life. You are in charge of your body and what you put into it. Don't give in to peer pressure to do harmful things with your body. Instead, be a hero for God and treat your body well by getting enough exercise, sleep, good food, and water, and you'll be a winner in life!

SELF-CONTROL

An ordinary Man

When Pat Tillman walked away from a multimillion-dollar contract with the National Football League to join the Army Rangers, many people were surprised—but not the people who knew hiim best. To them he was always known as someone who put others ahead of himself.

In June 2002 Pat joined the Army Rangers instead of the Arizona Cardinals, and became a soldier instead of a football player. He passed up $3.6 million because he wanted to serve his country. He showed self-control by putting the good of others ahead of his own.

Pat never wanted anyone to make a big deal out of his decision. People join the military every day, and he knew that he was no better than any of them just because he made a lot of money playing football. He knew that doing the right thing is more important than money or anything it can buy. Although he planned to come back to football after his time in the military, Pat was killed in action in Afghanistan in April 2004.

Pat never tried to be a hero—he just did what he thought was right, even when it wasn't the easy thing to do. He is a hero, not just because of the way he died but because of the way he lived.

Live your life today as a hero for God!

Present your bodies a living sacrifice, holy, acceptable to God, which is your reasonable service.

Romans 12:1.

SELF-CONTROL

28
AUGUST

*See, I have set
before you today
life and good,
death and evil,
in that I command
you to . . .
keep His
commandments,
. . . that you may
live and multiply;
and the Lord your
God will bless you
in the land.*

Deuteronomy 30:15, 16.

An Important Decision

Ben and his friend were listening to the radio when they got into an argument about what to listen to. Ben got so angry when his friend tried to change the station that, without thinking, he pulled a knife out of his pocket and tried to stab his friend in the stomach.

Luckily for both of them, the knife hit the boy's belt buckle instead. Ben was so upset about what he'd almost done that he locked himself in the bathroom. He spent several hours reading the Bible and praying, and when he came out, he was changed. He realized that no one "makes" you angry. You have the power, with God's help, to control the way you act—even when you're angry.

Ben could have blamed others for the way he acted. He was from a poor family. They lived in the inner city. Ben got such bad grades in school he was known as the class dummy. But he knew that he was responsible for how he reacted to things.

And do you know what Ben, the "class dummy" who almost murdered a friend, does now? He's Dr. Benjamin Carson, one of the most well-known doctors of our time. He was able to turn his life around because he decided to take responsibility for himself and not blame others. Then he was able to begin using the gifts God gave him.

God gives each of us gifts—things we are good at. God also gives us the ability to make choices. To be a hero for God, we need to ask Him to help us use our gifts for Him and to make wise choices.

250

SELF-CONTROL

Stop and Go

*D*oes your family have a car? You, your parents, and probably even your grandparents and great-grandparents have always had cars, or at least been around them. But cars were a new invention in the early 1900s. Cars had to share the road with bicycles, people who were walking, and horse-drawn carriages. Because there weren't many traffic rules, there were a lot of bad accidents. It was very dangerous to be on the road, whether you were riding, driving, or walking.

Garrett Morgan saw a bad accident himself one day and wanted to do something to make the roads safer. Any guesses on what he did? He invented the first traffic signal.

Today we have traffic lights with a green light that tells us to go, a yellow light that tells us to be careful, and a red light that tells us to stop. The Morgan traffic signal had three positions too, but it didn't use lights—it used signs. The signs looked like three little arms on a T-shaped pole. The word "stop" was written on one of the little arms. Another sign had the word "go." The third sign was used to get traffic to stop in all directions.

Soon roads all over England, Canada, and the United States had the Morgan traffic signal. Because people obeyed what the signals said—stopping when it said to stop, going when it said to go—everyone was safer, and there were fewer bad accidents.

God's book, the Bible, is like a traffic signal for our lives. If we follow what it has to tell us—stop doing bad, go on doing good—we will live happier, safer lives.

"I will direct all his ways . . . ," says the Lord of hosts.
Isaiah 45:13.

SELF-CONTROL

30
AUGUST

Love your neighbor as yourself.
James 2:8.

Ditto

Ditto has worked during many disasters. As a search-and-rescue dog, she has searched bombed buildings, she has worked after hurricanes, and she was on standby in case anything happened at the Atlanta Olympics. Once she and her handler were sent to Kansas to help find some workers who had been trapped when a grain elevator collapsed. Ditto loves her job and always does it well.

She knows when it's time to work, but Ditto loves to relax, too. She likes to hang out with the other rescue workers. When they pet her and play with her, it seems to help them relax.

Thanks to Ditto and her friends, many lives have been saved. They work together to help many people, even when they are tired, hungry, and want to go home.

Self-control means knowing that you can't always do what you want when you want. It means doing what is right, even when you may not feel like it. God's heroes should have self-control in their lives and remember to help others whenever they can.

SELF-CONTROL

Vasco da Gama

Those who wait on the Lord, they shall inherit the earth.
Psalm 37:9.

Vasco da Gama was sent to sea to find a way to sail from Europe to India. The king had promised that whoever found the route would be given honor, glory, and riches beyond their wildest imaginations.

Vasco decided that he would be that man. He hired a crew, got the supplies they would need, and set off. The journey was very long and hard. Many of the crew got sick, and they didn't have enough food. His men started to grumble and wanted to turn around and go home. Vasco wouldn't hear of it. They were going to India! They'd gone too far to turn back now.

As their ship rounded the Cape of Good Hope at the southern tip of Africa, the men were afraid because the sea was rough and stormy. The ship was tossed back and forth until they could hardly stand on deck. They told their captain that they wanted to go home. They didn't care about the riches, honor, and glory. What good would these things be to them if they were dead?

Their leader listened to them complain. Then he said, "Take courage! We are destined for glory! Even the sea trembles at us!"

Whether a situation is good or bad often depends on how you look at it. There may be some bad parts, but there's always good to look for too.

Vasco da Gama and his men rounded the Cape and found the route to India after the longest ocean trip of their time (11 months). Because they didn't give up, they were given the honor, glory, and riches promised by the king, and they changed the entire course of history by uniting the east and west.

Jesus changed history by not giving up when things got hard. We never know how our actions might affect others. Always look on the bright side, and don't give up!

SELF-CONTROL

1

Christ Jesus came into the world to save sinners.

1 Timothy 1:15.

The Bravest Man Ever

Do you know someone who is brave? Maybe your dad or mom, or some other family member. Who do you think was the bravest person ever? If you guessed Jesus, you're right.

Jesus lived in heaven with God the Father, the Holy Spirit, and the angels. Life there was perfect. There was no sickness, no lies, no pain, no death, no sorrow. Everything in heaven was happiness, love, and goodness. Until Lucifer got jealous.

Lucifer was the head angel, and he decided that wasn't good enough. He wanted to be God. Of course he couldn't be, since God created him, but he was proud and thought he deserved it. When he didn't get his way, he convinced one third of the angels that God was mean and unfair, and they left heaven.

After the earth was created, Lucifer convinced Adam and Eve to sin too. He's been working on all of us ever since.

God, Jesus, and the Holy Spirit were sad that Lucifer had made that choice. They made a plan to rescue the good people on earth. Their plan meant that Jesus would have to leave His perfect home in heaven and come to earth as a baby. He would grow up as a human, then die for the sins of everyone on earth.

It was a hard assignment, but Jesus loved us so much that He went through with it. There were times He was scared, but Jesus trusted God to work out His plan. Thanks to His bravery, we can all go to heaven and live in a perfect world with Jesus, God, the Holy Spirit, and the angels. Will you have the courage to ask Him to take you there?

COURAGE

Bold for Truth

The men had spent many long days trying to get the words just right. They were writing an important document—the Declaration of Independence. They wanted to make sure that the words they put down explained exactly what they wanted to say. Finally they had it. It was just how they wanted it.

This piece of paper would be sent to the king in England. It said that the people in America wanted to be free; they no longer wanted to be a colony of England. The king wouldn't be happy to read it—he might even order the men who signed it killed.

Would you have put your name on this piece of paper if you believed in what it said? John Hancock did. In fact, his signature is the biggest one there. As he signed, he said that he wanted the king to be able to read it "without his spectacles on." He believed in what he was doing and wanted to do what was right no matter what happened.

When you stand up for truth, you may not make other people happy. Remember that we need to follow God no matter what others say. If you are standing up for truth, ask God to help you to be bold like John Hancock.

In God I have put my trust; I will not be afraid. What can man do to me?
Psalm 56:11.

COURAGE

255

3

SEPTEMBER

Brave Beauty

And who knows but that you have come to royal position for such a time as this?

Esther 4:14, NIV.

One day the king's men came and took Esther to the palace, where the king chose her to be queen. Her cousin Mordecai told her never to tell anyone that she was Jewish. He was afraid that it would make some people angry. Haman, one of the men who worked for the king, hated Jews. Haman especially hated Mordecai, because he would not bow down to him when he passed. Mordecai would bow only to the God of heaven.

Haman made a plan to kill Mordecai and all the people like him. He didn't know that Queen Esther was Jewish. Esther was upset when she heard of Haman's plan. She tried to think of a way to stop him. She had to tell the king! But how? There was a rule that no one could go before the king without an invitation. If she went to see the king without being invited, she would be killed—unless he chose to hold out his golden scepter to her.

But if she didn't try, all of her people would be killed.

Esther spent time praying about what to do, and her friends and family prayed with her. Mordecai told her the words in today's Bible text. He suggested that perhaps God had let her be queen so that she could do something about this problem. So, bravely, Esther risked death and went before the king. He held out his scepter to her, and she was able to make her request. The king said that her people would be spared.

Esther was brave to go before the king, but she trusted God. When we ask God to lead us, He will lead us wherever it is best for us to go. And who knows? Perhaps you too will be in a position to make a big difference one day.

COURAGE

Riding Shotgun

Rain pounded the little tugboat and winds whipped it as it struggled in the stormy seas. Two men were aboard as the little ship began to sink. The water was too rough for them to swim or try to row the lifeboat.

On shore Albert Smith sat on his pony, Shotgun. It was dangerous weather, but, having seen the men in trouble, he had to try to help. Albert and Shotgun plunged into the cold water. The wind's roar was so loud that Albert's voice couldn't be heard above it. They struggled the quarter mile to the boat.

The men on the boat couldn't believe their eyes. They strained to look again; sure enough, there in the rough waters was a man and a horse, fighting their way to them. Finally they were near enough to shout. Albert yelled for them to lower the lifeboat so Shotgun could pull them in. Throwing a line to Albert, they tied one end to the lifeboat while Albert tied the other end to Shotgun's saddle.

When Albert gave her the signal, Shotgun whinnied and pulled toward shore. She fought until the water was only chest-high, then knee-high, then just a puddle around her hooves. She didn't stop until the boat was safely on the shore.

Finally all three men and the little brown horse were safe.

We should listen to God and do what He asks us to do without delay. Just as the men on the boat listened to Albert, we should listen to God. Our lives depend on it.

Be strong and let us fight bravely for our people.
1 Chronicles 19:13, NIV.

5

A Fiery Prophet

The wicked man flees though no one pursues, but the righteous are as bold as a lion.

Proverbs 28:1, NIV.

No rain had fallen for three years. The grass was dead, and the branches of the leafless trees rattled in the wind. King Ahab and the people of Israel had turned their hearts away from God. They worshipped Baal.

Elijah, the people of Israel, and the prophets of Baal met together on Mount Carmel. Elijah was a prophet of the true God. There on the mountain two altars were built—one for Baal and one for the God of heaven. A sacrifice was placed on each altar. Elijah told the prophets of Baal to pray to their god, then he would pray to his. Whoever answered was the true God.

All day the prophets of Baal prayed. They danced and jumped around the altar, shouted and cut themselves. Nothing happened.

Finally it was evening. Now it was Elijah's turn. The people watched closely as he dug a ditch around the altar and asked to have water poured over it not just once, but three times. The sacrifice was wet, the wood was wet, the altar was wet, and there was still enough water left over to fill the ditch. Reverently Elijah knelt down and prayed. He asked that God would show the people the truth. Flash! Just like that, fire zoomed down from heaven and burned up the wet sacrifice, the wood, the stones, and even the water in the ditch. There was no doubt who the one true God was. They all shouted, "The Lord, He is God! The Lord, He is God!"

The prophets of Baal thought that Elijah was outnumbered. They didn't understand that he had God on his side. No matter what the odds against us are, with God on our side we are always in the majority.

258

COURAGE

Lo Mo

A friend came to visit Donaldina Cameron's family. She told fascinating stories of young Chinese girls rescued from slavery by her friend, Miss Culbertson. Donaldina listened in amazement. When a chance came for her to work with Miss Culbertson, Donaldina jumped at it.

At that time many little girls were held as slaves in San Francisco's Chinatown. They had been kidnapped and smuggled into the United States. They had no way of escape and no one to protect them. Miss Culbertson, and now Donaldina, worked to rescue these girls and give them a better life.

Donaldina was good at finding the places the slave owners hid the girls. She found girls beneath false floors, under trapdoors, and in empty cupboards. The slave owners began calling her Fahn Quai, or White Devil. Sometimes she was afraid, but the thought of those little girls always made her work even harder.

Eventually the rescue home had so many children that a second house had to be built. One house was used for the younger children and the other for the older. All of the children lovingly called Donaldina "Lo Mo," or the Mother.

Donaldina could have stayed on her family's sheep ranch and lived a quiet life. Instead she chose to follow her heart and do something to help people in need. Doing the right thing isn't always easy, but courage means choosing to do the right thing, even when you don't feel brave or strong.

Have I not commanded you? Be strong and courageous. Do not be terrified; do not be discouraged, for the Lord your God will be with you wherever you go.

Joshua 1:9, NIV.

COURAGE

faithful King

He trusted in the Lord God of Israel. . . . He held fast to the Lord; he did not depart from following Him, but kept His commandments.

2 Kings 18:5, 6.

Israel had many kings who didn't follow God. Sometimes they claimed to, but they really didn't. They didn't follow God's commandments, they worshipped idols, and they listened to people more than God. Then Hezekiah became king.

King Hezekiah loved God. He cleaned out the idols from the Temple and started a revival in Israel. For a very long time he was the only king who loved God. His courage to stand up for God and what was right set him apart from the other kings. His bravery helped him to make great changes in his country.

If we have courage to stand up for what is right even when we are in the minority, we can help make great changes in our lives, families, and countries, too.

COURAGE

A Strange Dream

While Peter was waiting for lunch one day, he went up on the housetop to pray. God sent him a strange dream. In it he saw a big sheet held by the four corners being let down from heaven. The sheet held all kinds of animals, bugs, reptiles, and birds. A voice told Peter to get up, kill one of the animals, and eat it. There were some animals Peter didn't eat because of the Jewish health laws. Peter answered the voice, saying that he couldn't, because he had never eaten anything unclean. The voice spoke again, telling Peter that if God has made it clean, he must not call it unclean. Then the dream was over.

Peter thought and thought about the meaning of his dream. He realized it didn't mean that he could now eat whatever he wanted to. God's laws about the things we eat were given to help us stay healthy. No, that wasn't what God was telling him.

In Peter's day the Jews thought that they were the only ones who could be saved. They thought that anyone who wasn't Jewish was out of luck. But Jesus came to save everyone. God was telling Peter in this dream that His love is for everyone, whether they are Jewish or non-Jewish.

Sometimes we think that our way is the only way. It takes courage to remember that God loves everyone. We should treat everyone the same, regardless of what they believe or who they are.

What God has cleansed you must not call common.
Acts 10:15.

COURAGE

261

The Forbidden School

Do not be afraid; do not be discouraged. Be strong and courageous.
Joshua 10:25, NIV.

Soheila couldn't fight the Taliban, her country's cruel government. She was a woman, and the Taliban treated every woman as a second-class citizen. Women were not allowed even to go to the grocery store unless they were with a man—it could result in a severe beating if they were caught. Soheila waged her own quiet rebellion from the walled garden of her home. There, with two small blackboards, she did something forbidden by her rulers. She taught a school for girls.

The Taliban didn't want girls to work or learn. If Soheila had been caught, her punishment would have been harsh. But she bravely fought her quiet battles day by day, hour by hour, teaching the girls and helping them to learn. The students were taught that if they were stopped by the Taliban, they should explain that they were going to visit her. After school they left in small groups so as not to attract attention.

Now that the Taliban government is no longer in power in her town of Herat, Soheila's school is reopening. Her girls can learn without fear. Sohelia can now teach without hiding.

Thankfully, we live in a country where anyone who wants an education can have one. Because of Sohelia's courage, many girls in her country will have a better life. What can you do today to make the lives of those around you better?

COURAGE

Water Rescue

Whenever I am afraid, I will trust in You.
Psalm 56:3.

Uncle Tom invited Rachel and her parents to spend the Fourth of July on his boat, out in the Pacific Ocean outside of San Diego, California. Rachel saw the *Star of India,* a big sailing ship, and enjoyed the salty smell of the ocean breeze. She even "barked" at some harbor seals, and they barked back!

That evening there were fireworks on the shore. Uncle Tom suggested that they could see the fireworks best from the ocean, so they stayed on the boat and ate strawberry shortcake while they watched the exciting reds, golds, and blues of the fireworks exploding in the night sky.

When the fireworks were over, the boat's motor wouldn't start. Uncle Tom would have put up his sail, but there were no winds to move the boat. The boat began to rock wildly as other bigger boats zoomed past theirs. Rachel was scared. Uncle Tom called the Coast Guard for help, but they were busy helping other boats and couldn't come. Rachel asked her mom if they were going to drown. She was very scared.

Rachel's parents comforted her. Rachel and her mom were already wearing life jackets, and they made sure that everyone else put them on. Then Rachel's parents prayed with her. They prayed that God would protect them and help them to get home safe.

Finally some people on another boat stopped and helped tow Uncle Tom's boat back to the harbor. Rachel and her family were so happy to be safe on shore! They thanked God for keeping them safe and for helping them while they were out on the water.

If you're ever afraid, ask God to help you. He will protect you and keep you safe, as He did Rachel and her family.

COURAGE

11
SEPTEMBER

*For the Son
of Man has come
to seek and
to save that
which was lost.*

Luke 19:10.

Courage
Under Fire

Ray Downey was a nice guy. He was the father of five kids and husband to Rosalie. He lived his life to the fullest every day.

One thing Ray loved the most was being a firefighter with the New York City Fire Department. He became their most decorated fire chief and the world's leading expert on urban search and recovery. He even wrote a book about saving people who were trapped under collapsed buildings.

So when the World Trade Center buildings fell down on September 11, 2001, all of his family knew where he would be.

People who were there told his family that after the first building fell down, Ray stood up, dusted himself off, and went back in to help people. His sons spent the next eight months looking for him, but Ray had died there at the World Trade Center.

Ray Downey didn't just tell others to do what was right; he did it himself—even when it cost him his life.

Jesus is an expert in search and rescue too. He searches for each of us, asking if we want to be saved from the rubble of sin. When He came to live on earth, He did what was right too, even though it cost Him His life. Because of His sacrifice, we can live with Him in heaven forever.

COURAGE

A Giant Problem

The whole Israelite army was in a panic. Goliath, the Philistine giant, came out every day and threatened them, called them names, and challenged them to send a man out to fight. No one would go fight him. If they lost, the whole nation would become the servants of the Philistines. Besides, Goliath was so big that everyone was afraid to fight him.

Everyone, that is, but a boy named David. David's father, Jesse, had sent him to check on his brothers. When David got to camp, he saw Goliath and heard the things he said about Israel and their God. He couldn't believe that no one would fight him, so he offered to go himself.

King Saul and David's brothers tried to convince him not to go. He was, after all, just a boy, and Goliath was a trained soldier and a giant! There was no way David could win. But David knew that it was the right thing to do and that God would be with him.

As David made his way toward the giant, Goliath laughed. What were the Israelites thinking, sending a little boy out to fight him? But David stood strong. He knew that even though Goliath was a trained soldier, God would bless him and give him the victory. And He did!

People may try to discourage you the way Saul and his brothers tried to discourage David. Just remember that with God's help you can stand strong for what is right. God's opinion is what matters most, and we should always do what is right according to Him regardless of what others say or think.

You come to me with a sword, with a spear, and with a javelin. But I come to you in the name of the Lord of hosts.

1 Samuel 17:45.

COURAGE

13
SEPTEMBER

Be strong and very courageous. Be careful to obey all the law . . . , that you may be successful wherever you go.

Joshua 1:7, NIV.

Moon Walker

Can you imagine what it would be like to put your foot down on the ground and know that no human had ever stepped on that spot before? What would it be like to know that you were about to do something that no one had ever done before?

That's what Neil Armstrong did. He did something that, to this day, very few people have done. He walked on the moon.

On July 20, 1969, Neil Armstrong and Buzz Aldrin were part of the United States' first attempt to land on the moon. They landed on the portion of the moon called the Sea of Tranquillity. Neil bravely went first, and his words when he touched the surface are now famous: "That's one small step for a man, one giant leap for mankind."

It took courage to step out of that lunar module. The men knew they were relatively safe if they stayed inside, but they didn't know for sure what would happen once they stepped outside.

Sometimes we have opportunities to do new things in our lives too. It can be scary to step outside of our comfort zone, but God has promised that He will be with us wherever we go—even to the moon. And one day soon He'll come back to take us on the most amazing space flight ever!

COURAGE

No One Would've Guessed

We ought to obey God rather than men.
Acts 5:29.

As a Nazi, Oskar Schindler was the last person you'd imagine would want to help the Jews during World War II. But the Nazis didn't suspect it either, so it was a perfect plan.

In Krakow, Poland, Oskar took over two companies. He had mostly Jewish people working for him. Because they were working for him, they weren't as likely to be taken away and killed. He tried to have as many people as possible working at his different factories and shops so that they would be safe.

If he had been found out, he could have been killed for helping the Jews. But he knew that the Jews didn't deserve to be treated the way they were in the war. He risked his life and his family to save people he didn't know.

Even years after the war Oskar didn't want anyone to make a fuss over what he had done. He had just done what was right.

God asks us to obey authority unless it goes against Him or His Word. Governments can be wrong—the Nazis were wrong. As God's heroes we should obey God no matter what the people around us are doing.

COURAGE

15
SEPTEMBER

A Courageous Woman

Do not merely listen to the word, and so deceive yourselves. Do what it says.
James 1:22, NIV.

Hulda Roper was a fighter. She didn't get into fistfights, but she was one tough woman. The first female police officer in Lincoln, Nebraska, she refused to carry a gun. She figured that between her and God she didn't need one. And she never did.

Hulda was a Christian, and her entire life was spent serving others. Besides her police work, she helped start and run an orphanage. She took care of mentally disabled people. She gave money and time to worthy causes. Hulda became so well known for helping in her community that the city named an elementary school after her. Everything she did was for others, and people respected and loved her for it.

Hulda didn't have an in-your-face attitude. Her courage was strong and quiet, flowing through her entire life. When you have faith in God to protect you and be with you in your life, you can have the peace and quiet courage that only God can give.

COURAGE

It's All Relative

Albert Einstein is considered to be one of the smartest men who ever lived. His discoveries shook up the scientific world of his day. Even though some of his ideas were new, they helped solve some of the problems and questions scientists had been asking for many years.

It took courage for Einstein to try to prove his theories—they were so different from what everyone thought was true. He was sure of them, though, and set out to prove them and get other scientists to look at things in this new way.

In our everyday lives it takes courage for us to live what we believe. Knowing that we serve an awesome and loving God should give us courage in our day-to-day lives as well.

It is important to keep in mind that although Einstein was really smart, his intelligence doesn't even begin to match that of God's. Einstein had some good ideas, but God created the universe that Einstein tried to explain.

For the wisdom of this world is foolishness in God's sight.
1 Corinthians 3:19, NIV.

COURAGE

17

SEPTEMBER

cat Nip

The Lord is my helper; I will not be afraid. What can man do to me?
Hebrews 13:6, NIV.

One hot summer day Melissa, the fluffy white 3-year-old cat, was curled up in her favorite corner of her home, a book and music store. Melissa lazily listened to the normal store sounds as Diane, one of the owners, helped customers.

Suddenly Melissa heard a stranger's rough voice and Diane's unsteady answer. Diane sounded afraid. Melissa quietly padded around the corner. What she saw made her back arch and her fur stand up in anger. A man with a knife had backed Diane into a corner. He was demanding that she open the cash register. Diane told the man to do it himself. She didn't want to get any closer to him or that sharp knife!

Melissa sprang into action. Her long white fur standing on end, claws out, and tail standing straight up, she jumped onto the counter and stalked toward the man, snarling with every step. He shouted at her to get back, but she kept on. He waved the knife at her, but her eyes just narrowed, her growl deepened, and she kept on. Melissa growled louder, continuing to move closer, her eyes locked on him.

The man looked around for something to protect himself with. He threw a chair at Melissa, but she just ducked and kept coming. Because of the distraction, Diane was able to slip out of the store and call for help. The man was so afraid that he ran out of the store too, without even emptying the cash register. Melissa's bravery had saved the day—and possibly Diane's life.

It doesn't matter how big you are. (Melissa was really a rather small cat.) God can use you to be a hero for Him.

COURAGE

The Pilot Who Wasn't

Sergeant Clifford White was a machine gunner, not a pilot. But when his airplane was hit over Poland in World War II, the copilot was killed and the pilot was knocked unconscious. There was no one to fly the plane, and nine other men were on board. What could they do?

Clifford didn't have a pilot's license, but he'd done a little flying in his army training in the United States. He'd never flown an airplane this big before, but he didn't have a choice. He ran to the cockpit and took over the controls, wrestling the airplane out of a tailspin and turning it back to England, 700 miles away.

When they neared England, the radio operator told the men to parachute to safety. Everyone but Clifford obeyed orders and jumped out of the plane. Clifford refused to leave the pilot, who was still unconscious. With only two working motors left on the plane, he belly-landed it on the army base in England. Emergency workers ran to the plane and pulled out the pilot, who eventually recovered from his injuries. Clifford had barely gotten away from the plane himself when it exploded and burned. For his heroism he was awarded the Distinguished Flying Cross.

There may be times we need to do something hard, but God is always with us. Take courage from Him. He'll help you get through whatever you face.

Yea, though I walk through the valley of the shadow of death, I will fear no evil; for You are with me.
Psalm 23:4.

COURAGE

19
SEPTEMBER

No Fear

Do not be afraid of those who kill the body but cannot kill the soul.
Matthew 10:28, NIV.

John Huss was making the church leaders very angry with him. He was preaching that God alone has the power to forgive sins. He was teaching people that they should look in the Bible to find what to believe. The church of his day taught that church leaders had the power to forgive sins and that their teachings were on the same level as those of the Bible. The church leaders didn't like it when John taught something different. They wanted to kill him.

They tricked him into coming to some meetings. Then they set up a trial much like the one Jesus had, complete with phony witnesses and false accusations. The penalty was death by burning at the stake. John was given one last chance to say that what he had preached was wrong and that the church was right. But he couldn't say that—he knew it wasn't true. Even though it meant his death, he was not afraid, because he knew that he was right and that God would be with him.

Sometimes it's hard to stand up for what is right. But the Bible tells us that if we accept Jesus as our Savior, we have nothing to fear, not even death, because He is stronger than death. When He comes again, Jesus will raise up those who love Him. He will put an end to death and sin forever.

COURAGE

Ringo the Babysitter

Two-year-old Randy wandered the streets of his town for two hours with his big dog, Ringo, by his side while his worried mother and the police searched for him.

Randy came to the edge of a busy road with a blind curve and watched with excitement as the cars whizzed past. At the first break in traffic he stepped off the curb and waddled to the middle of the road, where he bent down to touch the shiny yellow paint. He didn't hear the car coming, but Ringo did. Ringo raced around the curve, barking ferociously. The driver saw him and honked, but Ringo wouldn't move. With the car safely stopped, Ringo ran back around the curve and led Randy off the road.

Back and forth the big dog continued until nearly 40 cars were stopped on that corner. No one could go around him, and people didn't dare get out of their cars.

Eventually a man at the end of the row of cars got out to see what the trouble was. He saw Ringo stopping cars; then he walked around the curve. There was Randy, laughing, right in the middle of the road. The man saw Ringo run back around the corner and try to lead Randy off the road. The man understood what was happening. He spoke kindly to Ringo, who let him pick up Randy and move him to the side of the road. Ringo finally relaxed, knowing that the man would not let Randy go back out into the road. Ringo had saved the little boy's life.

Little Randy didn't even know he was in danger. If it hadn't been for Ringo, he would have been killed. Thanks to the big dog, he was saved. God has promised us that He will send His angels to watch over us and protect us, even when we, like little Randy, don't know we're in danger.

For He shall give His angels charge over you, to keep you in all your ways.
Psalm 91:11.

COURAGE

21
SEPTEMBER

Blessed are those who hear the word of God and keep it!

Luke 11:28.

My Conscience Is Captive to the Word of God

Martin Luther had been called before the king, who wanted to know two things. First, had he written the books on the table in the room? Martin told the king that he had written the books. Next the king wanted to know if Martin would recant. The king wanted him to take back the things he'd written and say they weren't true. Martin said that he would need more time to study before giving a final answer to this second question. He wanted to make sure he said the right thing. He was given one day.

He spent that day in prayer and study. He was called before the king late in the afternoon. Many people had gathered to hear what he would say. Would he recant?

He didn't. He told the king that he could not accept any authority other than the Bible. He told them, "My conscience is captive to the Word of God. I cannot and I will not recant anything, for to go against conscience is neither right nor safe." Martin Luther knew that the Bible should be the highest authority in his life, and he would not listen to anyone who told him otherwise.

The Bible should be our final authority, too. There are other good books out there, some of which give good advice. But if any book contradicts the Bible, we shouldn't pay attention to it. The Bible is God's word to us, and it should be our guide in life, just as it was for Martin Luther.

COURAGE

The Shrimp Who Became a Whale

William Wilberforce was small and sickly. As he began to speak to the House of Commons in England, a hush came over the crowd. Although he was not a strong person, he was a very strong speaker. One man described him as a "mere shrimp of a man" who, when he began to speak, "grew into a whale." William spent three hours that day trying to convince the government that slavery was wrong.

John Newton, the man who wrote "Amazing Grace," had showed William thumbscrews, iron collars, metal whips, and other things used against slaves. William was convinced that slavery was evil, and he spent the rest of his life trying to fight it.

There were many people who didn't want to do away with slavery, because it raised a lot of money for England. But William was convinced it was wrong, and he was willing to do whatever it took to get rid of slavery. He spent a lot of time in prayer and study preparing his case before going before the House of Commons. Once there, he told the men of government everything he knew about slavery, and why it was wrong. He told them that they couldn't just ignore it anymore. Something had to be done.

William was discouraged when the House decided to delay action, but a friend reminded him that what he was doing was right, and "if God is with us, who can be against us?" It encouraged him, and he spent the rest of his life fighting slavery. He lived long enough to see some progress made, and slavery was abolished in England exactly one year after his death.

Sometimes we may get discouraged when things don't seem to be going well, but if God is on our side, it doesn't matter what the opposition is. If God is with us, no one can win against us!

If God is for us, who can be against us?
Romans 8:31.

COURAGE

A Bright Light

Papeiha (Pa-pay-ee-ha) was not afraid of the natives of Rarotonga, even though people said they were cannibals. To him, sharing God's love was more important than his own safety. He left everything he owned on the ship except for his clothes and Bible, and bravely went ashore to talk to the natives. He went alone—everyone else went back to the ship.

Papeiha told the people of Rarotonga that he had come to teach them of the one true God of heaven. He told them that soon they would take their gods of wood, feathers, and cloth and burn them. This made the people angry; they thought their gods protected them. If they burned the gods, there wouldn't be anyone to protect them, and then what would happen to them?

But there was something in the way Papeiha spoke that kept the people from killing him. They let him stay, and eventually many of the natives did become Christians. As he had predicted, they did burn their idols in great bonfires that could be seen from far away.

Today the flames of love that Papeiha shared with the natives still glow and have kept spreading, as the people share their God with the islands around them.

Some days it may seem as if the light of our witness is more like a candle than a bonfire. But it's still a light, and God can use it to warm others' hearts and bring them out of darkness and closer to Him.

COURAGE

The Wright Way

For with God nothing will be impossible.
Luke 1:37.

Everyone said it couldn't be done. They said, "If God had meant for humans to fly, He would have given them wings." But the Wright brothers, Wilbur and Orville, weren't so sure. They had always loved flying toys when they were children, and they worked for a while building kites. They hoped to build a kite that could carry a person.

The brothers played together as boys and worked together as adults. Everything they did was done well. It didn't matter that people laughed at them and their ideas; they just kept quietly working.

And then, on December 17, 1903, at Kitty Hawk, North Carolina, the Wright brothers did what couldn't be done—they flew. All of a sudden the people who had been laughing at them were giving them honors, medals, and money.

Because of their patience, determination, and skill, the Wright brothers made travel faster than ever. They made the world a better place. Today airplanes are used for passenger travel, mail delivery, mapmaking, forest protection, and exploration, among other things. This all happens because the Wright brothers didn't believe it when they were told it couldn't be done.

COURAGE

The Hero of Hawaii

Many of the people of Hawaii were new Christians who had been taught their whole lives to fear the fire goddess Pele. They believed Pele lived in the volcano and made it erupt when she was angry. Even though they now believed in the God of heaven, it was hard not to be afraid of Pele. But Kapiolani, the chief, was not afraid. She told the people that she would climb the mountain where Pele lived and that God would protect her. Pele wouldn't hurt her because Pele didn't exist. God made the volcano.

People begged her not to go. They just knew she would be destroyed. But she knew that God would protect her, and she climbed the mountain. As she neared the top of the volcano, she saw a bush with berries on it. They were "Pele's berries." No one could touch them without first asking her permission. To the people's horror, Kapiolani broke off a branch and ate the berries. The people wondered how much more Pele would take before destroying her.

Closer and closer Kapiolani went, until she was at the very edge. There she pulled out a Bible and read to the people about the God of heaven. Then she actually climbed down into the mouth of the volcano and threw the branch of berries into the lava! The people just knew that she would be destroyed now. But nothing happened. She climbed out of the crater and told them that the power of Pele was gone. From that moment the people decided to follow Kapiolani's God.

God probably won't ask any of us to climb into the mouth of a volcano to prove to our friends that He is God. But it can take just as much courage to stand up to the people around us and stand strong for God.

COURAGE

Slave Turned Speaker

Frederick Douglass was a former slave. As he stood before the large group of people to talk to them about why slavery was bad, he was nervous. Why should they listen to him? He was a former slave. Unlike some of the other people on the platform, he wasn't famous. What was he doing here?

But he put aside his fears and spoke to the crowd anyway. Because he had been a slave himself, he could tell people firsthand what it was like. The audience listened carefully.

Mr. Douglass became one of the most famous speakers of his time. He traveled widely in his lifetime and spoke against slavery to many thousands of people. He gathered his courage to help bring an end to slavery and a better life for former slaves.

When we focus on the negative side of things, it is hard to be brave or do something we aren't comfortable doing. But if you do your best even when it's not easy, as Frederick Douglass did, you may have a huge impact on someone for good.

Do you see a man who excels in his work? He will stand before kings.
Proverbs 22:29.

COURAGE

27
SEPTEMBER

*Therefore whoever
confesses Me
before men, him I
will also confess
before My Father
who is in heaven.*
Matthew 10:32.

Tell
the World

Solomon Ginsburg had a deep desire to share Jesus with anyone he could talk to. It didn't matter who they were. He just wanted to be sure that they knew about Jesus. He told friends, family, and even strangers. It didn't matter!

Solomon didn't care who people were or where they came from. Whether they were rich or poor, he wanted to share Jesus with them. He even went to the homes of former prisoners and convicted killers. If they wanted to know about Jesus, he wanted to tell them. He never backed down or refused an invitation, even though he was beaten and threatened for his faith.

Jesus asks us not to be afraid to share Him with others. Whether they listen or not, it's our job to share His love with everyone we meet.

COURAGE

The Brave Nurse

The big hairy man grumbled under his breath as he lay in the hospital bed. Who did this nurse think she was, anyway? She had told him no! He was used to getting his way, and he wasn't used to people telling him no—especially a woman!

Miss Cushman, the nurse he was grumbling about, was a small American woman working at a hospital in Turkey. The big man had ordered her to take a picture of Jesus off the wall, and she'd politely refused. She told him that the picture wasn't moving, but he was welcome to leave the hospital if he'd like. The big man knew he wouldn't get well if he left the hospital, so he just lay in bed and grumbled.

The man was rude to the other nurses as well, and Miss Cushman kindly reminded him that they were there to help him and deserved his courtesy and respect. Again, the man lay in bed and grumbled, but he was nicer to the nurses after that.

In time Miss Cushman was in charge of delivering food and clothing to some needy people in Turkey. And guess who helped her? The big hairy man! He had been won over by Miss Cushman's kindness and courage. He saw that her Christian love was better than his rude and mean ways.

Miss Cushman's bravery wasn't the type that won medals or honors on earth, but God recorded it in heaven. When Jesus comes again, He'll give Miss Cushman, and everyone who has been brave for Him, the best honor of all.

My eyes shall be on the faithful of the land, that they may dwell with me.

Psalm 101:6.

COURAGE

29
SEPTEMBER

*And this is
eternal life,
that they may
know You,
the only true God,
and Jesus Christ
whom You
have sent.*

John 17:3.

The Heroes of Flight 93

The bright, clear morning was like any other as people boarded their planes. Some were headed for work, others for vacations or to visit families. And a few were there to do the devil's work.

A handful of evil men boarded four airplanes and hijacked them while they were flying. They crashed three of the planes into buildings, killing many people. But the hijackers in the fourth plane were not able to go through with their plan to crash into a building, thanks to the bravery of some of the passengers.

Several people on board the fourth plane, Flight 93, found out about the other plane crashes. They decided to take action, even though it could mean their own death. A group of them ran to the cockpit, where the hijackers had taken control of the airplane. Their bravery resulted in the plane crashing into a field in Pennsylvania rather than into a building, which would have caused many more people to die.

The passengers on Flight 93 faced a hard decision, but they chose to put the safety of others ahead of their own.

Our planet was hijacked by Satan. Jesus did not fear for His own life, but fought to give us a chance to be saved and go to heaven and live with Him. His death and resurrection means life for everyone who chooses Him!

COURAGE

God's Railroad

Harriet Tubman decided to escape. For weeks she planned how she would do it, and one day she put her plan into action. Traveling at night and hiding during the day, Harriet slowly made her way from slavery to freedom.

Once she was free, she didn't rest. She was very brave. She helped start the Underground Railroad—a chain of people who helped slaves escape to freedom. Harriet made 19 trips back to the South. She helped more than 300 slaves to freedom, including three siblings and her parents.

Harriet knew that freedom was worth fighting for. With every trip she risked her life to help others so that they could be free too. She said once that, with God's help, her Underground Railroad had never run off the track or lost a passenger.

God's railroad to heaven will never run off track or lose a passenger either. Are you on board?

The Lord has anointed Me to preach good tidings to the poor; . . . to proclaim liberty to the captives, and the opening of the prison to those who are bound.

Isaiah 61:1.

COURAGE

1

OCTOBER

I AM

And God said to Moses, "I AM WHO I AM."

Exodus 3:14.

Moses was watching his sheep when he saw a strange sight—a burning bush. This wasn't just any burning bush, though. There were flames, but the bush wasn't burning up. He moved closer to see what was going on, and the bush spoke to him! (Actually, it was God speaking to him, but Moses didn't know that at first.) The voice told him to take off his shoes, because he was standing on holy ground; then God introduced Himself.

God told Moses that He was the God of Abraham, Isaac, and Jacob. God told Moses that He would use him to lead the Hebrews out of Egypt. It was a lot of information for Moses, and he didn't think that Pharaoh or the Hebrews would believe him. It seemed a little far-fetched, really, that the great God of heaven had spoken to a shepherd from a bush.

The Egyptians had many gods with many different names, so Moses asked God His name. He was sure that the Hebrews would want to know who had sent him. God told Moses He is "I AM." God didn't say "I was" or "I will be." God is "I AM"—eternal and unchanging.

In our society today laws and morals are constantly changing. It's good to know that we have an unchanging God. He is the same God today as He was when he talked with Moses. Dealing with changes in our lives can be hard, but we can face change with confidence, since we know our God never changes. We can trust Him to care for us today, just as He cared for the people in the Bible.

DEPENDABILITY AND RESPONSIBILITY

The Famous Ride

Threquiet of the night was broken by the thunder of a horse's hooves on the cobblestone streets and a man's voice yelling, "The British are coming! The British are coming!"

Paul Revere rode through the streets shouting his warning, and men jumped into action to defend their town.

The time was the American Revolution, when Americans were fighting to become a free country. It was Paul's job to keep watch and tell the people of the town if he saw the British coming to attack. It was late at night, and Paul was probably sleepy, but he knew that he had an important job.

Because he took it seriously and did what he was supposed to do, the Americans were able to wake up and defend themselves from the British. If he hadn't done his job, history might have turned out differently.

Can you, like Paul Revere, be counted on to do your job? Your warning might help wake someone up and save them for the freedom of heaven.

It is high time to awake out of sleep; for now our salvation is nearer than when we first believed.

Romans 13:11.

DEPENDABILITY AND RESPONSIBILITY

3
OCTOBER

The Man Who Ran From God

Do your best to present yourself to God as one approved, a workman who does not need to be ashamed and who correctly handles the word of truth.

2 Timothy 2:15, NIV.

Nineveh was a wicked city. The people who lived there were very sinful. God told Jonah to go to Nineveh and tell the people that if they didn't repent, He would destroy their city. Jonah loved God, but he didn't want to go. So he ran away and got on a boat going in the opposite direction.

Out at sea a strong storm came up, and the boat began to sink. Everyone on board was afraid, but Jonah knew that God had sent the storm. He told the captain to throw him overboard and then the storm would stop. The captain didn't want to throw Jonah overboard; he would surely drown in the rough seas. But the storm got so bad that the captain didn't know what else to do. So into the cold, dark water Jonah went with a splash.

Sure enough, the seas calmed down and the boat stopped sinking. Jonah sank down, down into the water, where God sent a big fish to swallow him up. Jonah was probably very afraid.

But God didn't give up on Jonah. He gave him a second chance. After three days that big fish spit Jonah out onto the shore. Maybe the light hurt his eyes, since he had been in the dark that long. And no doubt he really needed a bath. But he was safe. He was alive. He was glad to go to Nineveh and warn the people. The whole city repented because of the message Jonah brought, and the people were spared.

A hero for God is dependable. Sometimes we are asked to do things we might not want to do, but obedience is the best way. Can God count on you to do what He asks you the first time? Or do you sometimes need a second chance, like Jonah?

DEPENDABILITY AND RESPONSIBILITY

Doing Your Best

She did what she could.

Mark 14:8, NIV.

When General George Washington was looking for someone to make the first American flag, he called on a woman by the name of Betsy Ross. Betsy lived in Gloucester, New Jersey, where she spent her days sewing clothes and linens. She couldn't fight in the American Revolution with a weapon, but she did what she could to fight it with the skills she had. General Washington knew that she was good at what she did, so he counted on her to help.

What Betsy did may not seem very impressive. She just sewed some fabric together. But because she did her best, her sewing skills created one of the most recognizable flags in the world. The new flag helped unite the new nation.

Heroes for God will always do their best at whatever they do. We may not think that the things we do every day are very impressive, but we never know what impact they may have.

DEPENDABILITY AND RESPONSIBILITY

5
OCTOBER

A Young Example

Be diligent to present yourself approved to God, a worker who does not need to be ashamed.

2 Timothy 2:15.

Timothy and Paul became good friends. In fact, they were so close that Paul said Timothy was like a son to him. They worked together to spread Christianity and start the early church.

Timothy was young when he worked with Paul. There were people who didn't respect him because he was young. They thought he couldn't do a good job because he wasn't as old as they were.

Timothy also was quiet and reserved. Some people looked down on him and thought he couldn't do a good job because he was so quiet. But Paul and Timothy continued to work together, and God used them both for the good of many people.

Timothy set a good example for us as God's heroes. You know that even if you are young, God can use you if you let Him. Even if you are quiet, you can do your best for Him in everything you do.

DEPENDABILITY AND RESPONSIBILITY

A Stubborn Dog

Alix is stubborn. The big brown dog knows she isn't supposed to get on her owners' bed, but time after time they catch her up there, even though she has her own squishy pillow on the floor at the end of the bed. She knows that she shouldn't pull food off the counter when her people aren't looking, but whenever she gets the chance, she does it anyway. She knows that she shouldn't bark at other dogs, but whenever one walks by her house, she puts up a huge fuss.

Alix knows that she will be punished when she does bad things, but it doesn't matter. She does them anyway. That doesn't make much sense, does it?

Sometimes we do that with God. We know what we are supposed to do. We just don't want to do it. Even though we know there may be a punishment involved, we charge ahead and do our own thing. It's not very smart, is it?

Alix's owners aren't trying to keep good things away from her. They are trying to teach her to be a well-behaved, happy dog. They know that she will make a mess of the bed, that some people food will make her sick, and that other dogs have the right to walk on the street.

Rules work the same way for us. God doesn't make up rules to make us miserable or unhappy. He knows what is best, and His rules will help us to be well-behaved, happy people.

I desire to do your will, O my God; your law is within my heart.
Psalm 40:8, NIV.

289

7
OCTOBER

*The steps of
a good man
are ordered by
the Lord,
and He delights
in his way.*
Psalm 37:23.

Working With God

Samuel was an answer to prayer. When his mother, Hannah, prayed that God would give her a baby, she promised that she would dedicate the baby to God's service. That's exactly what she did.

Samuel spent his whole life in service for God. He grew up helping Eli, the high priest, in the tabernacle. Then Samuel became a prophet. He allowed God to use him, and he listened to God's voice. He asked God for direction, then followed through by doing what God asked him to do.

Many times we may ask God for direction in our life, but then we do what we want to anyway. Or perhaps we don't ask for direction and then ask God to bless us when we do our own thing. Ask God today for direction in your life and be willing to follow through with what He tells you to do.

DEPENDABILITY AND RESPONSIBILITY

Pressing Responsibility

Imagine what the world would be like without books. At first you might think that wouldn't be so bad—no schoolbooks and no homework assignments, right? But think about it carefully. That would also mean no bedtime stories. There would be no medical books, so doctors couldn't learn how to help you when you're sick. There would be no cookbooks for your mom to cook your favorite meal. There would be no Bibles. Maybe it wouldn't be so great after all.

In Johannes Gutenberg's day the only books that existed had been copied by hand. Books took months, and sometimes even years, to make, so only the very wealthy could afford them. Johannes knew that people could learn more things and live better lives if books were available to everyone—even the common people.

He felt a great responsibility to make books available to everyone. He spent a great deal of time experimenting with how to make them quickly and inexpensively. Eventually he made the first printing press, which did exactly that. Johannes took his responsibility seriously, and he made the world a better place for everyone.

If you see a need, or think of something that might make the world a better place, it is your responsibility to do what you can to make it happen. With God's help, you can do great things to help those around you.

My people are destroyed for lack of knowledge.

Hosea 4:6.

DEPENDABILITY AND RESPONSIBILITY

9
OCTOBER

*The righteous man
walks in
his integrity.*
Proverbs 20:7.

Living
the faith

The way Stephen lived his life showed others what he believed. He didn't just say the words, but lived out his beliefs in everything he did. Stephen was chosen as one of seven leaders of the early church to help give needy families food. This job was given to him because he was responsible and caring, and he always did his best.

Stephen died because he was a Christian. The Jewish leaders didn't like it when he told them they were wrong. The way he lived his life made it clear to them that their hearts and lives needed to change. It was a reminder they didn't want to hear. In the end he became the first martyr for Christ. (You can read his story in Acts 6:3-8:2.)

Stephen's sense of responsibility wouldn't let him deny his faith to make things easy on himself. He was faithful to his Savior no matter what it cost. To this day his story is told. He is still a witness for Christ.

The way we do things—both big and small—can reflect on our faith too. God needs heroes to stand strong for Him. He needs helpers He can depend on no matter what. You may be the only contact with Christianity that some people ever have. Will you be dependable for God today?

DEPENDABILITY AND RESPONSIBILITY

Six Impossible Things Before Breakfast

People thought Lewis Carroll was weird. The stories he came up with were really, really strange: stories of the Mad Hatter, the White Rabbit, and little girls who had adventures underground. Lewis was a gentle man, but it was said that he could think of six impossible things before breakfast. His imagination was very active.

As a young man Lewis thought of becoming a minister, but he was very shy and tended to stutter. He decided that perhaps a life of public speaking might not be best for him. Even so, he lectured and continued to have a love for Jesus all his life.

Instead of becoming a minister, Lewis wrote many books. Some were made up for his young friends. Others, such as his books on math, were for older audiences. He is best known for his book *Alice in Wonderland,* the strange story of a little girl's dream.

Lewis didn't worry that he wasn't able to become a professional minister. Instead he focused on sharing God's love with people on a daily basis. He used the gift of writing that God gave him to entertain and teach generations of people. What gifts has God given you that you can use to help others?

You have been faithful with a few things; I will put you in charge of many things.
Matthew 25:21, NIV.

DEPENDABILITY AND RESPONSIBILITY

A Quiet Hero

Righteousness guards him whose way is blameless, but wickedness overthrows the sinner.
Proverbs 13:6.

Boaz was a rich farmer living in Bethlehem. When he found out that his relative, Naomi, was back in town with her daughter-in-law Ruth, he did what he could to help them. They were both widows. He let Ruth pick up grain in his field for herself and Naomi. In fact, he told his workers to drop extra grain for her. After some time, he and Ruth married. They loved each other very much.

A hero for God can be counted on to do what is right and to treat others with kindness. Boaz didn't mean to be a hero. He just did what was right in the right way. He had no way of knowing that one day he and Ruth would be ancestors of both King David and Jesus.

God can use our little kindnesses to others in a big way. Ask Him today to help you to make the right choices and do the right things.

DEPENDABILITY AND RESPONSIBILITY

He Will Come

Trust in the Lord forever, for the Lord, the Lord, is the Rock eternal.
Isaiah 26:4, NIV.

Ice pressed against the little ship from all sides. The captain, Sir Ernest Shackleton, and his crew did everything they could to free the *Endurance*, but nothing helped. The ship was being crushed. They had to take what they could and go out onto the ice.

Now what should they do? The 27 men in Shackleton's crew had plowed their way through 1,500 miles of ice. And now they were stranded on an iceberg in the middle of the ocean, hundreds of miles from land. The brave crew set up tents and began to think of a plan.

No matter how worried he was on the inside, Shackleton never complained. He remained brave, calm, and cheerful. They had three small boats with them and, after three days of thinking, Shackleton decided to take the biggest boat and five men and try to reach a whaling station 800 miles away. It was their only hope.

He promised his men he would be back, and after several months and much hardship, he did come back. Later the stranded men told him that each day Frank Wild, the one in charge, told them, "Perhaps the boss will come today." When they finally saw the boat, they instantly recognized their boss and cheered. They had been on the island for more than four months and had suffered terribly, but they knew that their boss would come back for them, as he had promised. They knew that he was a man of his word and could be counted on to do what it took to rescue them.

Jesus, our boss, is a man of His word too. He can be trusted to do what He says. Sometimes it may seem that it's taking a long time for Him to come and rescue us from this island of sin, but He promised, and He will come for us. Will you recognize Him when He gets here?

DEPENDABILITY AND RESPONSIBILITY

295

13
OCTOBER

A Good King

And he did what was right in the sight of the Lord . . . ; he did not turn aside to the right hand or to the left.

2 Kings 22:2.

Israel suffered through a long line of very bad kings. One bright spot among all the bad kings was King Josiah. Josiah was only 8 years old when he became king, but he reigned for many years. Even though he was very young when he became king, he still did what was right.

During Josiah's time as king, he worked hard to bring the people of Israel back to God. He got rid of the idols that were in the Temple, and he promised to keep God's commandments. Josiah knew what was right and he did it, even when he was a child.

Can you be depended on to do what is right instead of what is popular? It's not enough just to say we believe something. If we don't live it, it doesn't do us or anyone else any good. Ask God today to help you to do what is right, no matter what your age.

DEPENDABILITY AND RESPONSIBILITY

New Uses for Old Crops

George was the son of slaves. He worked hard to put himself through school. He did odd jobs, housecleaning, laundry—whatever he could find that was honest work. Eventually he earned a college degree and began working at Tuskegee Institute with Booker T. Washington. These two men worked very hard to improve the lives of the African-Americans of their day, who were, for the most part, very poor and without many opportunities.

George thought that poor people could improve their lives if they were taught to use the land well. He set to work looking for ways to help.

In his experiments George found more than 100 ways to use a sweet potato—dyes, flour, glue, coffee, candy, starch, vinegar, inks, shoe polish, and rubber, to name a few. He found even more uses for the peanut. George discovered ways to use pecans, tomatoes, and corn that no one had thought of before. Because of all these new products, demand for these crops increased, and many people were able to live more comfortable lives.

George could have become rich from his many inventions, but he always used them for the good of others. His payment was the satisfaction of knowing that he had helped many people gain self-respect and independence through his work.

George Washington Carver never did anything carelessly. He believed that anything worth doing is worth doing well. Being a hero for God involves working to help others and doing your best at everything you do.

He who has mercy on the poor, happy is he.
Proverbs 14:21.

DEPENDABILITY AND RESPONSIBILITY

A Man of His Word

*And he carried
out his vow.*

Judges 11:39.

Jephthah was a judge and warrior in Israel. He promised God that if He helped the Israelites win a battle against the people of Ammon, he would give an offering. He promised that his offering would be whoever came out of his house first when he got home. It wasn't a very wise promise, perhaps, but that's what he said.

God did give Jephthah the victory. The Bible says that "Jephthah advanced toward the people of Ammon . . . , and the Lord delivered them into his hands" (Judges 11:32). The whole nation celebrated the victory God gave to Jephthah.

When he went home after the battle, his daughter, who was an only child, came out to meet him. Jephthah was so upset! He loved his daughter very much. But we are told that he kept his promise. We don't know if he actually gave her as a sacrifice or if he set her apart as a living offering. But he kept his promise, even though it was hard.

Can you be counted on to do what you say, like Jephthah? How dependable are your promises? God's heroes should be trustworthy and willing to do what they say, even when it's hard.

DEPENDABILITY AND RESPONSIBILITY

A Dependable Guide

*Your word is
a lamp to my feet
and a light to
my path.*
Psalm 119:105.

The explorers Lewis and Clark would have been in big trouble if it had not been for their Indian guide, Sacagawea. She was a young Indian woman who traveled with them on their entire journey. She cooked food from what they found in nature, she showed them paths through places she knew, and she helped to translate and trade when they met other Indians.

Many of the Indians they met had never seen White people, and they were suspicious of Lewis and Clark. The Indians were afraid they might be on the warpath until they saw Sacagawea and her baby son. The Indians knew that war parties didn't bring women—especially women with babies. Because of Sacagawea, most of the Indians were willing to make friends with the strange White men. She was a big help to Lewis and Clark in many ways.

Did you know that we have a guide we can count on for our adventures in life? It's the Bible. God gave us the Bible to be our guide. Reading the Bible will help us to get to know God better. The Bible is like a lamp lighting the way on a dark night. Don't stumble around in the dark. Let God's lamp guide you!

DEPENDABILITY AND RESPONSIBILITY

Water or Rock?

The Lord is my rock and my fortress and my deliverer; my God, my strength, in whom I will trust.

Psalm 18:2.

What shape is water? Is it round like an orange, or square like a box? Unless it's frozen, water doesn't have its own shape. If it is in a round container, it's round; if it is in a square container, it's square.

Joseph's brother Reuben was a lot like water. In fact, his own father said he was as "unstable as water." He never stood up for anything; he followed the crowd, whether it was good or bad. When his brothers wanted to kill Joseph, Reuben talked them out of it, but he went along with their plan to throw him into a pit. Secretly he planned to come back and get Joseph, but the other brothers sold him into slavery first. You can read the rest of the story in Genesis 37.

Someone once said that if you don't stand for something, you'll fall for anything. Being good, kind, patient, and loving won't do us any good if we act that way only some of the time. Your life should always be consistent, whether people are watching or not. Trust in God, who is as stable as a rock. And don't be all wet, as Reuben was.

DEPENDABILITY AND RESPONSIBILITY

Good Priest, Bad Dad

18
OCTOBER

He who is faithful in what is least is faithful also in much.
Luke 16:10.

As high priest of Israel, Eli had a very important job. He was in charge of the Temple and the sacrifices for the people. It was his job to take care of the lamps and candles, to offer the sacrifices, and to perform the different ceremonies.

Eli was a good priest. But he was a bad father. Eli's sons, Hophni and Phinehas, were wicked. They didn't respect Eli, the Temple, or God. Even though they were priests too, they disobeyed God by cheating and stealing from the people. If they had done the good work that they were supposed to, it would have brought people closer to God. But their wickedness caused many people to despise the Temple and the things that happened there. Eli was sad that his sons weren't honest.

Eli should have corrected his sons, but he didn't. He was a good priest, but his sons were not. Because he didn't discipline his sons, he let them ruin their own lives and the lives of many other people, too. It would have been better if Eli had corrected his sons from the beginning and helped them to be good priests and good people. Because he didn't, all three of them died.

In order to be a hero for God, we should ask Him to help us be dependable. We should do our best, not just in our chores or schoolwork, but in every area of our lives. Then we can be a blessing for Him to others.

DEPENDABILITY AND RESPONSIBILITY

301

The Hero of Scutari

Florence Nightingale's family couldn't believe that she wanted to be a nurse. In those days nursing was not respectable work. Because Florence's family was wealthy, they didn't think that nursing was good enough for her. But she had a strong desire to help people, and she wouldn't give up her dream.

Finally they gave in, and she was allowed to attend a new nursing school. There she scrubbed floors, did laundry, and did, without grumbling, whatever else was asked of her, even though it was work that she was used to having servants do for her.

During the Crimean War Florence was given the biggest job any nurse ever had to do. She was sent to Scutari, where hundreds of wounded men, thousands of miles from home, needed nurses to care for them. There weren't enough doctors, so she set out with a group of nurses to help. They cleaned, did laundry, and cooked in addition to taking care of the soldiers, all in the most horrible conditions. She used the money she was paid for her work to start a school for nurses. Florence Nightingale helped make nursing a respectable and honored work.

Florence could have lived a very different life. But she believed in doing what was right instead of doing what was easy. She did what needed to be done without grumbling, and she helped many thousands of people.

DEPENDABILITY AND RESPONSIBILITY

Murphy's Law

Murphy is an old, old cat. He's been around almost as long as anyone can remember, quietly padding around Ron's house and watching out the window as people come up the walk. Murphy is 22 years old and still perfectly healthy.

And Murphy is sneaky. When Ron's wife, Trish, went down to the basement, Murphy was perfectly able to jump up on the back of the couch or the counter to see what she was doing. He liked to walk between her feet, stick his head in the washer to see what was in there, and just generally make a nuisance of himself.

But whenever Ron came into the room, Murphy put on a show. He acted as if he were too old and feeble to climb up on anything, let alone jump. To watch him, you'd think he could barely walk. Ron felt sorry for his poor old cat and even built a ramp for him so he could get to his favorite spot without jumping. Trish tried to tell Ron it was all a show, but he didn't believe her. He thought that he knew Murphy better than she did.

Then it happened. Ron came around the corner just in time to see Murphy jump up on the washer and dryer. I don't know who was more surprised, Murphy or Ron! All this time Trish had been telling the truth, and Ron hadn't believed her.

Unlike Murphy, God never changes. We can find out what God is really like by reading about Him and spending time with Him. He tells us in the Bible that He is the same yesterday, today, and forever. Are you sneaky like Murphy, or can you be counted on to be the same, no matter who's watching?

Jesus Christ is the same yesterday and today and forever.
Hebrews 13:8, NIV.

DEPENDABILITY AND RESPONSIBILITY

21

OCTOBER

Empire Builder

*Do not labor
for the food
which perishes,
but for the food
which endures to
everlasting life,
which the Son of
Man will give you.*

John 6:27.

James Jerome Hill always remembered what his teachers and parents told him: think, plan, and make use of opportunities to do bigger things. He wanted to be someone they would be proud of, so he worked hard as a store clerk and studied in his free time. Although he had plenty of temptations to do wrong with his friends, he always kept his parents' and teachers' advice in mind.

After working as a store clerk, he started his own shipping company, then worked for the railroad. People told him he was dreaming too big, but he didn't listen, and he eventually became a wealthy man of integrity. His parents and teachers would have been proud of him. In spite of the discouragement, his dreams came true with hard work and integrity.

It's good to think and plan ahead for the future. Do your best at everything you do, and with God's help you can reach your dreams. What kind of plans are you making today?

DEPENDABILITY AND RESPONSIBILITY

Nearsighted

Jacob Kindleberger was in a dead-end job—it would never take him anywhere. Because his eyesight was so poor and he couldn't afford glasses, he'd had to drop out of school and work at the local paper mill.

One day Jacob went with some friends to a tent meeting to make fun of the preacher. He didn't expect it, but something the preacher said caught his attention. He said that your tomorrows depend on what you do today. Jacob thought about that. He realized that all of his tomorrows would be just like today if he didn't get an education.

He didn't want that, so he saved up to get a pair of glasses. He often said that those glasses opened up a whole new world to him. He spent as much time as he could learning. Even though he was older than the other students in elementary school, he started where he'd left off. With hard work Jacob ended up being the owner of a paper company that created many new products. Being able to see clearly changed his life.

We can be so spiritually nearsighted that it can be hard for us to see a way through our problems. But if we ask God, He'll act as our "glasses" and make the way clear.

Show me Your ways, O Lord; teach me Your paths. Lead me in Your truth and teach me, for You are the God of my salvation. Psalm 25:4, 5.

DEPENDABILITY AND RESPONSIBILITY

23

Khama

*Talk no more
so very proudly:
let no arrogance
come from your
mouth, for the
Lord is the God
of knowledge; and
by Him actions
are weighed.*
1 Samuel 2:3.

The men sat around the campfire, their eyes glittering in the light, as they all bragged about what they would do when they caught the lion. It had been harassing their village and killing their cattle for some time now. Although they hadn't had any success at catching the lion so far, they did a lot of talking about what would happen if they did catch it. Off to the side stood Khama, whose father was the chief of their tribe. He didn't join in the bragging. He just listened to the men.

One by one the men went to sleep beside the fire, and Khama quietly slipped off into the dark African night. As the morning light began to awaken the men from their sleep, they were shocked to see Khama walking up to the camp with the skin and mane of the lion slung over his shoulders. They had spent the evening bragging about what they were going to do if they caught the lion, but Khama, who had done no bragging, went out all by himself and did what needed to be done.

Who are you like? Are you like the men around the campfire, who sat and bragged about what they could do? Or are you more like Khama, who just went out and did what needed to be done?

God's heroes don't need to brag. They aren't filled with all kinds of foolish talk. They quietly do the things that need to be done without needing to be noticed.

DEPENDABILITY AND RESPONSIBILITY

Best Friends

John Wesley lived in England in the 1700s. When he was young, he and his friends laughed at people who tried to do what was right. Until he was nearly out of college, John just went along with the crowd. But then he started to study the Bible, and he became a Christian.

John realized that his friends had a big influence on him, and he decided to choose his friends more carefully. He was friendly to everyone, but he wanted his close friends to be a good influence on him.

He and his friends tried to earn their salvation by doing good things. But then John realized that all he had to do was trust God and accept His gift to be saved. He couldn't wait to tell his friends—and everyone! He began preaching in churches, in fields, and anywhere anyone would listen.

John was right—his Friend had a big influence on him, and he had to tell people of his choice to have Jesus as his friend.

Our friends do have a big influence on us, whether we know it or not. If Jesus is our friend, it will show in our lives.

But we all, . . . beholding . . . the glory of the Lord, are being transformed.
2 Corinthians 3:18.

DEPENDABILITY AND RESPONSIBILITY

25
OCTOBER

Love in Any Language

Since you are zealous for spiritual gifts, let it be for the edification of the church that you seek to excel.

1 Corinthians 14:12.

One thing people knew about William Carey was that he was determined. When he was a boy, he was clumsy. Many times he fell out of trees and got hurt, but he always tried again. That determination stuck with him his whole life. If he ever failed at anything, he just kept trying until he got it right.

William finished his schooling at age 12, but he always enjoyed learning and studying. His friend John Warr offered to study with him, and John shared Jesus with him. William accepted Jesus as his Savior and Friend.

One of William's favorite things to study was foreign languages. He read everything he could about them. In 1793 he went to India with his family as missionaries. In India he learned the Bengali language, and he began translating the Bible for the Bengali people. God used William's love of languages, and by the end of his life William had translated all or parts of the Bible into 34 languages. He brought the gift of God's love to thousands of people.

If we dedicate our lives to God, He can use for good the things we enjoy, just as God used William's love of languages to reach so many people.

DEPENDABILITY AND RESPONSIBILITY

Germ Warfare

Louis Pasteur was a thoughtful and careful boy who liked to learn. His father hadn't been able to attend school as a child, so Louis brought his lessons home, and they would learn together.

As he grew, Louis showed a special interest in science. He did many scientific experiments. His success in science didn't make him proud, however. It just made him want to try harder for more results so he could help more people.

Microscopes helped Louis to see things that were too small to be seen by the naked eye. His work with microscopes helped him to make one of his greatest discoveries—germs. The more he learned about germs, the better able he was to find out how to prevent diseases caused by them. Because of this discovery, he helped to save millions of lives and make all of our lives better and safer.

Jesus doesn't need a microscope. He can see everything without one—including our sins. If we ask Him to, He will act like a microscope for us in our lives to help us find sin germs before they can hurt us.

> *There is no creature hidden from His sight, but all things are naked and open to the eyes of Him to whom we must give account.*
> Hebrews 4:13.

DEPENDABILITY AND RESPONSIBILITY

27
OCTOBER

*Fear God
and keep His
commandments,
for this is
man's all.*
Ecclesiastes 12:13.

Praying John Hyde

John Hyde was known as a man who loved God with all his heart. Everyone knew that he had a deep, sincere love for God and others, and that he spent much time in prayer. In fact, he prayed so much, people started to call him "Praying John Hyde."

But John didn't just pray. He also spent time talking to people or sharing blankets, coats, and food with people in need. He put his love and faith into action and never forgot the value of every person.

When someone asked John why he spent so much time praying and helping people, he said, "I know but one word—obedience. I know how a soldier will obey an order even to death, and how can I look Jesus Christ in the face and obey Him less than a soldier does his commander?"

Who is the commanding officer of your life? Is it Jesus or yourself? Whom do you obey?

DEPENDABILITY AND RESPONSIBILITY

Erring Aaron

Moses had been gone a long time, and the people of Israel were getting restless. God had been leading them through the wilderness, and Moses had gone up to Mount Sinai to talk with Him. The people wanted something to worship—something they could see. They knew it was wrong, but they wanted it anyway. They pestered and bothered Aaron until they persuaded him to build them an idol.

Aaron also knew it was wrong. He knew that they should worship only the God of heaven—the God who was leading them right now. But he was afraid of what the people would do, so he gave in. The people brought him their gold and jewelry, and they melted it down to form a golden calf. Then they all bowed down and worshipped this idol.

Moses was very angry when he came down the mountain after talking to God. He was so angry, in fact, that he threw down and broke the tablets of stone God had given him—the tablets that had the Ten Commandments written on them. God was angry with the people too. He was disappointed that they hadn't wanted to have Him as their one and only God.

There are many temptations in life to disobey God and follow the crowd as Aaron did, but with God's help we can stand strong for the right and help others to do the same.

Do not turn aside from following the Lord, but serve the Lord with all your heart.
1 Samuel 12:20.

DEPENDABILITY AND RESPONSIBILITY

Night Sounds

He who keeps you will not slumber. . . . He . . . shall neither slumber nor sleep.

Psalm 121:3, 4.

Mike's gentle, calm voice is on the radio every night. When most people are asleep, he's at work playing Christian music for other people who have to be awake late at night. Mike loves Jesus and wants to make sure that everyone has a chance to hear about God—whether they are awake in the daytime or at night, whether they are early birds or nightowls.

No matter what time it is or where we are, God is awake and ready to listen. He tells us in the Bible that He never sleeps or even takes a nap. So whenever you are awake, God is too. He's always there, always ready to listen.

DEPENDABILITY AND RESPONSIBILITY

Beautiful Music

Wolfgang Amadeus Mozart always loved music, and he was really good at it. By the time he was 6 he could already play several instruments, and he was even writing his own music.

As he grew up, Mozart practiced, performed, and wrote music. Music was his life. By the end of his life, in 1791, he had written more than 600 pieces of music, many of which are still enjoyed by music lovers today. He is considered to be one of the greatest geniuses ever to live.

Has God given you a special talent—something you can do well? Perhaps you are good at music, sports, or school. Maybe you are especially good with people or animals or something else. Whatever your talent is, ask God to help you use it in a beautiful way that will inspire others and help them to live for Him.

My heart greatly rejoices, and with my song I will praise Him.
Psalm 28:7.

DEPENDABILITY AND RESPONSIBILITY

31

Sew Carefully

*Do all things
. . . that you
may become . . .
without fault
in the midst
of a crooked
and perverse
generation,
among whom you
shine as lights in
the world.*
Philippians 2:14, 15.

In 1813 Mary Pickersgill and her daughter, Caroline, were asked to make a flag. This was going to be a special flag. It would fly over Fort McHenry in the Baltimore, Maryland, harbor. They wanted it to be so big that "the British would have no trouble seeing it from a distance."

This flag wasn't just big. It was huge. They used 400 yards of fabric. That's enough to cover four football fields! Fifteen stars were cut out (that's how many states were in the United States then) that were two feet across from point to point. Eight red stripes and seven white stripes were cut, each two feet wide.

Mary and Caroline carefully stitched each piece together. It took most of the summer to get it done. The finished flag was 30 feet wide and 42 feet long—bigger than the first floor of many houses.

Their flag was flying over Fort McHenry the night the British attacked and Francis Scott Key wrote the words of "The Star-Spangled Banner." Although the flag is tattered and torn, it can still be seen at the Smithsonian Institution in Washington, D.C.

What are you making with the pieces of your life? Stitch them together carefully with threads of prayer. Ask God to help you make good decisions, and let your life be such a good example that others can "see your colors" and tell that you're a Christian "from a distance."

DEPENDABILITY AND RESPONSIBILITY

What Do You Want?

Have you ever worked hard for something you really, really wanted? When you finally got whatever it was, you probably almost forgot all about the hard work, because you were so happy to finally have it.

Jesus did that for us. He left His perfect home in heaven to come down to this old earth, hoping that you and I would choose to love Him. He came to where we live because He wants to be our friend. Jesus wants us to live with Him in heaven. In heaven there is no violence, sadness, or sickness. No one ever dies. We won't even have a reason to cry anymore. Not one reason. Ever.

He didn't have to, but Jesus left heaven because He wants you to be there with Him. He did it because the thought of being in heaven without you hurt Him even more than leaving heaven. Jesus died for you because He wants you to choose Him and be in heaven with Him. That thought makes Him happier than anything.

Let us fix our eyes on Jesus, the author and perfecter of our faith, who for the joy set before him endured the cross.
Hebrews 12:2, NIV.

HAPPINESS, CONTENTMENT, AND GRATITUDE

2
NOVEMBER

A friend Like Maria

A cheerful heart is good medicine, but a crushed spirit dries up the bones.

Proverbs 17:22, NIV.

Maria is a good friend. She is thoughtful, fun to be with, a wonderful listener, and very funny. People enjoy being around her because her happiness is contagious. She has a knack for making people feel loved and special when they are with her.

One day Maria saw a girl who was having a really bad day. It seemed that everything was going wrong! The girl's long face and slumped shoulders told Maria all she needed to know. She came over to her and put her arm around her, and they began to talk. Soon they were not only talking but laughing, and before long the girl had almost forgotten all of her problems.

Maria can make people laugh. Her happy smile and ready hug always help them to feel better—even if they were feeling good to begin with.

The Bible says that a cheerful heart can act like a medicine. Your laugh, hug, or smile could go a long way toward making someone's day.

HAPPINESS, CONTENTMENT, AND GRATITUDE

The Greatest Gift

*She gave
all she had.*
Luke 21:4, NCV.

Jesus and His disciples were standing in the Temple watching as people dropped their offerings into a box. One by one people walked past the box. Some spent a long time there, dropping many coins in. Their money clinked and clanked as it fell into the box. A few people made a big show of giving their offering. They wanted everyone to know what they were giving.

Then shyly, quietly, a woman began to creep toward the box. She was a widow, and she had only a tiny bit of money to give. She was embarrassed that her gift was so small, but she wanted to give what she could, so she went up to the box and dropped in two small coins before hurrying away. Jesus noticed her gift and told the disciples that she had given the most of anyone. The amount she gave was small, but she gave it because she loved God.

God loves to give us good gifts. In fact, He gave us the greatest gift of all in His Son, Jesus. It makes God happy to give us gifts, and it makes us happy to give to others, too. Our gifts don't have to be big or wrapped in a package. They can be gifts of kindness, friendliness, or time. What gift can you give to God or to someone you know?

HAPPINESS, CONTENTMENT, AND GRATITUDE

4
NOVEMBER

A friend loves at all times.
Proverbs 17:17.

Everybody's Poet

Henry's parents loved books, and they encouraged all of their children to read. By the time he was 6 years old, Henry could read, write, spell, add, and multiply. But what he really loved to do was write poetry. As he sat in school, lines of poetry just popped into his head. Sometimes his teacher would get after him for writing poetry instead of doing his schoolwork.

When he was about 13, Henry tried to get his first poem published. It was published, but his father didn't take notice, and a friend of his father's criticized the poem. But Henry didn't give up. He kept on writing, and before long many of his poems were published. Henry Wadsworth Longfellow became one of America's most famous poets. He is known as "everybody's poet" because nearly everyone enjoys his poems.

As Christians we should be known as everybody's friend because of our kindness toward people. We may get discouraged when people don't respond as we'd like them to, but keep on trying and be everybody's friend today.

HAPPINESS, CONTENTMENT, AND GRATITUDE

The Goldie Rule

More than 100 years ago Goldie grew up in a poor family on a farm in Iowa. She was one of nine children, and it seemed there was never enough money. But they didn't go hungry and always had a roof over their heads, and Goldie was content.

As a child Goldie never went farther than a few miles from her home. But she didn't mind. She was happy for her home and family and the blessings they shared.

When Goldie grew up and had a family of her own, they still weren't rich, but she had more than when she was a little girl. She was thankful for the blessings of her life.

Goldie lived to see children, grandchildren, great-grandchildren, and even one great-great-grandchild. No one in any of those generations could remember hearing her complain about anything, not even once, despite the hard life she had lived. Every day of her life was lived to the fullest, whether it was sitting on the porch rocking a great-grandchild or going for a motorcycle ride on her eightieth birthday. Goldie was a happy woman.

Most of us have more than we realize. We have more than enough food, more toys than we can play with at once, a roof over our heads, friends, family, and on and on. We have so much to be thankful for! Today, instead of complaining about the things you don't have, try taking a look at the things around you and counting your blessings instead.

I have learned the secret of being content in any and every situation, whether well fed or hungry, whether living in plenty or in want.
Philippians 4:12, NIV.

HAPPINESS, CONTENTMENT, AND GRATITUDE

6
NOVEMBER

The people who know their God shall be strong, and carry out great exploits.
Daniel 11:32.

Flying High

The first time Amelia saw an airplane, she wasn't impressed. It looked like a pile of rusty wire and wood. This tomboy was much more interested in climbing trees, hunting, and playing outside.

About 10 years after she first saw an airplane, Amelia's interest in airplanes began to get stronger. And after she actually rode in one, she was hooked. As soon as she could, she took flying lessons, and she began to save up enough money to buy her own plane.

Amelia Earhart became part of the first group of people to fly over the Atlantic Ocean. She is the most famous woman pilot of our time.

Just looking at an airplane didn't do much for Amelia, but that first ride in an airplane changed her life. It's the same way with religion. If you just look at it, it's OK, but really knowing Jesus will take you to new heights.

320

HAPPINESS, CONTENTMENT, AND GRATITUDE

A Happy Hero

Mattie Stepanek was born with muscular dystrophy, a disease that attacks his muscles. Because of his disease he can't do many things that other kids do. But he does his best at what he can do.

One of Mattie's favorite things to do is write. Even before he was a teenager he had several books published and was on national TV programs. Mattie always has a smile on his face. His happiness and the message of his writing have encouraged many people.

Mattie knows that happiness comes from inside. It doesn't matter what your circumstances are. It doesn't matter whether you're rich or poor, sick or healthy, young or old—you can be happy if you make up your mind to be. Ask God today to help you be a happy hero for Him.

A merry heart makes a cheerful countenance.
Proverbs 15:13.

HAPPINESS, CONTENTMENT, AND GRATITUDE

10
NOVEMBER

Give thanks to the Lord, for he is good; his love endures forever.
Psalm 107:1, NIV.

The Man Who Wished People Laughed More

His wife held out a rose for him, and as he reached for it everything went black. That's how Mark Hotchkiss describes losing his sight when he was 50 years old. Although it was hard for him to accept at first, he knew that he had a choice to make. He could think of it as a disaster and let the loss of his sight overwhelm him, or he could use the new opportunity to show that, even though he was blind, he could still do worthwhile things.

He decided to do worthwhile things. Mark started a company, the Hotchkiss Products Company, Inc., that made things to help road construction crews. He had several patents on inventions, and he ran a good business.

His favorite thing, though, was to make people laugh. Since he could no longer see people smile, he loved to hear laughter. He often said he wished people would laugh more.

Mark could have easily become sad and depressed when he lost his sight, but instead he chose to have a positive outlook. We choose our attitude. No one "makes" us angry, sad, or happy. We make that decision.

No matter what our circumstances are, we have two choices. We can either give thanks to the Lord for the new opportunities we have, or we can be sad and depressed about it. What decision will you make today?

HAPPINESS, CONTENTMENT, AND GRATITUDE

I'm Happy

Happy are the people whose God is the Lord!
Psalm 144:15.

Every week at church Mr. and Mrs. Beagles greet people with a big hug and a smile. Many people really look forward to seeing them each Sabbath because of the happiness and love they share.

Whenever Mr. Beagles is asked how he is, he says, "I'm happy." No matter what is happening around him, that's always his answer. He's happy. His reasons for being happy are usually different each week, but he always finds some reason to be happy.

Their life isn't perfect. Mr. and Mrs. Beagles deal with sickness, bills, and the regular things of life, just like everyone else. But they make the choice to be happy and to share that happiness with the people around them. People love them for it and look for them at church every week, just to soak up some of their happiness.

People looked for Jesus for the same reason. He was happy, and He shared that happiness and love with everyone He met. Because of that, people loved to be with Him. What about you? Whom can you share happiness with today?

HAPPINESS, CONTENTMENT, AND GRATITUDE

The Richest Man

He who has pity on the poor lends to the Lord, and He will pay back what he has given.

Proverbs 19:17.

John D. Rockefeller believed that every little bit of good helped. Sometimes he could do a lot of good. Other times he could only do a little. But he tried to do as much good as possible whenever he could.

John believed that work is honorable. He believed that neither time nor money should be wasted, and he was very careful with both. These beliefs, along with good judgment and planning, helped him become the richest man of his time.

John was kind and friendly to everyone, regardless of what they did for a living or how much money they had. He gave away millions of dollars where he thought they would do the most good. He didn't do it so that people would praise him. He did it because it was the right thing to do.

As God's heroes we should also do as much good as possible wherever we see the need, and treat everyone the same, regardless of who they are. It's the right thing to do.

HAPPINESS, CONTENTMENT, AND GRATITUDE

Chaplain Number One

He was no longer known as Frank Novak; he was Prisoner 6156. Frank had made some bad decisions and had been sent to jail for robbery. His life had totally changed. Instead of freedom, his life was a cycle of routines in a small jail cell. Little did he know that his life was about to change again, this time for the better.

While he was in prison Frank became a Christian and accepted Jesus into his heart. He asked for forgiveness for his sins and turned his back on his old ways. He even began preaching to the other prisoners. People were surprised at the change they saw in Frank.

After some time Frank was released from prison. He became a chaplain to other prisoners. He was so well liked that instead of Prisoner 6156 he became known as Prison Chaplain Number One.

When we get to heaven, God will give each of us a new name. You will have a name that He has picked out especially for you. God will wash away all of our sins so that we can live a new life with our new names.

To him who overcomes I will give . . . the hidden manna. . . . I will give him . . . a new name.
Revelation 2:17.

HAPPINESS, CONTENTMENT, AND GRATITUDE

God's Plan

*Rejoice always,
pray without
ceasing, in
everything give
thanks; for this
is the will of God
in Christ Jesus
for you.*

1 Thessalonians
5:16-18.

Joni Eareckson Tada was only 17 when a diving accident paralyzed her from the neck down. At first she spent a lot of time questioning why God let this happen to her. She was sad that she couldn't walk, run, or do most of the things that other people do. She even had to have help to comb her hair and eat.

That was more than 30 years ago. Now, although she is still paralyzed, she is president and founder of Joni and Friends Ministries. She and her husband, Ken, do what they can to help other people who are going through hard times. They give support, encouragement, and comfort. They also help with practical things: for instance, they hold retreats for families of people with disabilities, give wheelchairs to people who need them and can't afford them, and teach churches how to help people who have disabilities. Instead of feeling sorry for herself, Joni has turned her accident into a blessing for both herself and others.

Sometimes it can be hard to see God's plan when bad things happen to us. But God does have a plan, and He is in control no matter what. Trust Him and ask Him to make a blessing of your life—the good parts and the bad.

HAPPINESS, CONTENTMENT, AND GRATITUDE

Where Jesus Walked

*The joy of
the Lord is
your strength.*
Nehemiah 8:10.

Bruce Machiano was a struggling actor living in California when he was offered a role to play Jesus in a movie. At first it was just another job. He didn't really think much of it, even though he had recently become a Christian.

When he got the part, he started to do research. He wanted to show Jesus as He had been in real life. None of the movies he'd seen in the past about Jesus' life had seemed quite right. In those movies Jesus had seemed unhappy. He wanted his Jesus to be real. The movie script was taken from the book of Matthew, so Bruce studied Matthew to get it right.

The more he studied, the more Bruce thought that Jesus must have been a happy person. People don't like to be around someone who is a grump, and people came to see Jesus by the thousands. Bruce studied and prayed, and the Jesus he played in the movie was the happiest Jesus anyone had ever seen. He wasn't silly, but the love He had for the people around Him came out in everything He did. He smiled a lot, gave people hugs, and was just generally a nice guy.

People who watched the movie fell in love with Jesus all over again. And so did Bruce. This Jesus was someone he really wanted to know better. If we know and love the real Jesus, it will show in our lives too, by the happiness we show.

HAPPINESS, CONTENTMENT, AND GRATITUDE

The Encourager

When he came and had seen the grace of God, he was glad, and encouraged them.

Acts 11:23.

Have you ever been discouraged and sad? Has there ever been someone who came along and helped you to feel better? Or have you ever helped someone who was feeling bad to feel better? Then you've done what Barnabas did. He's known in the Bible as being an encourager. He cheered people up and cheered them on to do what needed to be done.

Barnabas encouraged a lot of people. He encouraged Paul and Mark to keep on doing good for God and not give up. He also encouraged the early Christians in their faith. When Paul was in Damascus right after his conversion, only Barnabas was willing to go to him and see if he could help. Everyone else stayed away because they thought Paul might be trying to trap more Christians.

Sometimes it's easier to criticize people and cut them down rather than encourage them. But encouragement really helps people who are discouraged. Do you know someone you could encourage today?

HAPPINESS, CONTENTMENT, AND GRATITUDE

The Happiest People

Everywhere they go Lynn and Mike spread smiles. Whether it's at church, work, or the grocery store, they leave behind happy people.

They don't do anything out of the ordinary and aren't silly about it. But they are friendly to everyone they meet and honestly interested in them. No matter what is happening in their own lives, Lynn and Mike greet people with a smile.

Lynn and Mike know God, and that makes them happy. They are heroes for God because they help make people's lives better by the way they live their own lives.

When we truly know God, He will help us to be happy and friendly. As you go through life, do you leave behind people who are happy or unhappy?

Whoever trusts in the Lord, happy is he.
Proverbs 16:20.

HAPPINESS, CONTENTMENT, AND GRATITUDE

Everyone the Same

It wasn't fair that some people were treated differently just because their skin was a different color. W.E.B. DuBois wanted to do something to change this attitude.

As an African-American living many years ago, W.E.B. DuBois knew what it meant to be treated differently. He had to use different drinking fountains and sit in separate areas. There were some jobs he wasn't allowed to have and some neighborhoods he couldn't live in.

He was determined to work to help everyone be treated the same. He helped to start the National Association for the Advancement of Colored People, or the NAACP. He spent his life working for equality.

God is happy when we treat everyone with love, kindness, and respect. Can you think of someone who is treated differently? What can you do today to help that person be happy?

HAPPINESS, CONTENTMENT, AND GRATITUDE

The Real Winner

John and his cousin Dale grew up around racing. Both of their fathers loved to race cars, and the boys spent much of their childhood around races. They loved the noise, the dirt, and especially the speed. It was a huge part of their lives.

As adults, the cousins still spent much of their time around racing, but in very different ways. Dale Earnhardt raced cars and became one of the best-known NASCAR drivers in its history. His cousin John, although he wasn't as well known, became a chaplain for the racers. He helped the drivers in their spiritual lives.

Dale tried to make it to the victory line, and John tried to help all of them make it to the spiritual victory line. Winning the spiritual race will make us the biggest winners of all.

Therefore, whether you eat or drink, or whatever you do, do all to the glory of God.
1 Corinthians 10:31.

HAPPINESS, CONTENTMENT, AND GRATITUDE

A Young Girl's Diary

You will keep him in perfect peace, whose mind is stayed on You.

Isaiah 26:3.

Have you ever played hide-and-seek? Which do you like better—to hide or to look for your friends?

Anne Frank and her family had to play a dangerous game of hide-and-seek. When Anne was only 13, the Nazis had already invaded her country. Because her family was Jewish, and the Nazis didn't like Jews, they went into hiding so the Nazis couldn't find them. For two years they hid in a small space with four other Jewish people. Can you imagine living with seven other people in a space no bigger than two rooms? They couldn't leave their hiding place, and they had to be very quiet so that no one would know they were there.

During their time in hiding, Anne kept a diary in which she wrote her thoughts and feelings and told about the things that happened in their lives while they were in hiding. After the war her diary was published as a book titled *Anne Frank: The Diary of a Young Girl*. Even though she and her family were forced to hide for their lives, Anne wrote in her diary, "In spite of everything, I still believe that people are really good at heart."

It would have been easy for Anne to be grumpy and complain about having to stay in those small rooms. She couldn't go to school, play with her friends, or even go outside. Even with so many of her freedoms taken away, she still believed people were good.

There are many things in our everyday lives that we take for granted. We can go outside and play, go to school, or travel wherever we want. What can you think of today that you are happy about? Take a minute to thank God for the good things He's given you.

HAPPINESS, CONTENTMENT, AND GRATITUDE

Hope and Happiness

My hope is in You.
Psalm 39:7.

Bob Hope lived to be 100 years old. In his long life he was known for acting in movies, singing, and telling jokes. What he will most be remembered for, though, is visiting the troops.

Every year at Christmas Bob Hope would travel overseas to visit American soldiers. He traveled to some very dangerous places through the years, but knew that his work was important.

By making the troops laugh, he helped them relax. He helped take their minds off the fact that they were away from home at Christmas. He gave them hope just by giving of himself. Even though he was putting himself in harm's way, he always went to visit and make new friends overseas.

Everyone needs hope. Do you know someone you can share hope with just by being a friend?

HAPPINESS, CONTENTMENT, AND GRATITUDE

Nothing Compares to Jesus

He who lays up treasure for himself . . . is not rich toward God.

Luke 12:21.

Charles Studd was born into a very wealthy family. His father had made a fortune in India and moved to England. When Charles was in his middle teens, his father became a Christian, and it changed everything. Instead of spending lots of money on things that didn't matter, Mr. Studd used his money to serve and honor Jesus.

Charles, or C.T., wasn't impressed with his father's new religion, but Mr. Studd still took Charles and his brothers to church and to hear evangelists. In 1878 C.T. gave his heart to Jesus and spent the rest of his life working as a missionary in China and Africa.

C.T. said that he'd done almost everything there was to do in the world, but nothing compared with helping people give their hearts to Jesus. He enjoyed what he had, but he didn't let anything become an idol to him. He knew that in heaven none of those things will matter. All that matters is that we will be there with our family and friends—and God.

Being a Christian means being unselfish with what you have. God's heroes will share what they have with others and let Jesus use it the way He thinks is best. Will you let Him use you today to bring someone closer to Him?

HAPPINESS, CONTENTMENT, AND GRATITUDE

Gertrude Bell

Gertrude Bell had always loved adventure. When she was young, she and her brother, Maurice, were always looking for new and exciting things to do.

As an adult Gertrude never lost that love of adventure, and it took her all over the world. Eventually it took her to Iraq, where she learned the language, made friends with the people, and studied the culture. She became such an authority on the area that she drew maps for England during World War I.

Gertrude was the happiest when she was in Iraq. She wrote to her father that she had a "wild feeling of joy" in her life in Iraq, even though they didn't have many of the things she had grown up with in England. The people of Iraq loved her so much that the king named a museum in her honor after her death.

We are all travelers and adventurers in life. How the trip goes is up to you. Will you have a joyful trip or an unhappy one? Your adventures may take you to different places on earth, but if you're God's hero, the greatest adventure of all is waiting for you in heaven.

*Lead me,
O Lord . . . ;
make Your way
straight before
my face.*
Psalm 5:8.

HAPPINESS, CONTENTMENT, AND GRATITUDE

Not Just a Slice

For your Father knows the things you have need of before you ask Him.

Matthew 6:8.

The old grandmother was worried. She needed food for her grandchildren, but her cupboards were as empty as her purse. She didn't know what to do. When her granddaughter asked what they would eat that evening, the grandmother told her, "The Lord will provide." Then they knelt down to pray. The little girl asked God to send them a whole loaf of bread, not just a slice.

All day they worked around the house doing their chores. When their stomachs growled with hunger at suppertime, there was still no food. It looked as if they would have to go to bed hungry.

Just before bedtime there was a knock at their door. There in the doorway stood an old friend. Snow was falling all around him and gathering in little piles on his head and shoulders. He apologized for coming so late. He had walked 18 miles to get there. He didn't really know why he had come, except that he'd felt that he should. The little girl danced in front of him as he asked, "Do you know what I brought you?"

"Yes! I do," cried the little girl. "A loaf of bread! Not just a piece, but a whole loaf!"

The man looked surprised as he asked her how she knew. The girl told him of their prayer as he pulled a long loaf of fresh bread from under his coat.

To walk 18 miles, the man would have had to leave his home before the little girl even prayed for bread. God knows what we need too, before we even ask. He will always take care of us. He doesn't want us to have just a slice of life. He wants us to enjoy the whole thing with Him.

HAPPINESS, CONTENTMENT, AND GRATITUDE

Prayer Works

If the missionaries in Maya's village had ever wondered if prayer works, they found out one day in a big way. Just as they were sitting down for breakfast one morning, a villager burst into their hut, begging them to come quickly. Maya was having trouble breathing.

The missionaries raced to Maya's home. As they neared the hut, the villager told them that Maya had had this trouble before. The evil spirit must have come back. The missionaries looked at each other with worry. An evil spirit!

When they went into her hut, they wondered why three strong women were holding Maya down. All of a sudden Maya let out a wild yell and struggled to get free. When she finally calmed down, the hut was quiet except for the loud breathing of the three women.

The missionaries knelt down beside Maya and began to pray that God would help her and make the demons leave. Almost before they said "Amen" Maya relaxed, sat up, and asked for her baby. The others in the hut were amazed.

Maya stood up and asked why everyone was looking at her. She didn't know what had just happened, but everyone else did. They said an extra-special thank-you prayer for the way God had helped Maya.

Prayer works. God is happy when we spend time talking to Him, and He loves to answer our prayers.

Call to Me, and I will answer you, and show you great and mighty things, which you do not know.
Jeremiah 33:3.

HAPPINESS, CONTENTMENT, AND GRATITUDE

No Place Like Home

Behold, I stand at the door and knock. If anyone hears My voice and opens the door, I will come in to him and dine with him, and he with Me.
Revelation 3:20.

Who lives at your house? Parents? Brothers and sisters? Maybe aunts, uncles, or grandparents? Your family. A house is just a house until a family moves in. Then it becomes a home. The outside of a house isn't what matters. It's the family inside that counts.

Alcyon was just a regular girl. When she was growing up, she worried about kids who didn't have families. She loved her family and wished that every kid could grow up in a family. It made her sad to think of all the boys and girls around the world without a mom or dad. She decided that when she was grown, she would help boys and girls who didn't have families.

And that's exactly what she did. Alcyon and her husband, Ken, went to Guatemala and started an orphanage. They helped the orphans find loving homes. At the time, Guatemala was having a civil war; the rebel soldiers watched their every move. It was a dangerous time, but God protected them and the children they cared for.

International Children's Care, started by the Flecks, still takes care of many children every year. Their goal is to give children not only a building to live in but also a family and a home.

Did you know that Jesus is looking for a home and a family? He wants to live at your house with your family. Ask Him today to make His home in your heart.

HAPPINESS, CONTENTMENT, AND GRATITUDE

What Really Matters

Have you ever worried about what someone thought of you? Maybe the cool kids at school, or a group of friends? I know I have, and so did Ginny Owens, until she got to thinking.

Ginny, a Christian singer, wrote and played her own songs on the piano. She also happened to be blind. But even though she couldn't see people, she still worried about what people thought of her. She still got her feelings hurt if someone said something unkind about her or her music.

Then Ginny got to thinking. She thought about how much her family and friends love her. She thought about how God loves her even more than they do. She realized that it really doesn't matter what anyone else thinks.

Ginny still wants people to like her and her music, but she knows that she is doing God's will for her life. And now, even if someone says something mean about her or her music, Ginny knows that it won't change God's plan for her life.

We all want to be liked, but we shouldn't try to be someone we aren't just so that people will like us. God loves you for who you are. Be true to Him and to yourself by being the person He's made you to be.

I know the thoughts that I think toward you, says the Lord, thoughts of peace and not of evil, to give you a future and a hope.
Jeremiah 29:11.

HAPPINESS, CONTENTMENT, AND GRATITUDE

28
NOVEMBER

Bear one another's burdens.
Galatians 6:2.

A Tale of Two Kitties

Two mama cats lived on the same farm with their kittens. Both mama cats hid their babies in the same barn, high up in the hay to keep them safe.

One day when the people on the farm went to work, they accidentally brought one of the mama cats with them in their truck. They didn't know she was there until lunchtime, and they worried about her babies for the rest of the day.

After work they drove home quickly so that the mama cat could get back to her kittens. When they let her out, they expected her to run to the barn to be with her kittens, but instead she ran to the garden and dug in the dirt. While they had been gone, something had found and killed the mama cat's kittens. The children had buried them in the garden, and her instinct told her where they were.

When she found her dead kittens, the mama cat went to the back porch and started to cry. The other mama cat came up on the porch too, and cried with her. Then she ran to the barn and came back with one of her own kittens. She laid it on the porch, then ran back to the barn. One by one she brought all of her kittens and laid them on the porch. From then on, the kittens had two mothers instead of one.

What good friends those mama cats were. They weren't just friends when everything was happy; they were friends when things were sad, too. Since we're God's heroes, we should be friends to people in bad times as well as good. Can you think of something you can do to help a friend who is sad?

342

HAPPINESS, CONTENTMENT, AND GRATITUDE

True Happiness

Eleanor Roosevelt was a hero to many people. She was the wife of President Franklin D. Roosevelt and was a great help to him after he had gotten polio and become disabled. Some people loved her, some people hated her, but almost everyone respected her.

Eleanor was from a rich family, but she spent her life helping the poor of every religion, race, and nation. She could have spent her life in wealth, comfort, and privilege, but instead she spent it in service to others, traveling the world and working to make it a better place.

She was known for her charming friendliness and integrity, and her entire life was dedicated to others. She knew that was where the greatest happiness could be found. She once said, "You get more joy out of the giving to others, and should put a good deal of thought into the happiness you are able to give."

It's fun to make people happy, and it makes God happy when we think of others. Take a minute and think of something you could do today to make someone you know happy.

It is more blessed to give than to receive.
Acts 20:35.

HAPPINESS, CONTENTMENT, AND GRATITUDE

The Most Important Choice

What would you do if you had to make a choice between keeping the Sabbath or being paid a lot of money for doing something you love? It's a choice that Trevor Bullock had to make.

Trevor loved baseball and had been playing since he was about 6 years old. He knew about the Sabbath from his mom, but she let him choose whether or not to play on Sabbath. He always did play on Sabbath, and he figured it was no big deal. He played in Little League, high school, and college.

Then he signed up to play with a minor league team that sent players to the Philadelphia Phillies. His dream was coming true. He was on his way to the big leagues. Trevor was a great pitcher. He loved baseball and was having a lot of fun playing.

Trevor started studying the Bible and decided that he wanted to be baptized. Even though he believed in the Sabbath now, he kept playing baseball on God's special day. His conscience bothered him, but he told himself it was OK. God kept working on Trevor's heart, though, and he came to the decision that he couldn't keep playing baseball on Sabbath. As much as he loved the game, he loved God more, and he wanted to follow Him with all his heart.

When Trevor resigned from baseball, Satan really started making things hard for him. Offers from baseball teams all over the country started coming in, offering him more money than he'd ever seen in his life. Trevor decided that no price was too high for salvation. He knew that he was giving up a lot of money, but he also knew that he was putting his relationship with God first, and that is the most important decision of all.

What profit is it to a man if he gains the whole world, and is himself . . . lost?
Luke 9:25.

HAPPINESS, CONTENTMENT, AND GRATITUDE

Alive Again

The people at the funeral walked slowly out of the city, crying loudly. The mother of the young man who had died stumbled behind them in shock. First her husband had died, and now her only son. She was so sad!

Jesus and His disciples saw the funeral and the sad mother. The Bible says He "had compassion on her" (Luke 7:13). It made Him sad to see her cry. He walked over, put His arm around her, and said, "Don't cry." Then He reached over, touched her son, and told him to get up.

Everyone there knew that Jesus had done miracles before, but could He raise the dead? They couldn't believe it when the young man opened his eyes and blinked. Jesus helped him up so that his surprised and very happy mother could give him a hug. The event that started out as a funeral turned into a party!

That young man didn't do anything to earn the gift of new life. In the same way, we can't do anything to earn salvation. Jesus gives it to us as a gift. All we have to do is accept it and thank Him for it. He will give us a new life and turn our sadness into joy.

But because of his great love for us, God, who is rich in mercy, made us alive with Christ even when we were dead in transgressions—it is by grace you have been saved.
Ephesians 2:4, 5, NIV.

KINDNESS, COMPASSION, AND MERCY

2
DECEMBER

There will always be poor people in the land. Therefore I command you to be openhanded toward your brothers and toward the poor and needy in your land.

Deuteronomy 15:11, NIV.

Saint of the Gutters

Her name was Agnes Gonxha Bojaxhiu. When she was a little girl, she became interested in overseas missions. When she was a 12-year-old public school student, she decided to spend her life helping the poor.

She was a teacher and principal in a large city for many years. Then she felt that Jesus was calling her to give everything up and follow Him to the slums, where she would serve Him among the poor. She took medical training in order to get ready for her new job, and she started a school for underprivileged children in the slums of her city. She spent the rest of her life caring for the people that everyone else wanted to forget. We know her as Mother Teresa.

By 1996 Mother Teresa was operating 517 missions in more than 100 countries. Each mission was devoted to helping those who were poor, blind, disabled, and old. She ran schools and orphanages, homes for the needy, and homes for people with AIDS. Mother Teresa was possibly the best-known and most-loved public figure in the world.

What made this tiny woman so powerful? Why did the whole world listen when she spoke? She was living her faith, showing kindness to everyone—not just the popular or pretty people. She didn't listen when some people told her that one person couldn't make a difference. She went out and, one at a time, changed the lives of thousands of people.

KINDNESS, COMPASSION, AND MERCY

Burning Compassion

Antoine came from a rich and influential family in France. His family was so rich that their home had glass in the windows, a luxury that few people could afford in the 1700s. As a law student Antoine was set to live a comfortable life.

He quit law school, though, to pursue his first love: science. He wanted to know why things burned. The popular idea of his day was that things had "fire particles" in them that came out when they were heated. Antoine didn't think this was so, and he set out to prove it wrong. He eventually discovered that things burn because of their chemical makeup, not because of any fire particles. Because of his many contributions to science, he is considered the father of modern chemistry.

Antoine's experiments required money, so he became a member of the General Farmers, where his job was to take taxes from the people. Tax collectors weren't very well liked; they were generally thought of as thieves who stole money from the people. Antoine, though, became known for being honest and fair and trying to lower the taxes, rather than raise them.

Everything Antoine did was for others. He supported the idea of free public schools so that everyone who wanted to could go to school. He taught farmers how to be more productive. He created the industrial arts courses, so that people could be taught skills to get a job. He even created the metric system, a standard system of weights and measures.

The gifts given to us from God should be used to help others. That is just what Antoine-Laurent Lavoisier did.

Therefore, as we have opportunity, let us do good to all people.
Galatians 6:10, NIV.

KINDNESS, COMPASSION, AND MERCY

The Good Samaritan

*And who is
my neighbor?*

Luke 10:29.

The man glanced nervously around him as he and his donkey traveled down the steep trail. Suddenly a noise caught his attention. He glanced up just in time to see men jump from behind a rock. They pulled him off his donkey, beat him, took everything, and left him, bleeding and alone, on the side of the road.

When he heard footsteps, his hopes rose. Surely this person who was coming would see him and stop to help. It was a priest! He knew a man of God would help. The priest did see the man, but instead of stopping, he hurried by. The poor man lay there, wondering why the priest hadn't stopped to help him.

Then he heard footsteps again. He could see that it was a Levite, a man who worked at the Temple. The Levite also walked right by the poor, hurt man.

Footsteps rang out a third time. When he raised his weak head to see who it was, he saw a Samaritan. Samaritans and Jews hated each other. He knew the Samaritan wouldn't stop to help him.

The Samaritan's footsteps slowed, and then stopped. He stooped down, bandaged the man's wounds, and gently lifted him onto his own donkey. Slowly they made their way into town, where the Samaritan took him to an inn and paid the innkeeper to take care of him.

Who do you think acted like a neighbor? Was it the priest or the Levite? Or was it the Samaritan, who was supposed to have been his enemy?

There is no reason to be anyone's enemy. If we are heroes for God, we will do everything we can to be kind to everyone, even to people who don't like us very much.

348

KINDNESS, COMPASSION, AND MERCY

Kindness Returned

*A kind man
benefits himself.*
Proverbs 11:17, NIV.

The woman of Shunem and her husband lived near a well-traveled road. When the prophet Elisha and his helper passed by their home, she noticed how hot and tired they looked. She invited them in to rest and eat. They gladly accepted. The woman of Shunem invited them to stay the night, but they couldn't. They thanked her and her husband for their kindness.

After Elisha left, the woman of Shunem and her husband decided to build a room on the roof of their house for Elisha to stay in the next time he passed by. When it was finished, they added a bed, a table and a chair, and a candlestick. It was all ready for the prophet to stay in.

The next time Elisha visited, he was so happy with the new room! He wished there was some way he could thank his friends for their kindness, but they didn't want any money. They were just happy that Elisha was pleased.

Elisha tried to think of something he could do to repay their kindness. His helper noticed that they didn't have any children. Elisha told them he would pray that God would send them a son.

The next year Elisha's friends had a new baby son. They were so happy with their beautiful boy.

The woman of Shunem didn't expect a reward from Elisha. She wasn't nice because she wanted something in return. That wouldn't be right. We shouldn't do nice things for people with the hopes that they will do something nice for us. But kindness has a funny way of being repaid, just as it was for the woman of Shunem.

KINDNESS, COMPASSION, AND MERCY

6
December

*Go into all
the world and
preach the gospel
to every creature.*

Mark 16:15.

Jungle Music

As a child Albert Schweitzer sat in many church services listening to his father tell stories of missionaries in Africa. The tales of lions, crocodiles, and tribal wars thrilled him. But more than that, he wanted to help the people there. The mission stories told about men and women who didn't have a doctor and didn't know Jesus. Albert wanted to help change that.

Albert's ideas of mission work faded as he went to college, got married, and worked at a job. He was nearly 30 years old when he remembered the stories of Africa and decided to go to medical school to be a doctor. His friends and family were unhappy. Why would he go to the jungles of Africa when he had a perfectly good job and a bright future? But Albert and his wife had made up their minds. They were going to Africa.

It was a long and exciting trip to Africa, but even more excitement was waiting there for them. Most of the people had never seen a doctor who could pull teeth or do surgeries. Dr. Schweitzer was always patient and kind, helping whenever and however he could. In the first year he treated nearly 2,000 patients!

Dr. and Mrs. Schweitzer loved working in Africa. They were able to help many people, and they made many friends with their kind and gentle ways. They could have made a lot of money if they had stayed in Europe, but they knew the value of service to others. They were rich in what really mattered—happiness and friendships.

KINDNESS, COMPASSION, AND MERCY

A Home for Everyone

One day little Jacob Riis put a box for the birds outside his bedroom window in Denmark. A starling made its home in the box, and Jacob was so excited when the little bird laid some eggs and raised a family there! When the box began to fall apart, he replaced it with a wooden box. Soon sparrows began to crowd out the starlings. When Jacob saw this, he put a note on the box saying, "This box is for starlings, not sparrows."

Throughout his life Jacob wanted to help those who didn't have a home of their own. One Christmas he was given some money. Instead of spending it on himself, he took it to a poor section of his city. He asked a man there to please use the money to clean up the place and give the children a better place to live. The man looked surprised, but the next time Jacob walked by, he noticed that it looked a little cleaner and that the children looked happier. It made Jacob happy to help people.

When Jacob was older, he moved to the United States. It made him sad to see people living in poor conditions, and he worked hard to try to help them. He wanted to help people live better lives. He once said, "I love to mend and make crooked things straight."

God loves to do that too. He loves to take our shabby, unhappy hearts and make them clean and happy. He wants to help us to live better, happier lives. Will you let Him help you today?

Trust in the Lord with all your heart and lean not on your own understanding; in all your ways acknowledge him, and he will make your paths straight.
Proverbs 3:5, 6, NIV.

KINDNESS, COMPASSION, AND MERCY

351

8

Frist Aid

*Serve one another
in love. . . .
"Love your
neighbor as
yourself."*
Galatians 5:13, 14,
NIV.

One minute they were speeding down the interstate; the next minute their twisted, mangled car lay on the side of the road. The family was far from help, and the road wasn't well traveled. Would another driver come in time to help?

Luckily, one did. And it was not just any driver. Senator Bill Frist, who was driving the same road with two of his sons, came upon the accident. Quickly pulling over, he jumped out to help. Senator Frist is also a doctor, so was able to help the family in the car until the ambulance crew arrived. His help saved at least one life.

Senator Frist could have kept driving. He could have said he was too busy and too important to stop. He could have just called 911 on his cell phone as he drove by. But he knew that he had skills that could help those people, so he stopped and did what he could.

God's heroes know that they can use the skills God gave them to help others. Heroes will use their skills for good whenever and however they can.

KINDNESS, COMPASSION, AND MERCY

our Daily Bread

Do not withhold good from those who deserve it, when it is in your power to act.
Proverbs 3:27, NIV.

The king wanted Elijah dead. He didn't like being told that he was wrong. Elijah the prophet had told the king that it was the God of heaven who sent the rain. Elijah had said that God had told him there would be no more rain until the people stopped worshipping Baal. Then Elijah escaped by hiding beside the brook Cherith.

Because there was no rain, the crops, trees, and grass died. But God had not forgotten His servant Elijah. He told the prophet to go to the city of Zarephath, where a widow would give him food and shelter.

When Elijah came to the city, he found the widow and her son gathering sticks. He asked her for a drink and something to eat, but the woman told him that they had very little left. In fact, they were just gathering some wood for a fire to bake their last loaf of bread.

Elijah told them to trust him, and that God would not let the food run out. So the widow baked a small loaf of bread and gave it to Elijah. Sure enough, every day, just as God promised, there was enough flour and oil to make bread, and enough water to drink. During the long dry time, Elijah, the widow, and her son had enough to eat and drink.

Although she didn't have much, the widow of Zarephath shared what she had with Elijah. We too should help people in need whenever we can. When we share and show kindness to other people, we show our love for God, too.

KINDNESS, COMPASSION, AND MERCY

The Lepers' Hero

Defend the poor and fatherless; do justice to the afflicted and needy. Deliver the poor and needy.

Psalm 82:3, 4.

William Anderson listened with interest to the sermon about mission work with lepers. He wanted to help, and he gave some money as an offering to help the mission. But then he didn't just forget about it.

When the chance came for William to work with lepers in Chandkuri, India, he eagerly accepted it. He found the conditions there to be even worse than he'd expected, but he worked hard to change that. The mission he worked at became known as "Fairyland" because it was so well kept, clean, and peaceful. People with leprosy could come there and live an orderly, peaceful life.

William wasn't content with just one mission. By 1924 there were 98 stations in 15 countries caring for 19,000 lepers. His work helped to bring hope, health, and happiness to people whose lives had once consisted of pain and rejection.

When Jesus was on earth, He cleansed the lepers. Jesus did everything He could to help people who were suffering. He will help us, day by day, to help those around us as well. We can show the same kind of kindness and compassion that William Anderson showed.

KINDNESS, COMPASSION, AND MERCY

Ma Slessor

Mary Slessor grew up with a mother who knew the importance of mission work, and this love for missions rubbed off on Mary and her brothers.

Finally the day came when she could sail to Africa. Mary noticed that her boat was full of kegs of rum, but it was carrying only one missionary. She would have a lot of work to do!

In Africa Mary worked hard to help the people. She did everything she could to teach them about the Bible and to show them a healthy way of life. They came to respect her so much that she was often asked to be a judge in any disputes between the natives. Perhaps her most important work, though, was with the children.

In her village twins were considered to be a curse. The mother of twins became an outcast in society, and the twin babies were usually killed. Many mothers, knowing of Mary's kindness, brought their twin babies to her in secret, and she raised them. Even when she went back to Scotland to visit, she took these adopted children with her so that nothing would happen to them while she was away. She became known as "Ma."

Mary became well known and loved in Africa because she treated the people with kindness and respect. As heroes for God we should always treat others with kindness and respect too.

And if anyone gives even a cup of cold water to one of these little ones because he is my disciple, I tell you the truth, he will certainly not lose his reward.
Matthew 10:42, NIV.

KINDNESS, COMPASSION, AND MERCY

Watch Your Words

Keep your tongue from evil and your lips from speaking lies.

Psalm 34:13, NIV.

Dave had gone to the same tiny church his entire life. It was a small country church with a traveling preacher, 14 pews, and not many more members. He and his family came faithfully every week. Dave liked going to church with his family, and he was happy when the head deacon asked him to help take up the offering. He liked to help.

When Dave was a teenager, his hair was a little long and he wore stylish clothes. He still liked to come to church and help take up the offering.

One day as Dave reached the back of the church after taking up the offering, one of the grown-ups leaned over and told him that he shouldn't be allowed to help take up the offering when he had long hair and stylish clothes. Dave was sad. He handed the offering plate to the grown-up and walked out the door. That was almost 40 years ago, and Dave hasn't been back since. He still loves God and likes to help people, but he doesn't go to church.

God's heroes should be very careful about their words and actions. They have a much greater impact on the people around us than we might think. God loves people whether they have short hair, long hair, or no hair. He loves them whether they have red, brown, or purple hair. He loves people in nice clothes, in dirty clothes, and yes, with no clothes! No matter what someone looks like or wears, we should do our best, as God's heroes, to be kind in the way we treat other people.

356

KINDNESS, COMPASSION, AND MERCY

Beautiful Inside and out

Beauty is passing, but a woman who fears the Lord, she shall be praised.
Proverbs 31:30.

The road to the well was long and dusty, and the sun beat down as Rebekah carried her pitcher to get water for her family. A bead of sweat trickled down her cheek as she neared the well. She noticed a stranger there. He had many camels, and they all looked hot and thirsty too.

As was the custom, Rebekah offered the stranger a drink, and he gratefully accepted. Then she offered to get water from the well for his camels, too. She knew that they drank a lot of water and that it would be hard work. But she thought of how tired and thirsty everyone got in the hot sun, and she didn't want the animals to suffer.

Time and again the beautiful girl lowered her pitcher into the well and poured the water out for the camels to drink. The hot sun still beat down on her, but she was thankful to be able to help the stranger and his animals.

Rebekah was beautiful both inside and out. Appearance is important to our society today, but how much effort do you put into making your inside beautiful too? Beauty isn't just about how we look on the outside. Our attitudes and behaviors can be beautiful too. Are you ugly on the inside, or beautiful like Rebekah?

KINDNESS, COMPASSION, AND MERCY

14
DECEMBER

Honor all people.
1 Peter 2:17.

Looking for Gold

Andrew's Scottish mother knew that hard work wasn't something to be avoided. She taught him that work was admirable and God-given, and it was a lesson Andrew never forgot. When Andrew's family moved to America from Scotland, he remembered his mother's lesson and worked hard to help his family.

In that day there were no public libraries from which people could borrow books. In his free time Andrew loved to read, and he was very impressed when a family friend, Colonel Anderson, opened his personal library for people to visit. The man's generosity had a big impact on Andrew, and many years later he helped open the first public libraries.

Throughout his life Andrew Carnegie remembered the values of hard work and generosity he'd learned when he was young. He worked very hard and planned wisely, eventually becoming very, very rich. He used his money to make other people happy by building schools, hospitals, and libraries.

Someone once asked him how he was able to bring out the best in everyone he met. He said that dealing with people was like panning for gold. When you're panning for gold, you look for the yellow gold instead of the dirt. When you're dealing with people, you should always look for the good instead of the bad. You'll find what you're looking for!

KINDNESS, COMPASSION, AND MERCY

It's the Pits

And we know that in all things God works for the good of those who love him.
Romans 8:28.

Joseph had many reasons to be angry with his brothers. His father had sent him to check on them, and they'd laughed at him and threatened to kill him. They threw him into a pit and then sold him into slavery. He was taken to live in a strange land where everyone spoke a different language and where he didn't know anyone. He could have been very bitter.

Joseph didn't understand why these things had happened to him, but he worked hard and did his best. Eventually he was made second in command next to Pharaoh. He went from being a slave to vice president. Because he allowed God to use him, Joseph helped save the people of Egypt from starving to death during a famine.

The famine affected his family back home as well. His father sent his brothers to Egypt to try to get food. When his brothers found out how powerful Joseph had become, they were afraid. They thought he would punish them for being so mean to him. But Joseph saw that his brothers had changed, and he forgave them. He told them, "What you meant for evil, God has used for good."

When someone does something mean to us, it's natural to want to be mean to them. Instead, we should let God take care of it. Even though they may have meant evil toward us, God can use it for good if we let Him!

KINDNESS, COMPASSION, AND MERCY

one Smart Donkey

A righteous man regards the life of his animal.

Proverbs 12:10.

Balak, king of Moab, was scared of the Israelites. There were so many of them. He was afraid that they would take over his land. So Balak hired Balaam to curse the Israelites. God spoke to Balaam, though, and told him that he would be able to say only the words the angel gave him.

As Balaam traveled to see Balak, an angel of the Lord stood in the way of his donkey. Balaam didn't see the angel, but the donkey did, and she went off the road and into a field. That made Balaam angry, and he hit her. Two more times the angel stood in the way, and two more times the donkey veered off the road and got hit by Balaam. Once she crushed his foot against a wall, and the last time she lay down underneath him. Balaam was so angry that he hit and hit the donkey.

Then God let the donkey talk. Balaam was so angry that he talked back without even being surprised that he was having a conversation with his donkey! Then Balaam's eyes were opened so that he could see the angel, and he realized that the donkey had saved his life. He realized that he had been unkind to her, and he was sorry.

Being a hero for God means being kind to all of His creation—not just people, but animals and the environment, too. Don't be like Balaam. Be kind to animals.

KINDNESS, COMPASSION, AND MERCY

The Sore Preacher

Horseback riding had never been something John Hatfield was very good at. He heard there was a cowboy in the area who was famous for being wild and mean. John asked if they could go riding together. To everyone's surprise, the cowboy agreed. The date was set, and off they went.

For 30 miles the preacher and the cowboy rode together through the hills and plains. By the end of the day John was so sore he could hardly walk. But he'd gained a new friend who eventually accepted Christ into his heart because of the friendship of the horseback-riding preacher.

We don't have to preach to everyone we meet in order to be a good Christian. Just be a friend. Have the courage to be yourself and do God's will for your life, and you'll end up not only having good friends, but being one, too.

Be wise as serpents and harmless as doves.

Matthew 10:16.

KINDNESS, COMPASSION, AND MERCY

18
DECEMBER

Surprise Ending

A soft answer turns away wrath, but a harsh word stirs up anger.

Proverbs 15:1.

The news raced through the village: The bandits were coming! Everyone must escape. They grabbed what they could and bolted out the back door. Everyone made it out in time except for two young girls. One hid in the closet, but the other was frozen in fear as the bandits burst through the door. As they ransacked the room, the leader grabbed her around the neck and demanded to know where her father was. When she told him that she didn't know, his grip tightened in anger.

Suddenly she had an idea. She offered to sing for him. At first he laughed, but he figured she might as well sing for him before he killed her. She called her cousin out of the closet, and together they sang "Jesus Loves Me" for the bandits. The leader was so moved by their song that he made his men put everything back. Then he gave her $2 from his own pocket before he left!

You too might be surprised by how your kindness affects people. Use kindness today and see if you come up with some surprise happy endings.

362

KINDNESS, COMPASSION, AND MERCY

Kidnapped Babies and Pickled Kids

The Goforth family were missionaries in China. None of their fellow missionaries allowed the Chinese people into their homes. They were afraid of people stealing their belongings. But the Goforths felt that kindness and hospitality were more important than their things, so they invited people into their home. They did have a few things stolen, but the good of making friends outweighed the bad of losing their things.

The people had heard wild stories about the missionaries. The Goforths led thousands of guided tours through their home to show that the stories they'd heard weren't true. They explained that their dolls weren't kidnapped babies. They showed their visitors that there were no children canned and pickled in jars in the basement. Once the native people realized that the missionaries weren't going to hurt them, they became much more open and friendly.

Sometimes silly stories can be started about us that don't make much sense. By being open and friendly to people, we can get rid of the rumors, make new friends, and share the truth of Jesus with those we come in contact with.

Keep your tongue from evil, and your lips from speaking deceit. Depart from evil and do good; seek peace and pursue it.
Psalm 34:13, 14.

KINDNESS, COMPASSION, AND MERCY

20
DECEMBER

*I was sick and
you visited Me.*

Matthew 25:36.

Being
Like Jesus

Every week you can count on a quiet smile and a firm handshake from Pastor Griffin. And Mrs. Griffin is always at church, ready to give a hug. The Griffins always show genuine interest in people. Their lives are a quiet, steady example of Christianity to everyone who knows them.

Whenever anyone is sick, the Griffins will visit with homemade soup, good conversation, a big hug, and prayer. They are never pushy; they just want people to know that they care.

When Jesus lived here on earth, He did much the same thing. He never pushed Himself on people, but was always there to love them and be interested in them. He did whatever He could to help. We can never go wrong by following Jesus' example. What can you do today to show Jesus' love to someone who is sick?

KINDNESS, COMPASSION, AND MERCY

A Berry Good School

I have no greater joy than to hear that my children walk in truth.

3 John 4.

O ne day as Martha Berry was sitting in her home, she felt as though someone was watching her. When she turned toward the window, she saw a little boy peeking in. She invited him in, and he came in with several other kids. When she asked what they were doing, the little boy told her they were looking in the windows.

She asked them if they'd ever been to church. They told her they hadn't because they didn't have any church clothes. So Martha asked them if they'd like to hear a story. They said they would, and she began to read them Bible story after Bible story. They wanted to hear more, so she told them to come back the next week for more stories.

Week after week the children came, bringing friends and family, until they had to move to a different place because they'd run out of room. That was the beginning of the Martha Berry Schools in Georgia.

Martha wanted to help people who didn't have an education. She began expanding her Bible stories into other kinds of learning. By the end of her lifetime all of her land was used to teach boys and girls how to read, write, and make a living. Her work changed the course of history in the South by helping people live better lives.

The kindness you show to others may not seem like much today, but let God use it, and you could make a huge difference! Since you're God's hero, ask Him today to use your kindness to help others have a better life.

KINDNESS, COMPASSION, AND MERCY

22
DECEMBER

Do not judge according to appearance.

John 7:24.

The Change

Loland had a rough time growing up. His father died when he was only 2 years old, and his mother died when he was 7. After that, he was passed back and forth between his aunts and uncles until he was old enough to live on his own.

Largely because of his sad childhood Loland grew up to be a gruff, difficult man. His wife was a Christian with a gentle, kind spirit. He often made fun of her for her beliefs, but he quietly began to change as he grew older.

Gardening was important to him, and he gave much of his garden's produce to a poor neighbor family. He found ways to quietly improve his neighborhood, such as trimming weeds and tree limbs from a one-way bridge to make it safer. He even started to respect his wife's beliefs by not mowing the lawn on Sabbath, which was a big change from the teasing he'd done in the past. Much credit for his changes can be given to his wife for her steady, kind, gentle Christian example.

The things that happen to us will influence who we are, but they aren't the final influence. We always have a choice as to how we behave. We never know what influence we may have on the people around us. God can use any of us to have an influence for Him.

KINDNESS, COMPASSION, AND MERCY

Miracle Meal

[He] is able to do exceedingly abundantly above all that we ask or think.
Ephesians 3:20.

There was a huge crowd gathered on the hillside. They had come to listen to Jesus. He'd talked to them all day, and now it was evening and the crowd was getting hungry. Jesus knew this, and He told His disciples to find them something to eat. They must have given Him a funny look. There were 5,000 men, plus women and children. How would they ever find enough food for all those people?

But Jesus had a plan. There was a boy in the crowd with a basket. In his basket were five loaves of bread and two small fish. The disciples asked the boy if he would be willing to share it with Jesus. When he said yes, they took the food to Jesus, and He blessed it. Much to the disciples' surprise, every time they put their hand into the basket, there was more food. There was more and more, until the entire crowd had been fed. They even had leftovers!

The gift the boy had to give to Jesus was small compared to the large number of people. But the boy was willing to give all that he had, and Jesus blessed it. The gifts we have to give may seem small too, but never underestimate God's power to use them to bless many people.

KINDNESS, COMPASSION, AND MERCY

Little Boat, Big Surprise

His merciful kindness is great toward us.

Psalm 117:2.

The tiny boat rocked gently in the water as it bumped back and forth among the bulrushes. Pharaoh's daughter came to the water with her maids and saw the tiny boat. She sent one of her maids to wade out into the water to get it and see what was inside.

When they opened the lid of the small boat, Baby Moses began to cry. He didn't like to be in the tiny boat. Pharaoh's daughter was surprised to find a baby! She wanted to keep him for her very own.

Just then Miriam came from the edge of the river and asked the princess if she would like to find someone to take care of the baby until he was older. Pharaoh's daughter said yes, so Miriam, Baby Moses' sister, was able to help their mother get her baby back! God used Pharaoh's daughter to help raise the man who would one day help to free the Israelites from slavery.

Never underestimate the power of kindness. God can use even the kindness of strangers to help His people.

KINDNESS, COMPASSION, AND MERCY

Christmas Presents

*The gift of God
is eternal life.*
Romans 6:23.

By age 12 Chang was an orphan and a slave. His mother had died, and his stepfather had sold Chang and his siblings as slaves. The man who bought Chang treated him cruelly. Life was not happy for him.

One day an old grandmother saw how badly the man treated Chang. She hid Chang where the mean man wouldn't find him—at the home of missionaries who were out of town. When the missionaries came back, they became friends with Chang.

The missionary family loved Christmas. They were looking forward to spending Christmas together with new friends from the mission. Little Anna was especially excited. There was a stocking hung in their house for Chang. She knew he was poor and had never had Christmas, so she couldn't wait to share their Christmas with him.

When Chang came up their front walk, Anna could hardly stand it and raced out to see him. Chang was excited to see her too, but he never even noticed the stocking with his name on it. Instead he handed Anna and her brother each a small toy. He had gotten the toys as gifts at school, and he wanted to share what he had with his friends.

Christmas shouldn't be focused on getting. We celebrate Christmas because Jesus came to earth and died on the cross to give us the gift of salvation. God shared Jesus with us; Chang shared his toys. What can you share this Christmas?

KINDNESS, COMPASSION, AND MERCY

TeamWORKS

*Whatever you
want men to
do to you,
do also to them.*

Matthew 7:12.

The woman was sick. She was sitting in the waiting room of the hospital emergency room when suddenly she stopped breathing. The nurses rushed out and immediately took her to where they had the medicine and equipment to help.

While they were working to help her, the woman's heart stopped beating. It didn't look good, but the team of workers in the emergency room didn't give up. Soon the woman was breathing, and her heart was beating again. She had almost died, but because of the teamwork of the ER workers, she lived.

Several weeks later, after she was well, the woman and her family brought pizza to say thank you to the ER workers who had saved her. She and her family were very grateful for the help they had been given there.

The hospital isn't the only place where teamwork is important. In our everyday lives it's important for each of us to do our part and work together as a team. Good things can happen when we do. Who knows—it might even save a life!

KINDNESS, COMPASSION, AND MERCY

Dr. Luke

When was the last time you went to the doctor? What are the people who work at your doctor's office like? Are they nice? If your doctor and the people who work in the office are kind, it makes going to the doctor a little easier.

Dr. Luke was kind. It didn't matter if he was taking care of a Jew or Gentile, a slave or free man, a man, woman, or child. He treated all people nicely. People liked Dr. Luke because he showed kindness to the people he took care of, and did the best he could to help them. You can read about Dr. Luke in the book of Acts in the New Testament.

How do you treat people? Today, ask Jesus to help you treat people with kindness and compassion, as Dr. Luke did.

Walk worthy of the calling with which you were called.

Ephesians 4:1.

KINDNESS, COMPASSION, AND MERCY

28
DECEMBER

You have turned for me my mourning into dancing.

Psalm 30:11.

A Nice Surprise

Laura and Patrick were working in their yard when Patrick had pains in his arms, chest, and jaw. Laura called 911, and the fire department came right away. They hurried Patrick to the hospital, where they found out that he'd had a heart attack. Thanks to Laura's quick thinking and the care of the fire department and hospital, Patrick would be OK, although he would have to spend some time in the hospital.

When Laura pulled into their driveway that night, she was tired from the stress of the day and worried about everything she still needed to do at home. Imagine how surprised she was to see that the yardwork had been finished and the tools had been put away. Even the sidewalks had been cleaned! The same firefighters who had taken Patrick to the hospital had come back and cleaned up for them.

Those firefighters didn't have to come back to clean up Laura and Patrick's yard, but they did what Jesus would have done. They did more than was expected of them. Jesus spent His life on earth helping others and turning their sadness into happiness. As heroes for Him we too should do more than is expected in helping others.

372

KINDNESS, COMPASSION, AND MERCY

Back to Life

Dorcas helped everyone she could. She was especially known for making clothes for people who needed them. People said Dorcas was "full of good works and charitable deeds" (Acts 9:36). Everyone loved Dorcas because she showed such love and kindness to them.

Then one day Dorcas got sick. Before long, she died. The people were so sad that their dear friend had died. They heard that Peter was in a town nearby and sent men to get him. Some of the women Dorcas had helped when she was alive were at her house when Peter got there. With tears in their eyes they showed him the clothes she had made for them before she had gotten sick.

Peter asked everyone to leave, then knelt down and prayed. We don't know what he said in that prayer, but when he was finished, he turned around and spoke to Dorcas. He said, "Dorcas, arise." She opened her eyes and sat up! Peter helped her up and took her to her friends who were outside. What a party they must have had to celebrate getting their friend back.

Dorcas, like all God's heroes, used the gift of kindness to help those around her who needed it most. What can you do today to show kindness to someone who needs it?

Let us not grow weary while doing good.
Galatians 6:9.

KINDNESS, COMPASSION, AND MERCY

Snow Angel

*Lo, I am with
you alway, even
unto the end
of the world.*
Matthew 28:20, KJV.

After many years in Africa as missionaries, Gerald and Mable Nash were back in America and excited about visiting family again.

On their way to Gerald's parents' home they found themselves in the middle of a terrible snowstorm. Gerald was scared. He wasn't used to driving in the snow. His family didn't have warm clothes, since they had just come from Africa. The blizzard howled, and the snow was blinding. They prayed and asked God to take care of them. They needed their angels.

The Nashes counted more than 80 cars in the ditch or stranded. They were afraid to keep going, but they didn't want to stop, either, since someone might slide into them. They had only summer clothes, so they didn't want to spend the night in a ditch!

The snow was getting deeper and deeper when a police officer stopped them and asked if they would like to get onto a better road. Of course they would!

"Follow me," said the officer. He took Gerald and his family to a road that was almost clear. Gerald followed him until they got close to Gerald's parents' house. How did the officer know where they were going?

Then the officer waved. Gerald went to say thanks, but there was no car and no police officer.

Gerald, Mable, and their family know that an angel led them safely through the storm. They had asked God for help, and He'd sent it. He'll take care of us the same way.

KINDNESS, COMPASSION, AND MERCY

God's Heroes

All this year we've been reading about heroes for God. Have you learned anything? I hope so. I know I have. I hope the things you've read will help you to be a hero for God, not just this year, but for the rest of your life.

More than anything, God wants you to be His hero and friend. He's writing a special book in heaven about your life just for you. Someday, when we get to heaven, He'll read you your story from your special book. So be a hero for God here on earth, and we can be heroes together in heaven forever!

See you there!

Rejoice because your names are written in heaven.
Luke 10:20.

KINDNESS, COMPASSION, AND MERCY